ROOSEVELT
AND *THE*
FRENCH

Franklin D. Roosevelt at his home in Hyde Park, New York, on July 4, 1937. From the Franklin D. Roosevelt Library in Hyde Park. Photo by UPI/Bettmann.

ROOSEVELT AND THE FRENCH

Mario Rossi

PRAEGER

Westport, Connecticut
London

E
807
R755
1994

Library of Congress Cataloging-in-Publication Data

Rossi, Mario.
    Roosevelt and the French / Mario Rossi.
      p. cm.
    Includes bibliographical references and index.
    ISBN 0–275–94613–4 (alk. paper)
    1. Roosevelt, Franklin D. (Franklin Delano), 1882–1945–Relations
with French. 2. United States–Relations–France. 3. France–
Relations–United States. I. Title.
E807.R755 1993
327.73044′09′044–dc20   93–12973

British Library Cataloguing in Publication Data is available.

Library of Congress Catalog Card Number: 93–12973
ISBN: 0–275–94613–4

First published in 1993

Praeger Publishers, 88 Post Road West, Westport, CT 06881
An imprint of Greenwood Publishing Group. Inc.

Printed in the United States of America

The paper used in this book complies with the
Permanent Paper Standard issued by the National
Information Standards Organization (Z39.48–1984).

10 9 8 7 6 5 4 3 2 1

For Richard, my son, my friend

For years he [Cordell Hull] has been unfairly criticized for his "Vichy policy," which in fact was Roosevelt's personal policy, and which the President often shaped without consulting his Secretary of State.

Robert Murphy
Diplomat among Warriors
(New York, 1964), 122

I know the President is running foreign affairs and I know the President will not let me help him anymore. . . . Since Pearl Harbor he does not let me help in connection with foreign affairs. . . . I just don't know what is going on.

Cordell Hull to Henry Morgenthau
John Morton Blum
From the Morgenthau Diaries: Years of War, 1941–1945
(Boston, 1967), 242

The Department of State regards its role at that time as nothing more than that of a messenger boy for the Pentagon and [was] accustomed to sneezing whenever the Pentagon caught cold.

George F. Kennan
Memoirs, 1925–1950
(New York, 1967), 162–63

Contents

Preface

When dealing with Franklin D. Roosevelt or the French, one can hardly remain indifferent. Both subjects elicit emotions in which this historian, at least, becomes inevitably entrapped. I might as well confess now, therefore, that one of my first jobs was with the Roosevelt administration and that ever since I have felt a not-uncritical admiration for the man without whom the West could well have been lost. As a child I had a French governess who taught me not only *pas les coudes sur la table* but also to love a certain France – the France of the Rights of Man, of 1848, of Victor Hugo and Emile Zola and Jean Jaurès. If my opinions appear to have been colored by my affection for that France, I ask the reader to bear with me.

This book concerns Roosevelt's relations with the French; it does not purport to examine all Franco-American relations during the Roosevelt era. My purpose is less to relate a sequence of historical events than to emphasize those constant themes in the president's view of the French that will help the reader understand the nature of his attitudes toward them.

Roosevelt was largely his own secretary of state, and U.S. policy regarding France was, in particular, his own doing. The French leaders knew this, as their efforts to penetrate the president's mind demonstrate. In this respect, of great value to them – and subsequently to historians – were Roosevelt's conversations with France's ambassadors to the United States. Equally important was the manner in which French policy toward the United States was perceived by Roosevelt. The contrast between the two perceptions – Roosevelt's perceptions of the French and the perceptions the French had of Roosevelt – has had consequences for Franco-American relations to this day. Roosevelt approached French leaders – whether those of the Third Republic, the Vichy government, or the Provisional government – in his own particular way, and his policies toward them were based on that approach. It is that view or approach, its foundations and its consequences, that will be examined in this book.

The dispatches to Paris from the French embassy in Washington naturally reflected the personality of the French ambassador, his understanding of the complex American scene, Roosevelt's attitude toward him, and the degree to which the ambassador understood the president—all elements that influenced the way information from Washington was perceived in Paris. French embassy dispatches proved important in another respect: Roosevelt was a very secretive man who put as little as possible on paper; his conversations with French ambassadors regarding important aspects of his European policies contribute much to our understanding of his presidency.

All research dealing with Roosevelt begins at the Franklin D. Library at Hyde Park, New York. William R. Emerson, the library director, was a wise guide and counselor. Archivists Frances M. Seeber and Raymond Teichman proved of great assistance with research. John E. Taylor of the Military Research Branch at the National Archives in Washington and Bernard F. Cavalcanti and Martha L. Crawley of the U.S. Navy Archives were also very helpful. In addition, Harvard University's Charles Warren Center for Studies in American History provided an ideal setting for research and exchange of ideas.

In Paris, I spent several months doing research at the Ministry of Foreign Affairs, where Madame Monique de Nomazy saved me from getting lost among the millions of documents stored at the Archives Diplomatiques. The personnel were invariably courteous and helpful. I found the same friendly assistance at the Institut Charles de Gaulle and at the Service Historique de la Marine.

Many people have been of assistance through the various stages of research and writing. I am particularly indebted to Roosevelt biographer Frank Freidel, whose advice and friendship have never failed me. His recent loss was a cruel blow.

Introduction

Franklin Delano Roosevelt became president of the United States at a time of serious crisis for much of the world. All but paralyzed by the Great Depression, the United States was, literally, a nation coming apart. In Europe, Hitler's rise to power was a premonition of the aggression that would lead to another world war. Fascism and authoritarianism were spreading throughout the Continent, in Italy, Portugal, Spain, the Balkans, and most of eastern Europe – the ruling parties often being sympathetic toward nazism even when fearful of German power. France and England, deeply divided within themselves and mindful of the enormous losses suffered during World War I, sought peace at almost any price. Japan was readying for aggression throughout the Pacific region.

Roosevelt belonged to that minority of Americans who realized that two oceans were not real protection against possible hostilities. He knew that the breakdown of civilized intercourse among nations would spell disaster; that fascism corroded and corrupted the very texture of society; that just as "a house divided against itself cannot stand," a Europe politically at odds with itself was surely headed for war. Although the first years of his presidency were dominated by domestic problems, a number of Roosevelt's early initiatives showed the direction his foreign policy would take. These included nonrecognition of territorial acquisitions by force, recognition of Soviet Russia, the Good Neighbor policy toward Latin America, the decision on Philippine independence, improved relations with Canada, efforts toward a settlement of the problems of the Pacific, initiatives toward disarmament, and economic cooperation with the European democracies.[1]

Vying with foreign matters for Roosevelt's attention, however, were America's pressing domestic problems. Roosevelt's first task was to provide the leadership that would make Americans realize they had nothing to fear but fear itself, the

"nameless, unreasoning, unjustified terror" that paralyzed needed efforts to convert retreat into advance. In addition to lifting the country from the depths of
despair, the New Deal produced an unprecedented expansion of the democratic
process. More and more Americans were brought into active participation in the
life of the commonwealth, a role until then reserved almost exclusively for an
Anglo-Saxon, white, male, Protestant, middle-class minority.[2] The cares and
concerns of millions of newly enfranchised Americans were to be taken into
account for the first time in U.S. history. They played a major role in producing
the kind of atmosphere in which Roosevelt's foreign policy decisions would be
made.

Destined within a few years to become the most powerful country in the
world, the United States in the 1930s was in the grip of an intransigent form of
isolationism. Americans were too involved in their everyday problems to be
concerned with events in the rest of the world. Europe was seen as a distant
continent, endemically in trouble and eager to involve the United States in its
problems. Isolationism was primarily a rejection of Europe: "The hell with Europe and the rest of those nations," Minnesota senator Thomas Schall shouted
during a Senate debate in February 1935. The United States was also a very
different country then, demographically speaking, than the country it became
later in the century. Until World War I, it counted 13 million immigrants, and as
many children of immigrants, in a total population of some 100 million; though
sentimentally attached to the "old country," these immigrants were determined
to leave behind its problems. Recent immigrants were eager to belong, to become part of the American scene, and in the process they often found refuge in
being "all-American." "The worst in the United States," a New York taxi driver
told me just before the start of World War II, "is better than the best in Europe."

Attitudes of this kind tended to breed conformism, provincialism, and ideological intolerance; diversity came to be considered un-American. Roosevelt
once referred to Europe's "ancient hatreds, turbulent frontiers, the 'legacy of
old-forgotten, far-off things and battles long ago' . . . [and] its new-born fanati-
cism."[3] The United States and Europe have radically different histories. The
roots of the U.S. economy and society were not feudal and clerical, as Europe's
had been, and that difference, Charles Beard wrote, was "a fact of immense significance." The philosophy of isolationism found its roots in the instinctive self-
protection of a people that could not hope to complete its national fusion
unless it was shielded from the passions and the divisions of its European ancestors.[4]

This isolationism also reflected a physical reality: the vast expanse of the Atlantic separating the United States from Europe. Given the relatively primitive
state of transportation and communications in the 1930s, the physical and
emotional distances seemed much greater then than they do today. To most
Americans, Europe was what one heard about on the radio or read about in
newspapers and magazines.

The Italians who had come to the New World had left behind the appalling poverty of the peninsula's southern regions; the Jews, the persecutions and anti-Semitism of Russia and eastern Europe; the Irish, near starvation in their British-dominated homeland; but what about the French? They had not faced the same dramas as other immigrant groups; nor had they felt, like them, the need to emigrate. Americans of French origin were relatively few and largely free of the love–hate relationship so many immigrants had with their countries of origin. Americans came to identify the French with style, culture, elegance, and the good life; many celebrated Americans writers had spent time in Paris after the Great War and recounted with emotion their experience of life in the City of Lights.

To many Americans, however, France presented problems that tempered its likability. In 1917, over 2 million young Americans had landed in France to join the "war to end all wars," but no brave new world had emerged–only disappointment and bitterness. The issue of the vast sums the United States had lent France during and after World War I was a periodic reminder of the ingratitude of a people who not only refused to repay their debt but resented being asked to. This controversy became so nasty at times that the Hoover administration would feel for the French a lack of respect bordering on contempt.

The French living in the United States were thus confronted with a dichotomy in public opinion: They were appreciated as individuals because of all that France stood for in terms of civilization, but they were resented as a people due to unpleasantness over the war debt and other contentious issues. As we shall see, Roosevelt shared this ambivalence to a certain extent. Under the circumstances, there was not much the French in the United States could do to assist their homeland. A European country under attack could normally count on the support of kindred national minorities, whose impact was proportionate to their numerical importance. The Italians and the Irish, for example, could mobilize very large numbers in support of their countries of origin; not so the French, who were too few to have much impact. The French tried to compensate for numerical unimportance with historical recollections, reminding Americans of France's contributions to the War of Independence and pointing to the many towns and streets named after Lafayette, the symbol of France's commitment to the American Revolution. This emotional appeal hardly sufficed at the polls, however.

Nevertheless, France was accepted as a potential ally in the preservation of a tolerable degree of world order, under threat of aggressors in Europe and in Asia; but it seldom occupied the center stage of American concern. The press usually followed the public's moods, and with few exceptions such as the Hearst newspapers, was neither deliberately friendly nor deliberately hostile toward France. Its coverage tended to vary according to the period and the subject.

Another shaper of public opinion, the churches, remained divided, Protestants being more favorable to the French than Catholics. Protestant churches had been engaged in social work in France, especially during and after World War I, and were sympathetic to France's problems. The Catholic Church's attitude reflected, instead, the hostility of American-Irish bishops to French *laïcité* and the confiscation of Church properties by the government. France's close ties to Great Britain were also resented by the Irish clergy, who largely controlled the U.S. Catholic hierarchy. This animosity abated somewhat when the Nazis came to power in Germany, brandishing their anti-Christian philosophy. Because of their hostility to Germany, Jews were generally sympathetic toward the French. Their attitude caused a certain reserve among the Anglo-Saxon population, who were anti-Semitic not in the European sense but in the sense that class and social prejudices existed to which even the young Eleanor Roosevelt, the future champion of human rights, was not immune.

Americans traveling to France in various capacities also influenced public opinion. Their impact was usually limited to the urban centers of the East and West coasts, for to citizens of the American heartland France was as far removed as the moon. Though fascinated by the country's beauty and the scope of its culture and civilization, American students in France complained upon returning home of their isolation, the difficulty of making friends, and the near impossibility of being invited into French homes. Feelings among World War I veterans about the country they had fought to defend were mixed. Former officers, who had been treated with respect, had pleasant memories, while former soldiers recalled the lack of hospitality, the dirt of the peasant homes where they were billeted, and their feelings of being taken advantage of in shops and restaurants. Veterans generally felt the French had taken U.S. military assistance for granted and would now rather forget their debt to the American soldier. French historians have identified this sentiment of rejection as the *complexe de Perrichon*, directed at those who, by intervening in World War I, saved France from certain defeat. No one was prepared to admit this: On the right, anti-Americanism was the expression of a nationalism that would not recognize France's debt to anyone; on the left, the United States was seen as a capitalist bastion against world revolution. Belonging as they did to every class and to every part of the country, the 2 million American veterans played a significant, though indirect, role in shaping public sentiment toward France, which was affixed with the label "ungrateful" for a long time.

Between the two wars, France had endeavored to maintain close political ties with the United States while at the same time resisting Americanization. "The world advances toward a kind of Americanism, which affronts our refined ideas," wrote the philosopher and historian Ernest Renan. A strong feeling of cultural and ideological anti-Americanism prevailed in France at the time. It was felt that American modernism and materialism threatened to compromise France's ancient traditions and its prestige around the world. France's political and intellectual leaders were obsessed with the specter of European decadence. They feared that a weakened Europe might be overwhelmed by the financial and political power of an America offering a different, more seductive form of civilization.[5] Politicians urged France to reject all forms of reliance upon the political and economic power of Anglo-Saxons in general and the United States in particular.

The United States was often depicted in French literature as an equalizing society, conformist and materialist, peopled by miserable creatures who were anxious about the future and gripped by boredom, deluded by a belief in collective illusions, and living as though in termite colonies. As we shall see, these ideas were diffused throughout the society in which de Gaulle grew up and were to have a perhaps unconscious impact on his conduct.

These ideas, so thoroughly permeated in French intellectual circles, might have had an impact on Roosevelt, although there is no evidence to support this assumption. In his youth he had traveled regularly to Europe with his family and was permanently influenced by what he saw, but the Roosevelts, like the other affluent Americans traveling to France, seldom took more than a passing interest in its people. "They live among themselves and don't know the French better than the Laplanders," a French writer complained. Even though less affluent Americans apparently loved the country (or at least its image), almost none of them really knew anything about France.[6] Referring specifically to the Roosevelts, Geoffrey C. Ward wrote:

The Old World was interesting to them for its comforts and its culture. The ordinary people among whom they lived for months at a time – the French and Germans, Italians and Swiss and Spanish – were barely worthy of notice. Visitors like the Roosevelts learned European languages so that they might make sense of the opera and the theater – and give clear directions to the servants. In fact, they had little need of European friends, for when they went abroad they took their own world with them. After the Civil War, a large segment of New York society reconstituted itself overseas each summer. There were always friends and acquaintances and sometimes kinsmen aboard the ships that took them across the Atlantic. And once ashore, the Roosevelts and their circle stayed at the same hotels . . . , dined at the same restaurants, wandered through the same palaces and picture galleries, attended one another's parties, worshipped together at the English or American chapels that offered Protestant services in nearly every city.[7]

Some of America's best-known writers – Ernest Hemingway, F. Scott Fitzgerald, Gertrude Stein, William Faulkner, John Dos Passos, Sinclair Lewis, T. S. Eliot, and others – had made their homes in Paris after World War I to escape the conformism and intolerance of American society. America was nearly always the subject of their stories and novels, however, and but for a few exceptions, they all eventually returned to the United States. They lived with other writers and artists of various nationalities in a world apart, making little contact with everyday France. They became known as the Lost Generation.

Franklin Roosevelt's contact with France was not significantly different. He had experienced it the way other Americans of his class had. He would eventually meet French generals, ministers, presidents, and ambassadors, but not the *people* of France – the collective incarnation of a thousand years of history and the subjects of its traditions and culture. We shall examine Roosevelt's education and youthful wanderings through France for clues to how his experience of the country affected him and to what extent his impressions influenced his later policies.

Like other visiting Americans, Roosevelt spoke some French, though not as much or as well as he believed. Receiving a French newspaper reporter at Hyde Park, he exclaimed: "France, France, I love her so much!" Writing to French scholars of the Ecole libre des hautes études, he proclaimed: "The light of French culture has enlightened the world; so long as it is maintained, France cannot die. . . . French thought was not made for slaves. Those who keep it alive work for the liberation of France."[8] Statements of this sort, made by a man who relished hyperbole, are too general to be indicative of his true feelings.

Roosevelt, it should be remembered, possessed a complex and almost impenetrable personality. "Beyond the screen, the real Roosevelt existed in mystery, even to himself," Arthur M. Schlesinger, Jr., wrote.

Underneath there remained the other man – tougher than the public man, harder, more ambitious, more calculating, more petty, more puckish, more selfish, more malicious, more profound, more complex, more interesting. Only intimate friends saw Roosevelt in these aspects, and then in enigmatic and sometimes terrifying glimpses. The eyes, friendly but impenetrable, the smile, genial but noncommittal, the manner, open but inscrutable – all signified the inaccessibility within. Detachment endowed him with a capacity for craftiness in politics and for calculation, sometimes even for cruelty, in human relations. . . . He seemed soft and complaisant, but he was terribly hard inside. . . . At bottom, Franklin Roosevelt was a man without illusions, clearheaded and compassionate, who had been close enough to death to understand the frailty of human striving, but who remained loyal enough to life to do his best in the sight of God.[9]

We can assume that Roosevelt loved an abstraction called France, but even he could not ignore the historical evidence that relations between the United States and France had never been entirely cordial. Suffering from what Britain's Anthony Eden has called the "Lafayette complex," the United States often gives the impression of knowing what is best for France. The French, for their part, generally seem to feel that the United States owes them eternal gratitude for assistance rendered during the American Revolution. Reference is periodically made to "traditional ties," enshrined by history, that found confirmation in American intervention during world War I and "Lafayette, nous voici!" No ceremony marking a major event in U.S. history is complete unless some of France's most distinguished citizens are present. Marshal Henri Philippe Pétain was delegated to the ceremonies marking the 150th anniversary of the battle of Yorktown in 1931. The 100th birthday of the Statue of Liberty in 1986 saw President François Mitterrand next to President Ronald Reagan, who duly shouted, "Vive la France!"

All this euphoria produces the impression – for some, the conviction – that the United States is honor-bound to rush to France's assistance in times of trouble. Of course, "traditional" among countries are only the interests, dictated by geography far more than history. France has threatened neither the security of the United States, nor its vital interests, nor the freedom of sea lanes, whereas the Germans and the Japanese have. Ideals are also insurance against aggressive intentions. If a community of ideals exists among the United States, Great Britain, and France, the basic reason is that in our age, democracies have tended to be allies.

It serves no purpose to prevail upon tradition to explain the relations between two countries at a given moment. It is all the more fruitless when at issue are the relations between an individual and a foreign country. Any individual, even the president of the United States, is a composite of emotions, prejudices, education, family background, and so forth. He or she may or may not adhere to the traditional view of the exceptional nature of Franco-American relations. President Roosevelt gave the impression that he did; his predecessor, Herbert Hoover, gave the impression that he did not. Roosevelt was fond of Léon Blum but not of Charles de Gaulle, and in both cases his policies reflected his feelings. "Traditional ties" were invoked only when warranted by particular circumstances. They were one diplomatic instrument of many, not an objective reality.

When Roosevelt proclaimed his love for France, which France did he mean? Did he love Léon Blum's socialist France or Charles Maurras's rightist, nationalist France? This is not a compelling question when two countries conduct their relations on the basis of objective evaluation of the interests at stake, but it is significant when a like objectivity does not obtain, as in the relations between an individual and a foreign country. To Roosevelt, France was his direct responsibility.

Having taken personal charge of U.S. relations with France, how well equipped was Roosevelt to understand so sophisticated and complex a people as the French? Probably not very. He based his actions more on intuition than on intellect. His appreciation of art was minimal. Following a visit to Venice's Accademia di Belle Arti during his honeymoon, he wrote his mother: "A few Paul Veronese and Titians etc.–chiefly indecent infants sitting on, or falling off clouds–or scared apostles trying to keep the sun out of their eyes."[10] He had little interest in music and preferred detective stories to classic literature.[11] His own writing fairly prosaic, he greatly envied Churchill's majestic prose. All kinds of junk cluttered his desk. He was better acquainted with U.S. history and traditions than were most American leaders before and after. He had a phenomenal understanding of the geopolitical issues of the time. He loved, and was loved by, the American people perhaps as no other president save Abraham Lincoln. Americans felt that though an aristocrat, he was one of them. But an understanding of American values and traditions did not necessarily prepare Roosevelt for a similar appreciation of European values and traditions. As we shall see, the United States and Europe did not share a similar historical process, and their fundamental historical differences were more marked then than now. Americans who, like the Roosevelts, had spent time in France often thought they knew the country well when in fact their knowledge was limited and often biased.

The French people's highly developed sense of historical continuity, of sharing common traditions and a common culture, might never have been fully understood by Roosevelt. When he became president, his knowledge of history hardly extended beyond that of the United States. "For want of wide-ranging historical reading," Joseph Alsop, who knew the president well, wrote, "his world view always retained something of the provincialism of the very provincial though privileged American group he came from."[12]

Because of his traditional American background, Roosevelt distanced himself and his family from European traditions. Reacting to a journalist's statement that "from his earliest years Franklin D. Roosevelt moved in a society which was in a real sense international and which was not conscious of any differentiation between the interests of the United States and the interests of Western Europe," he branded the assertion pure invention. He felt the author's

failure to investigate is rather pathetic, as is his knowledge of history. . . . If he could look into the question of "family ties" he would realize that the Roosevelt family, in the West Indian sugar business, was compelled to contend many years against the British and French interests in those lands – and that is what made them revolutionaries rather than tories in 1776. If he had ever read about the China trade of the Delano family, he would have realized that the great fight in those days was between the British and the American firms. And that I was brought up in the story of how the Delano's family principal competitors were British.[13]

Roosevelt's understanding of Europe, including France, was colored by his belief in the uniqueness of the American tradition. He agreed with the concept that the United States is both an extension of European culture and a New World civilization conscious of its individuality and needing to be distinct from the Old World – a dual nature deeply rooted in U.S. history.[14] The first Americans had intended from the start to establish a country different from all others, a country that, for this reason, cannot be explained in European terms. "We have it in our power," Thomas Paine wrote in *The Rights of Man*, "to begin the world over again. A situation similar to the present had not happened since the days of Noah until now." Roosevelt also shared Jefferson's conviction that a corollary to the Declaration of Independence was a new foreign policy that assumes that Europe's political interests "are entirely different from ours." Jefferson's "first and fundamental maxim" was "never to entangle ourselves in the broils of Europe" and "never to suffer Europe to intermeddle with cis-Atlantic affairs." Roosevelt the student of U.S. history could not fail to be influenced by these views. Although it was inevitable for the United States to become entangled in the turmoils of Europe, he did not assign a major role to Europe in the postwar world. He would have preferred that the United States not meddle in European affairs, leaving that chore to the British. A firm believer in the Monroe Doctrine, he would not tolerate European interference in the Western Hemisphere any more than his predecessors had.

The United States was to Roosevelt not only different but unique. He shared with his distant cousin Theodore a faith in America's "manifest destiny," as he frequently made clear to Europeans. But Franklin Roosevelt was at the same time a politician who possessed, to a supreme degree, the politician's ability to seduce, cajole, and even intimidate. He never forgot that one needs people to win an election. And "people" in the United States also meant immigrants and descendants of immigrants whose intellectual rejection of the Old World was often accompanied by a sentimental attachment to it. In this respect Roosevelt was no exception. Even though his family had been established in the United States for over three centuries, he took great pride in his Dutch ancestry. Four times he took the oath of office on a Dutch Bible, and passages from it were read at the Saint James Church in Hyde Park, New York, where he was a warden.

Many Americans shared Roosevelt's ambivalence about Europe. Their attachment to their countries of origin was not politically motivated, for had they agreed with the policies in force, they would not have left. Rather, they valued their homeland's cultural heritage. No politician could afford to ignore this political reality; no candidate for office could ever hope to carry New York City, for example, who did not sing the praises of Italy's culture, history, and traditions. Such flattery was and is a political necessity, whether or not it also reflects a candidate's true sentiments. Roosevelt himself was not averse to using these tactics and, as we shall see, some of his most unfortunate foreign policy decisions were made in view of their impact upon certain national minorities.

Did Roosevelt take this tack with the French population in America, even though their electoral impact was minimal? No one can say for sure, of course, but the possibility cannot be excluded. The French in the United States were nearly all Roman Catholic and generally quite conservative. Roosevelt might have considered the influential Roman Catholic hierarchy when dealing with them. The French had also exerted a great deal of cultural and political influence in Latin America, where the Napoleonic Code was still widely in force. The Good Neighbor policy toward Latin America was one of Roosevelt's top foreign policy priorities. The student of U.S. history might have not been indifferent to the role France had played in helping defeat the British in the War of Independence. Anti-British sentiment was very much alive in the 1930s because of historical recollections and Irish propaganda. All of these might have been contributing factors to Roosevelt's interest in the French, but we can only advance suppositions. To approach the truth, we have to examine Roosevelt's actions during the twelve years of his presidency.

ROOSEVELT
AND *THE*
FRENCH

A Young Man in Search of France

Franklin Delano Roosevelt was the product of his family, his social environment, and his time. He was born to a wealthy and socially prominent family at a time when huge fortunes were being built. His father, James, had amassed his fortune in the China trade. He then settled on an estate on the Hudson River, where many of New York's most affluent families also had homes, decorated, often with questionable taste, with European furniture, paintings, and arras. In the Victorian age, propertied society in the United States was very puritanical, far more so than its European counterpart. Frequent trips to Europe often lasting several months were *de rigueur*, with a net preference for England and France. For the socially fashionable, contact with the native population was usually restricted to the wealthy and the aristocratic, the lower classes working as domestics. Americans abroad were aware that they were representatives of a distinct breed, superior in wealth but inferior in culture. They were the "innocents abroad," and the aura of culture that enveloped the Old World could not fail to impress them.

The Roosevelts and the Delanos, Franklin's mother's family, visited Europe every year. Before or after a stay in Germany the family would usually make a stopover in France to visit with "Auntie Doe" (Dora Forbes), a sister of Franklin's mother, Sara, who had settled with her husband in Paris. In 1867 Sara stayed in Paris, in an apartment her father had rented overlooking the Bois de Boulogne, at the time of her sister's wedding. Sara was then twelve years old, and the Paris Universal Exposition had drawn to the City of Lights many of Europe's potentates. From her window she admired the resplendent uniforms of Tsar Alexander II of Russia and Emperor Wilhelm I of Prussia, who was accompanied by his prime minister, Count Otto von Bismarck. Sara would continue to visit her sister almost every year. After her son became president, she was coddled by presidents of the French Third Republic, prime ministers, and ambassadors, but she always managed to hold her own thanks to her irrepressible character. "You might as well have asked me to stop the flow of the Niagara as asked me to see to it that she did not accept a number of invitations. . . . She is, of course, having an immense personal success," Ambassador William Bullitt wrote the president.[1]

During a visit to Versailles, Sara was received by the mayor, G. Henry-Haye, who was to become the Vichy ambassador to Washington. She toured the Cincinnati Museum established in the old pavilion of the royal ministry of foreign affairs. "She manifested a great emotion in traversing the sumptuous gallery leading to the room where the diplomatic act consecrating the independence of the United States was signed," Henry-Haye wrote.[2]

Sara was still in Paris when France went to war in 1939 and, so the story goes, expected her son to send a warship to fetch her. She left, instead, on 24 August from Le Havre on the SS *Washington*, along with Roosevelt's son John and his wife, Anne. In her slightly accented French, she told the press: "I am quite upset about leaving France after a very interesting visit. I am very grateful to everyone who has done so much for me and shown me all those beautiful things." A reporter asked, "Mrs. Roosevelt, what do you think of the international situation?" She replied, in English, "I can only hope for peace, but I must say that after seeing that wonderful military review yesterday, I think that France is well prepared for anything and I can only hope and pray that it will be peace." What were her impressions of France? *"Pour moi, c'est toujours la belle France, sympathique et loyale."*

Franklin had been dearly loved by both his parents, and that love plus a solid religious faith had imbued him with a sense of mission and a serene, confident character. Butlers, servants, and nurses assured him of comfort and a well-regulated life. He delighted in the sea, stamp collecting, and U.S. history. He went riding with his father, who deeply influenced his character and sense of purpose, and was overindulged by a domineering mother whose will he never allowed her to impose upon him.

Like a proper upper-class American, Franklin learned French as a child from governesses brought over from Europe. Jeanne Sandoz, a Swiss governess hired in 1891, was his favorite. He was Frankie to her, and she stayed with the family until 1893, when she returned to Europe to marry. Franklin never lost touch with her. From the White House, in 1933, he wrote her: "The lessons in French which I began at that time stood me in good stead during all those years, and here in Washington it is a great pleasure to be able to converse with the members of the Diplomatic Corps in a common tongue." Two years later, he wrote her again: "I think it will interest you to know that it has been the greatest help to me to be able to speak French—not only during the war days when I was in France and Belgium, but also here in Washington where I meet so many foreigners and diplomats who cannot speak English." A niece of Mlle. Sandoz wrote to Roosevelt in 1935 to say that all through her childhood she had heard of the remarkable youth whom [Aunt Jeanne] had taught at Hyde Park, and for a long time there was a photograph of him in my father's stamp album, a photo that was most delightful to our eyes, for my brothers wore overalls and their feet were bare. But now and then Father would let us see the boy with such fine clothes, and such neat hair. "A fine gentleman," my father would remark. "And don't forget that a Swiss woman was his teacher, and a Sandoz."[3]

Franklin was taught at home by tutors until he was fourteen, and then in 1896 he was sent to Groton, a private boys' academy of distinction. He was not a particularly outstanding student. His main interests were socializing and athletics. Much of his correspondence with his family refers to frequent invitations to the homes of socially prominent families. He played tennis and golf with their children and took an active part in school sports. He saw Sir Henry Irving's Lyceum Theater production of Victorien Sardou's *Robespierre*, which delighted him. Shortly afterward he himself turned to the theater: "I decided to try for a main part, in which I have to appear constantly, have little to say, but lots of acting. . . . My chief work is kissing the heroine (I am her cousin) and thus I enrage the hero, her fiancé. The name of the play is *Wedding March*, a translation of the French *Un chapeau de paille d'Italie*, by Michel and Labiche."

Franklin's grades were never more than average, his main interests being U.S. and naval history. He spoke French and German fairly well and had no trouble passing the exams in those languages. To improve his knowledge of French, he asked his parents to send him a book on French composition by one Van Daeal. He must have applied himself diligently, for his first semester's grade in French was 95 out of a possible 100. To show off his knowledge, he would send letters to his family in a mixture of French, German, and English.

At that time the Dreyfus Affair was tearing France apart. Roosevelt proposed to write an article on the subject for the school paper, the *Grotonian*. On 23 April 1899, he reminded his parents to send him the *Dreyfus Case*, most likely a reference to the book by Frederick C. Conybeare. Two days later he wrote: "The Dreyfus case and the nail brush have come and thanks for them. I am sorry to say that Archie Brown does not want an article on Dreyfus, as he says they had one about a year ago."

Franklin's parents must have sent him copies from Europe of the *Paris Herald* and *The Times*, for he commented that both seemed like old friends. In 1899 he was working hard to accumulate the number of credits required for admission to Harvard and preparing for his entrance exams. He was successful. He wrote his parents, "I forgot to mention that I got at least 3, and possibly 4 or 5 honors in my preliminaries, in French, Advanced French, German, and maybe two others which I do not yet know of."

In the fall of 1900, Franklin entered Harvard, where his French courses were naturally more demanding. They included French prose and poetry (which covered the works of Corneille, Racine, Molière, Hugo, de Musset, and Balzac), French literature, and medieval and modern European history. He studied no

French in his sophomore and junior years, and his history and government courses dealt exclusively with the United States and Great Britain. He must have kept up his French on his own, for while aboard the SS *Celtic* on his way to Europe he informed his "dearest Mummy" (24 July 1903) that he had read 150 pages of *Notre Dame de Paris*. During his senior year at Harvard, Franklin took no French but studied the history of Continental Europe from the Peace of Utrecht and the history of Germany from the Reformation to the close of the Thirty Years' War. He also took a one-semester course in U.S. history, "The Development of the West," taught by Frederick Jackson Turner, whose work *The Frontier in American History* had a deep influence on future historians.

While still at Harvard Franklin became engaged to his distant cousin, Anna Eleanor Roosevelt, daughter of Theodore Roosevelt's younger brother. They were married on 17 March 1905.

A delayed honeymoon took the couple to Europe in June. Following a brief stay in London, they arrived in Paris, a city they both knew well, Franklin from his summers abroad with his parents, Eleanor from the time she had been a pupil of Mlle. Marie Souvestre, founder of an exclusive finishing school in England. Eleanor's report cards had shown a history of lively interest in French: "She works admirably in French and history and is the first out of a class of nine"; she "works at French with much intelligence and taste," "works with application," and is "well advanced."[4] She spoke French fluently, and her affection for France was sincere.

Eleanor's first concern in Paris was shopping: "A cloak and dress, a cloth skirt and coat, very dressy. Then we went to Combe and Levy and ordered thousands of dollars' worth of linen, 8 doz. tablecloths, 6 napkins, 1/2 doz. pillow cases and a handkerchief, all very attractive and full of holes, or *à jour* as they say here." The newlyweds visited various dressmakers, where "Eleanor got a dozen or so new dresses and two more cloaks and Franklin bought his wife lovely furs." One evening they went to the Opéra Comique to see *Manon*, which they found "very delightful and well rendered." The following day they visited the Alcazar on the Champs Elysées, "very funny and very vulgar." While Eleanor was shopping, Franklin went rummaging around old bookshops. He especially sought old books dealing with the U.S. Navy, first editions, and the then-fashionable miniature books.

After a trip to Venice and the Dolomites, the couple returned to France, staying at St. Moritz. "This place is lovely," Eleanor wrote her mother-in-law. "Franklin says it's the loveliest place we've seen yet." On their way to Germany, Eleanor began reading "a French book by Anatole France, but he occasionally disgusts me so that I have to stop, and yet it is a mild and proper book in French, devoted so far to the problems of our future life!" They returned again to Paris, staying this time at the Imperial Hotel, where Franklin learned he had failed two exams. (He was then studying law at Columbia University.) They shopped for socks at the Bon Marché and visited the Sainte Chappelle, Notre Dame, the Pantheon, St. Etienne, and Versailles. At the Comédie Française they saw *Le dé-*

pit amoureux and *Andromaque*, "both well given and the latter quite marvelous." Eleanor commented, "There is really nothing like an old classic and the French language to bring one to the highest pitch of excitement, is there?" A trip to Fontainebleau, an evening at the Théâtre Français to hear *Le Barbier de Seville* ("Wonderfully given and so distinct that even I could understand it"), three hours at the Louvre ("much interested in the Musée de la Marine, recently opened"), more shopping, more books – some "very handsome French historical works" left behind to be bound – and then on to London, where Franklin went off to his tailor. "We've had the most wonderful time possible," Eleanor wrote.

During their trip the Roosevelts behaved like typical upper-class American honeymooners, making the rounds of shops, museums, theaters, and so forth. They visited with friends and relatives and did not attempt to make friends among the French. Information about their trip can be gathered solely from correspondence with Franklin's mother, and quite possibly the young couple only mentioned things of interest to her. Yet their lack of contact with the French people, other than necessary business exchanges, seems to have been the rule rather than the exception.

Franklin Roosevelt returned to France in 1918 in an official capacity as assistant secretary of the navy. As a member of the Wilson administration, he dealt frequently with the French, as the historian Frank Freidel recounts:

A French mission came to the United States, not at all sure how much it could get, and first learned from Roosevelt that it could demand a great deal. The head of the mission was a rather touchy former premier, René Viviani; the naval representative was Vice Admiral Chocheprat, but Marshal Joffre, renowned in America as the hero of the first battle of the Marne, attracted most of the attention. Roosevelt was assigned to meet the French at Hampton Roads, and bring them up the Potomac on the presidential yacht, *Mayflower*. In consequence, he had "twenty-four hours of quite intimate conversation" with them before they reached Washington or saw anyone else. "My outstanding impression was that none of them had any real idea of what America was going to do to help in the war," he recalled. "The situation which they had left at home was a desperate one, and while of course they anticipated all kinds of financial and manufacturing and foodstuffs assistance from us, they had no information as to the amount of military or naval assistance they could expect. When I told Viviani and Joffre that we expected to go into the military and naval operations on the largest possible scale they seemed impressed and intensely gratified. As a matter of fact that was the primary object of their visit – to bring word back to France as to the exact military and naval help they could count on.[5]

Roosevelt's mission to France was to inspect stockyards, gather information, and enquire into any matters he deemed necessary. He sailed with his immediate staff on 9 July from Brooklyn aboard the USS *Dyer*, a newly commissioned destroyer. Other members of his staff sailed three days later on the HMS *Olympic*, a British admiralty transport. After stopovers at the Azores and in England, Roosevelt arrived in Paris and stayed at the Hôtel Crillon. His arrival had been preceded by a very warm letter of introduction to the minister of the navy from Capitaine de Frégate Blanpré, naval attaché at the French embassy in Washington:

Some very powerful forces within the Navy had somewhat feared the personality of Mr. Roosevelt, finding him very attractive and very removed. Up until now they had been able to block this trip that Mr. Roosevelt had wanted to make for a long time. However, thanks to President Wilson personally, Mr. Roosevelt finally won his case.

The letter went on:

Mr. Roosevelt is young, just 38, and a cousin of President Theodore Roosevelt. Although he has much of the keenness, generosity and broad ideas of his cousin, he is nevertheless distant from him, for he is a democrat and in this capacity is a member of the Cabinet. As Assistant Secretary of the Navy, he is in charge of the organization of the dockyards, administration, labor and salary issues. He has very little influence over purely military topics.

He was always extremely pro-Allied. Even before the declaration of war, he didn't hide his impatience over the slowness of President Wilson's decisions, nor over the inadequacy of the preparation to join the war. He felt U.S. participation was inevitable. As early as January 1917, I had very typical conversations with him about this.

Mr. Roosevelt is extremely personable, and he speaks French with ease. His home has always been open to all our officers. I know that our admirals particularly appreciate the attention he has given them. I therefore request that he be given an especially cordial welcome in Paris. He is most deserving of it, given his utter devotion to our cause. He will probably be called upon to play a considerable role in politics.

Other French naval officers described Roosevelt in similarly enthusiastic terms. On a visit to Washington in 1917, Admiral Grasset had written that Roosevelt, like his uncle Theodore, was a "convinced and active partisan of the immediate intervention on our coasts. He does not hide his sympathies in regard to France and I have found in him the best backing to support my requests."[6] Roosevelt's direct boss, Josephus Daniels, considered Roosevelt a "dangerous, war-mad lunatic."[7]

Captain Blanpré's letter of introduction, with its prophetic words about Roosevelt's future, could not fail to have a considerable effect on the French leaders. Copies were forwarded to the president, the premier, and the ministers of war and foreign affairs.[8]

Before undertaking his assigned tasks Roosevelt decided to visit the front. His French drivers consistently ignored orders to reduce speed from 85 kilometers to 60 kilometers an hour. "He says 'oui Monsieur' and does so for just three minutes before resuming 85 kilometers." Roosevelt was taken through recent war zones, defended mostly by the British.[9] On his first evening in Paris he was invited to dinner by Admiral de Bon, chief of the general naval staff. "One of the most delightful Frenchmen I have ever met," Roosevelt wrote.[10] The following day Roosevelt saw Minister of the Navy Georges Leygues. At the ministry he was impressed by the fact that the tapestry had been replaced with damask; in London or Washington the wall would have been left bare. "It is the same spirit," he commented,

which enabled the French during the "touch and go" days of 1914, when the government had gone to Bordeaux and the Germans were literally outside the gates, to keep on with the planting of the flower beds in the Tuileries and the repairing and cleaning of the streets. They seem to lose their heads even less than the Anglo-Saxons – very different from what we thought four years ago. It is this spirit that kept every village official in his own little village when the Germans overran northern France. Even though half or three-quarters of the population had fled southward, M. le Maire and M. le Curé were always at their posts.[11]

It is important to keep in mind these impressions of a courageous and fearless France, for they help explain the frightful disappointment Roosevelt suffered when the France he had so admired collapsed, physically and morally, in 1940. They also offer insight into Roosevelt's view of France once he became president.

After paying his respects to the minister of foreign affairs, Roosevelt met President and Mme. Poincaré at the Elysée Palace at a luncheon for forty people. "On the whole I thought the whole entertainment very much like similar ones at the White House except that here the wines were perfect of their kind and perfectly served." Later in the afternoon he called on Premier Georges Clemenceau.

I knew at once I was in the presence of the greatest civilian in France. He did not wait for me to advance to meet him at his desk, and there was no formality such as one generally meets. He almost ran forward to meet me and shook hands as if he meant it; grabbed me by the arm and walked me over to his desk and sat me down about two inches away. He is only 77 years old, and people say he is getting younger every day. He started off with no polite remarks because they were unnecessary; asked me three or four definite questions about our naval production and what I thought of the effect of the submarine campaign on the troop transportation. He seemed delighted at the present rate of progress and I told him that I was over here solely to learn how to make everything move even faster.[12]

After a "hair-raising description of the horrors left by the Boche in his retreat," the premier "spoke of an episode he had seen while following just behind the advance – a Poilu and a Boche still standing partly buried in a shell hole, clinched in each other's arms, their rifles abandoned, and the Poilu and the Boche were in the act of trying to bite each other to death when a shell had killed both"; and as Clemenceau told him this, "he grabbed me by both shoulders and shook me with a grip of steel to illustrate his words, thrusting his teeth forward toward my neck."

The following day Roosevelt met with Marshal Joffre at the Ecole Militaire. "He seemed very glad to see me and I came within an inch of getting my 'accolade.' I have escaped this charming little ceremony so far." The conversation turned to a visit to Washington the marshal had made in May 1917. The decision whether to send a large U.S. force to France had then hung in the balance. "Of course we did not talk much about the military operations for the marshal is not very much a part of that just now, but I think he felt, and rightly so, that only a small part of the million and a quarter Americans now in France would be here had it not been for his mission at the outbreak of the war."[13] A signed photograph of Marshal Joffre still sits on top of the fireplace in the Roosevelts' living room at Hyde Park.

On Sunday, 4 August, Roosevelt and his staff left for the front in three cars. Along the way they passed French troops heading to the front and German prisoners being moved to the rear. The Germans "did not impress me as being physically unfit, but there is an awful contrast between the amount of intelligence in their faces compared with the French Poilus." (Roosevelt usually referred to a French soldier as Poilu and a German soldier as a Boche or a Hun, both derogatory epithets.) Also encountered were refugees returning to their homes.

They went with big carts drawn by a cow or an ox and a calf trotting behind, bedding, chickens, household goods and children and sometimes a grandmother, piled on top, all of them taking it perfectly calmly, remembering always their good fortune in having gotten away before the arrival of the Boche, ready to start in again even from the ground up, but constantly impressing upon their children what the Boche has done to Northern France in these four years.[14]

The war had been in progress for five years, and "there is just such quiet determination in France to see this thing through to victory or to go down fighting as there was in the beginning. . . . These people show for the first time a complete confidence in the outcome." On his way to the front Roosevelt saw the path of destruction the war had left—homes in ruin, bridges blown up. The Americans had performed well, the Bois de Belleau having been rebaptized Bois de la Brigade de Marine in their honor. Roosevelt wanted to get closer to the front, instead of visiting safe areas according to the U.S. naval attaché's plan. "From now on for four days I ran the trip, especially as I had discovered that the plan called for late rising, easy trips, and plenty of bombed houses thirty miles or so behind the front."

To reach the Bois de Belleau, Roosevelt's party threaded its way past

water-filled shell holes and thence up the steep slopes over outcropping rocks, overturned boulders, downed trees, hastily improvised shelter pits, rusty bayonets, broken guns, emerging ration tins, hand grenades, discarded overcoats, rain-stained love letters, crawling lines of ants, and many little mounds, some wholly unmarked, some with a rifle stuck down in the earth, some with a helmet, and some, too, with a whittled cross with a tag of wood or wrapping paper hung over it and in a pencil scrawl an American name.

The Marines had to make their advance under extremely heavy fire. Very often food and ammunition could not be brought up, the wounded could not be brought out, the detachment could not maintain contact, and the only sure thing was fighting, without rest or sleep. The Marines had finally cleared the forest of forces three times greater than they.[15]

Crossing more devastated villages and fields, Roosevelt and his party got to within three miles of the front lines. "It is quite evident that we are on the battlefield. To our sensitive naval noses the smell of dead horses is not only evident, but very horrid. These army people do not seem to notice it at all." On the way to Château Thierry, they passed French soldiers heading toward the rear for rest. "The men looked pretty thoroughly tired and were trudging along at the same rate as the slow moving transport animals, but these Poilus after many days of constant fighting and shell fire still looked awake and intelligent, very different from the stolid, stupid look in the faces of the German prisoners, whom we also passed in small groups."

On 6 August Roosevelt reviewed the grounds of the decisive Battle of Verdun.

The first thing that met our eyes on one of the walls was the memorable original signboard which was posted near the entrance to the citadel during the siege, and on which, for the French people, will sum up for all time their great watchword of four years – "Ils ne passeront pas." Here too were representations of what the advance of Verdun had meant; the Legion of Honor conferred on the city and the great "Book of Privileges," in which statesmen of all nations had written their appreciation.

And then came the description of the battlefield:

For a few moments it didn't look like a battlefield; for there was little or nothing to see but a series of depressions and ridges, bare and brown and dead. Seen from even a short distance, there were no gashes on these hills, no trenches, no tree trunks, no heaps of ruins – nothing but brown earth for miles upon miles. When you look at the ground immediately about you, you realize that this earth has been churned by shells, and churned again. You see no complete shell holes, for one runs into another, and trench systems and forts and roads had been swallowed up in a brown chaos. This ridge . . . marks the final and successful stand of the French. In front is the "Valley of Death," and beyond it, crowning the second bridge, Fort Douamont. After the loss of the latter the French fell back into the valley and from then on, day after day, the Germans poured men down one side and the French the other, and it is possible that over a hundred thousand men were actually killed in this little stretch of valley.[16]

Marshal Pétain had been the hero of Verdun. Would Roosevelt's recollection of this memorable battle play a role in shaping U.S. wartime policies toward Vichy? All that is certain is that he was deeply marked by this experience.

Further visits to the front revealed additional scenes of desolation and death. After a brief visit to Rome to confer with Italian naval authorities, Roosevelt left for an inspection tour of U.S. facilities in France, including a powerful radio station the American navy was installing for the French government at Bordeaux. On 20 August he wrote Eleanor from Brest: "It has been a frightfully busy week – on the road each day from 6 A.M. to midnight – and we have done all manner of interesting things all the way from south of Bordeaux to here – all by auto, flying stations, ports, patrols, army stores, receptions, swims at French watering places, etc."[17]

One of Roosevelt's assistants, Livingston Davis, who accompanied him on the trip, wrote: "Such tireless energy as Roosevelt's I have never known, except perhaps in his kinsman, Theodore Roosevelt. I thought I was fairly husky, but I couldn't keep up with him. In a letter to my wife I complained bitterly that it didn't seem to matter to him what he ate, where or when he slept or if he even got a bath."[18]

At the end of his trip Roosevelt wired his "sincere gratitude and appreciation" to the minister of the navy for the assistance he had received. He also praised the friendship between the armed forces of their two countries, "which surely promises to contribute in no small degree toward the downfall of our common enemy and the successful termination of the war." In his reply, the minister of the navy, Georges Leygues, said: "I take great pleasure in thanking you at a time when the American Army has just won a brilliant victory and has liberated a piece of Lorraine soil. The feeling of gratitude that France holds for the U.S. at this historical moment goes toward both the American Army and Navy. Your naval units, whose courage and never ending labor we admire, are the auxiliaries of your magnificent soldiers."[19]

Roosevelt was to return to Paris at the time of the Versailles Peace Conference. Early in 1919 the president of the United States, eleven prime ministers, and twelve foreign ministers converged on Paris together with hundreds of other officials. Roosevelt had full authority to liquidate the U.S. Navy's large European installations. He sailed on 2 January 1919, accompanied by his wife. During the crossing they were saddened by the news of Theodore Roosevelt's death.

The Roosevelts stayed at the Ritz. "I never saw anything like Paris," Eleanor wrote her mother-in-law. "It is full beyond belief and one sees many celebrities and all one's friends! People wander the streets unable to find a bed and the prices are worse than New York for everything." After joining a French family for tea, Eleanor made the startling comment: "I've decided there is very little real beauty in France!"

During a luncheon with naval officers, Roosevelt noted that the conversation turned to the "attitude of the Germans in the Rhine provinces toward our troops. The Germans are being so nice to them. They are billeted in the best rooms, which is a contrast to French barns, and then the Germans are cleaner and bring them hot water, and the mayor had all the pre-war prices posted, and they cannot be changed more." Franklin gave a vivid account of the desolation and destruction he had viewed throughout France, which had obviously moved and saddened him. Eleanor wrote most of the letters home, which usually dealt with gossip, meetings with friends, luncheons and dinners, and clothing purchases for herself and the children. She seemed surprisingly little affected by the actual situation in Paris and the failure of Wilson's initiatives. "I got 6 pairs of gris pearl gloves and I have your bags, but I am so afraid they won't be what you wanted. Mrs. Meyer and Julia Brambilla are here, and they asked me to tea so I went at five and found Janet Auchincloss and we had a very nice time and Mrs. Meyer was sweet." Most letters contained page after page of such chatty remarks. It is regrettable that during this trip Franklin Roosevelt neither kept a diary nor had the time to do much writing home. Consequently, there is little record of how he perceived the Versailles Peace Conference, one of the most decisive events in modern history, which was to cause disappointment both in the United States and in Europe and which was to give rise to many of the problems Roosevelt was to face as president. On 15 February the Roosevelts sailed for home aboard the SS *George Washington* in the company of President and Mrs. Wilson. "The President is not very flattering about the French government and people," Eleanor noted.[20]

Roosevelt paid another brief visit to France in 1931 when his mother fell ill. With his son, Elliott, who had accompanied him, he went to Mareuil without even asking for directions. "We found the roads, the slope, the bushes, the wall and the broken roof [of a barn], exactly as I had described them, after 13 years. There was a new section of wall, and too, the new tile just where the hole had been." On 11 December 1944, Roosevelt would dictate a sequel. Referring to the episode in which the American gun crew had startled the visitors, he said: "After we had accepted the laughter of their gun crews we went into the thicket and the C.O. trained them [the French 155s] on a German-held railway junction about 12 miles north. I pulled the lanyards, and a spotting plane reported that one shell fell just short of, and the other directly on, the junction and it seemed to create much confusion. I will never know how many, if any, Huns I killed!"[21]

2

European Statesmen: "A Bunch of Bastards"

Adolf Hitler's rise to power was in full swing when Roosevelt became president. Roosevelt's European policies were dominated by the German question, and his attitude toward France cannot be understood without reference to the Nazi peril. During his first term in office Roosevelt was too absorbed in domestic issues to pay much attention to foreign affairs, but Germany was a constant concern from the start. It can even be said that for him Germany became a lifelong obsession.

Roosevelt's hostility to Hitlerism and the Junkers, the German military class responsible for three European wars in less than a century, dates back to the time when, as a youth, he spent several months each year at a spa in Bad Neuheim, where his father, James, underwent treatment for a heart condition. The family shared his antagonism, to the point that his mother objected to "feeding with German swine," preferring the company of British friends.[1] During his summer months in Bad Neuheim he received instruction in military reading and topography at a local public school. The discipline he received there, he would later recall, had given him his first glimpse of the German potential for aggressive militarism.

In August 1914, on learning that Germany had invaded France, he had written: "Rather than long, drawn-out struggle I hope that England will join in and with France and Russia force peace *at Berlin*."[2] Roosevelt was convinced that had the Allies dealt with Germany decisively then, the world would have avoided the Nazi threat. Dissatisfied with the way World War I ended, he was indignant that the Germans had escaped the penalties for their crimes.

In addition to his political beliefs, a profound religious conviction motivated Roosevelt's revulsion for nazism. Religion was an essential dimension of his personality, a means to go "from worse to better" and of "progress that was inevita-

ble because of God's will."[3] From this religious perspective Roosevelt saw Nazi
Germany as the incarnation of evil, and with evil no compromise was possible.
The Danish theologian Søren Kierkegaard, who explored the demonic in men
who abandon the path of righteousness, provided Roosevelt with an explanation of Nazi behavior. "Kierkegaard," the president told Secretary of Labor
Frances Perkins, "explains the Nazis to me as nothing else ever has. I have never
been able to make out why people who are obviously human could behave like
that. They are human, yet they behave like demons. Kierkegaard gives you an
understanding of what it is in man that makes it possible for these Germans to
be so evil."[4]

Roosevelt had little interest in political ideology and tended to see the world
in terms of good and evil. He tended to speak in biblical terms of "peace and
good will among men." "If civilization is to survive the Principles of the Prince
of Peace must be restored." "Storms from abroad directly challenge three institutions indispensable to Americans, now as always. The first is religion. It is the
source of the other two – democracy and international good faith." "Today the
whole world is divided between human slavery and human freedom – between
pagan brutality and the Christian ideal."

European understanding of democracy derives from the revolutionary tradition that had nothing to do with religion or the Bible. To Europeans, democracy
is an ideology, not an article of religious faith. In later years they would find the
American approach confusing and wonder whether Americans understood
what the real issues were. An almost theological, rather than historically motivated, aversion to nazism explains Franklin Roosevelt's relationship to Joseph
Stalin – the other world leader, he felt, who had seen through Adolf Hitler. It also
explains his urging at the Teheran and Yalta conferences that Germany be returned to a pre-Bismarckian confederation of states, his initial acceptance of the
Morgenthau plan to reduce Germany to a pastoral country deprived of heavy
industry, and, finally, his advocacy of Germany's unconditional surrender.

Roosevelt never made a secret of his sentiments. French ambassador André de
Laboulaye, a friend of the Roosevelts' for over twenty years, once noted the
"loathing he had, and not just for Hitler's Germany, but for all Germans."[5] During a fireside chat on 29 December 1940, his voice shaking with anger, he said
the Nazis have "in their background the concentration camps and the servants
of God in chains. . . . Shooting and chains and concentration camps are not
simply transient tools but the very altar of modern dictatorship."[6] As German
atrocities became known in all their horror, he warned Henry Morgenthau: "We
have to be tough with Germany, and I mean the German people not just the
Nazis or you have to treat them in such a manner so they just can't go on repro-
ducing people who want to continue the way they have in the past."[7] And in a 26
August 1944 note to Henry Lewis Stimson he wrote, "The German people as a
whole must have it driven home to them that the whole nation has been engaged in a lawless conspiracy against the decencies of modern civilization."

Roosevelt read all of Hitler's speeches and was aware of the dictator's intentions. On the inside leaf of an English translation of *Mein Kampf*,[8] he wrote in 1933: "This translation is so expurgated as to give a wholly false view of what Hitler really is or says – the German original would make a different story." Thomas Mann, the celebrated German author living in exile in the United States, was the private dinner guest of President and Mrs. Roosevelt at the White House on 30 June 1935. In a letter to Herman Hesse, he wrote:

But pacifism is a strange thing. It does not seem to be the truth under all circumstances. For a time it was a mask for fascist sympathies; in 1938 "Munich" was the despair of all friends of peace; I passionately longed for war against Hitler and "agitated" for it; and I shall be eternally grateful to Roosevelt, the born and conscious enemy of l'Infâme, for having maneuvered his all important country into it with consummate skill. When I left the White House after my first visit, I knew Hitler was lost.[9]

With France's heroic resistance to German ambitions during World War I fresh in his mind, Roosevelt again counted on France to stand up to Hitler in the 1930s. In a private meeting with Paul Claudel, serving at the time as the French ambassador to the United States, the president-elect expressed his affection for France and his desire to eliminate problems. In February 1933 he announced in a joint communiqué "Franco-American collaboration on world issues." Roosevelt and Claudel agreed that a closing of the ranks among the world's three great democratic and conservative nations, in opposition to the forces of change and destruction, had become necessary and urgent. "A close entente between England, France and America represents a needed warning to turbulent neighbors" and the only way to curb German and Japanese ambitions. Leaving his post and coming to say farewell, Roosevelt told Claudel: "The situation in Europe is alarming. Hitler is a madman and his advisers, some of whom I know personally, are even crazier than he. France cannot disarm now and no one will ask her to do so." The last sentence was underlined in Claudel's 5 April message to Foreign Minister Joseph Paul-Boncour.

Roosevelt's fresh attitude toward France brought about a change of atmosphere that was welcomed by the French, who had for some time been facing a negative world opinion. Herbert Hoover, for example, had felt for France an unmitigated scorn that he made no effort to hide. "I am not exaggerating," Claudel informed Paris late in 1932, "when I say that the state of American opinion is worse now than it has been for a long time. . . . Its origin dates back to the vote in the [French] parliament over the American debt. . . Far more serious is the lack of understanding in America with respect to France, and this has been going on for a long time."[10] A negative attitude evidently prevailed in other countries as well, for Ambassador Peretti della Rocca complained in December 1932 that "France gets truly a ghastly press in all countries. . . . We are portrayed as overflowing with gold, imperialists, corrupt, having no respect for treaties nor for word of honor. . . . One advocates boycotting our products, our books, our sea lanes. One discourages tourists by warning them they will be

badly treated." Sharing this concern, the French Ministry of Foreign Affairs instructed its agents abroad to "organize more forcefully action against the systematic defamation campaign of which France is the target in most foreign
countries."

Roosevelt's friendly overtures to France were welcomed for their candor as
well as for their representation of a break with past patterns. Claudel was elated
by his conversations with the president-elect. In a dispatch to Paris, he underlined "the tone of sincerity, and the desire to go as far as possible in our direction that his words conveyed. This friendly attitude with his open and cheerful
countenance was a pleasant contrast to the hostile and cold approach of President Hoover who of late hardly bothered to conceal his feelings toward our
country." Claudel added a word of caution, however: "We would be mistaken not
to take into account certain factors [a probable reference to the debt issue]
which prevent one from being too optimistic."

This rosy picture belongs to the period during which Roosevelt was preparing
to take over as president of the United States. Once Roosevelt was installed in
the White House, his attention was almost exclusively given to the tremendous
task of dealing with the Depression. Foreign policy of necessity took a back seat,
except for foreign initiatives likely to have an impact upon Roosevelt's program
of national reconstruction. For the New Deal to succeed, stability abroad was
also necessary—a stability threatened by obstacles to the free flow of trade
among nations and the crushing cost of armaments, both of which were politically and economically disastrous for all concerned.

Roosevelt was not particularly upset by France's failure to pay its war debt. He
had made a number of suggestions advantageous to France, but the country's
unwillingness to settle was politically motivated, and negotiations reached an
impasse. Although the controversy was bothersome, it was not a serious obstacle to friendly relations. A far graver issue was the harmonization of monetary
policies, without which worldwide economic stability was threatened.

An early measure by Roosevelt—taking the United States off the gold standard—caused serious strains with France. The celebrated British economist
John Maynard Keynes thought the president had been "magnificently right," but
the French, who held to the gold standard tenaciously, were indignant. The London Economic Conference (June–July 1933), far from proving the instrument of
harmonization for which it had been called, became the scene of a bitter confrontation, with France trying to sabotage the proceedings when it could not get
its way. As the controversy switched to the political arena, the executive officer
of the U.S. delegation, William Bullitt, described the French attitude as "obnox-
ious" and called French delegate Georges Bonnet "as cooperative as a rattle-
snake."

On 8 July Bullitt urged the president to "make it clear to the French that we
feel that they have rejected with contempt our efforts to collaborate with them
in foreign affairs, and that we should back such a statement by appropriate
actions." He added, "The whole French attitude toward us at the moment is one

of contempt and I think it would be healthy to let them know that our personal affection for them will not prevent us from refusing to support them in any way if they continue to behave as they are now behaving."

The London experience caused great consternation. Bullitt drew the conclusion that the United States "can do little in Europe and should keep out of European squabbles and that our future lies in the Americas and the Far East."[11] And Secretary of the Treasury Morgenthau, who would work hard through the years to stabilize the democracies' finances, had by that time reached the conclusion that France was a "bankrupt, fourth-rate power."[12]

The United States was badly prepared for the conference, and conflicts of authority within the U.S. delegation caused confusion. The impact of this situation upon public opinion, which ignored the details but saw emphasized U.S. isolation amidst European criticisms, was strongly negative. As Sumner Welles pointed out, "the sessions of the conference aroused a widespread hostility to the United States government which should at all costs, in those crucial days, have been avoided. . . . Foreign attacks upon the United States because of the breakdown of the conference increased American distaste for any form of international cooperation."[13] The French had been at the forefront of attacks on the United States, and Roosevelt was disappointed that his overtures had elicited such an unfriendly response. "It is important to keep in mind that Roosevelt's pro-French attitudes are exclusively due to his personal sentiments and those of a very small number of advisers," Claudel warned.[14]

Franco-American relations had gotten off to a bad start, compromising another program very close to Roosevelt's heart: the search for common ground concerning the arms race. The weighty issue of armaments caused political tension and economic disruption; it encouraged military adventurousness and economic autarchy; and it threatened a hard-won peace.

The issue of disarmament was to cause a great deal of misunderstanding between Roosevelt and the French. Paris was under the impression that Roosevelt, while appalled by the consequences of the arms race, paid little heed to its causes. The president apparently believed that irrespective of the causes, the arms race could only spell disaster. The only possible course of action, if peace was to be preserved, was disarmament and the strengthening of mutual confidence among nations through the expansion of international trade. Thus disarmament and world trade were the two recurring themes in Roosevelt's approach to Europe; however, they only caused confusion and did not contribute to France's determination to stand up to Hitler.

Roosevelt's foreign policies were dictated in the context of the domestic situation in the United States. In their efforts to secure Roosevelt's cooperation in implementing their policies, the French, as well as Europeans in general, failed to appreciate how far away their continent was from the conscience of Americans, how physical was the isolation that engendered isolationism. Nor were they sufficiently acquainted with the complex nature of the U.S. political scene: the opposing forces tearing the country apart; the president's efforts to achieve consensus; the split within his own cabinet between the advocates of an active foreign policy and those who feared that foreign entanglement would weaken the resolve to implement the New Deal; the impact of isolationism on the composition of the Congress; and the hostility of most of the press. Differing domestic considerations led the French and the Americans to see the same problems from different perspectives, and the synchronization of their resultant policies proved most difficult.

Pacifism was widespread in Europe, and isolationism was its U.S. counterpart. Both ideologies represented a refusal either to become involved in another country's problems or to face up to reality. Both engendered appeasement and, in France, an urge permeating society to come to terms with the dictators at almost any price. Were they not isolationist, however, Americans would not have followed had Roosevelt advocated a more aggressive foreign policy. As Roosevelt knew, Americans could take the reality of the world surrounding them only in small doses, a new dose not to be administered before the previous one had been digested. Acting before Americans were ready would have led to the kind of disaster Woodrow Wilson had faced when he tried to impose U.S. membership in the League of Nations upon an unwilling country and Congress. Indeed, Wilson's drama haunted Roosevelt throughout his presidency.

The 1930s produced a variety of disarmament plans. Roosevelt's consisted of three main points: (1) destruction of aged armaments, (2) suspension of new production for a three-year period, and (3) creation of an international control mechanism operating worldwide with U.S. participation. As the United States and the United Kingdom disposed of 75 percent of all raw materials essential to the war industry, receiving countries would be required to undertake not to use such materials for military purposes.[15]

The French position was that given the nature of nazism, they were entitled to permanent military superiority over the Germans. In April the Quai d'Orsay noticed to its dismay that none of the statements coming out of Washington bore out the president's assurance to Claudel that "no one will ask you to disarm," for that was precisely what the Americans were now asking. Ambassador de Laboulaye, Claudel's successor, assured Paris that the president was not asking France to disarm unilaterally, but did insist that all governments undertake radical measures to disarm, to reassure the masses and assist in balancing budgets.[16] Edouard Herriot, the distinguished French politician and parliamentarian who had visited with Roosevelt at the latter's invitation, informed Paris of his host's determination to work for an international organization dedicated to peace.[17] Roosevelt was already thinking of the project that was to become the United Nations.

A visit by a German envoy furnished Roosevelt with the opportunity to clarify his position on disarmament. To distract attention from their secret rearmament the Germans were loudly proclaiming their interest in disarmament. Early in May, Hitler sent Hjalmar Schacht, his economic wizard, to see the president and assure him of Germany's peaceful intentions. Roosevelt called the German delegate's attention to the situation in which Hitler had placed Germany: "You did so well . . . that no one can have any confidence in you." A proposal for German rearmament to match France's level was unacceptable: "You are for the moment at the bottom of the armament ladder. You must remain where you are. It is up to the other powers to take the progressive steps needed to come down to your level." Rejecting the argument that Germany felt threatened, the president believed that it was Germany that threatened its neighbors. "As to the security of Germany," he told Schacht, "trust me: I am prepared to guarantee a ten-year truce in which [Germany] can have confidence." De Laboulaye, who heard of the conversation from the president, commented that Washington's German policies had undergone a new orientation and no longer supported German claims, as they had in Hoover's time.[18]

Shortly after meeting with the German envoy, Roosevelt saw Morgenthau over lunch: "He [Roosevelt] greeted me in German. I asked him about Schacht, and he swung his arms around and said, 'Why, he is terrible. I am in an awful jam with Europe,' and jokingly remarked, 'I may have to call up the Army and the Navy as Great Britain and France respectively disown McDonald and Herriot. They are a bunch of bastards,' he said referring to European Statesmen."[19]

His reason for calling the French "bastards" was due in part to Roosevelt's irritation at their constant criticism of America's role at the Geneva Disarmament Conference. The French attitude, the president feared, could frustrate his efforts toward closer cooperation with European democracies and encourage further isolationism. The French, he told de Laboulaye, misunderstood his intentions for his disarmament plan, which was simply meant to ensure that Germany stayed disarmed. Should Germany proceed to rearm in defiance of his efforts, the European democracies would recover their freedom of action and, if need be, intervene militarily.[20]

Roosevelt's suggestion that German armament remain frozen and that France's armament be gradually reduced to the German level was rejected in Paris, for it implied equality of treatment between the two countries. France did not threaten the peace; the Nazis did, however, as the president was well aware. "It was not France that invaded Belgium," Premier Edouard Daladier told Norman Davis, an American delegate to the disarmament conference. "It was not French soldiers who behaved like *sauvages* in the occupied zones. A speech by Hitler is not sufficient to make us forget other speeches, nor his actions, nor his provocations."[21] The French pointed to their many suggestions at the conference, in particular a proposal to set up a control mechanism providing for inspection to guard against violations. If the mechanism worked smoothly for four years, and Germany did not rearm, other nations could then begin undertaking a disarmament program. No sooner had the British and the Americans accepted the French proposal than Germany withdrew from the conference. By a significant coincidence (if one keeps in mind future events), the German withdrawal occurred at the time Washington recognized the Soviet Union.

Convinced he was doing his utmost to preserve peace, Roosevelt resented the

French criticisms, and de Laboulaye found him bitter and hurt. "By a happy coincidence," the ambassador warned Paris, "the present president of the United States is, of all the presidents who preceded him, including George Washington, the one who has the strongest personal inclination for our country and all it represents. . . . That friendship is now disintegrating."[22]

Roosevelt was at times responsible for misunderstandings with the French because he sent out mixed signals. In September 1934, during a conversation with French minister of public works Etienne Flandin over lunch at Hyde Park, he mentioned how deeply developments in Germany worried him, since all information reaching Washington pointed to the Nazis' preparing for war. He hinted that under the circumstances the disarmament issue was no longer urgent.[23] After visiting with the president, Flandin went over to the State Department for a chat with Cordell Hull, who expounded on his favorite subject: "Conversations with Hull are almost exclusively focused on international trade. On everything else he is completely mum," the minister reported to Paris.

Flandin pointed to another subject causing concern and puzzlement for the French. According to the secretary of state, with Roosevelt in agreement, a country's best defense was not adequate armament but maximum development of international trade, the assumption being that obstacles to free trade represented a major cause for war. Hull's position was clarified in a State Department note to the British: "The Secretary feels, and feels very strongly, that a mere preparation for war is no way to prevent it, and no time should be lost in pressing forward the only possibility . . . of avoiding war, that is, to reestablish sound and substantial trade upon a firm basis of equality of treatment and exchange of opportunities for trade to the greatest extent each nation can possibly contribute."[24]

The Germans were not only rearming but relying on economic autarchy precisely to avoid having to rely on world trade. Secretary of the Interior Harold Ickes probably reflected the French point of view as well when he wryly noted that all Hull ever tried to do "in addition to his futile protests at continued encroachment by the dictators, was to negotiate reciprocal trade agreements. These were all right as far as they went, they might have led to something in ordinary times when peace was the principal preoccupation of nations of the world, but . . . with the world in a turmoil they were like hunting an elephant in the jungle with a fly swatter."[25]

One of the foundations of U.S. foreign policy in its approach to the world crisis was to act in concert with Great Britain.[26] London's timorous approach to foreign affairs, its readiness to compromise with the dictators, found a counterpart in the American determination to eschew foreign commitments, as demonstrated by Congress's refusal to let the United States join the International Court of Justice. The French considered this the first foreign policy defeat for the president.

Throughout the crisis caused by the Italian invasion of Ethiopia, the United States and Great Britain acted in unison, though electoral considerations also played a role in the United States. When hostilities broke out, Congress refused to grant Roosevelt the discretionary powers he had requested and on 21 August 1935 unanimously voted in the neutrality law. In accordance with that law, the president proclaimed the existence of a state of war between Italy and Ethiopia on 5 October and decreed an embargo on arms, ammunitions, other war instruments, and an assortment of raw materials. The ban did not include oil and other goods needed for waging war that Italy continued to receive in quantities well above peacetime levels. Roosevelt was upset that people could extract "blood money" from war; his heart went out to the Ethiopian victims of aggression; he rejoiced at every success of the Negus's troops – but he never forgot it was the Italians, not the Ethiopians, who delivered the vote in New York and elsewhere at election time. As the 1936 election neared, Italian-Americans were unusually active in support of their country of origin. Roosevelt followed the Geneva debates closely, but he warned Paris that the United States would not act in concert with the powers at the League of Nations.[27] Washington had done nothing to support collective security, and U.S. oil shipments had proved indispensable to the Italians, who could not have waged a war without them.

Even though the United States had failed a victim of aggression, and indirectly contributed to its demise, the selling out of Ethiopia caused an "immense deception" in Washington. De Laboulaye quoted Cordell Hull as saying, "Two great powers, members of the League, recognized being ready to accept the dismemberment of a country belonging to the same organization and to turn the pieces over to a third country, also a member of the League, as a reward for its aggression."[28] This sort of sermonizing tainted with hypocrisy did not go down well with the French.

Despite their domestic problems, Americans were becoming increasingly aware that the situation in Europe was threatening and that a response could not be avoided. Not only was Nazi arrogance a major cause for concern, but conditions within France seemed ominous. The country gave signs of being caught in a spiral of political and moral disintegration that bode ill for the future.

In a 13 February 1936 letter to Roosevelt, the U.S. ambassador to Paris, Jesse Isodor Straus, painted a devastating picture:

One must always remember that, if rumors and innuendos are to be believed, there is little honesty intellectual or moral among the politicians in France. Whether they are as dishonest as it is reported, I can of course not assert. The press is said to be, almost without exception, venial. Italian money is said to flow into some coffers in large amounts, Russian, German and Japanese into others. The signed articles of comment, criticism and opinion are in many instances said to be yieldful of munificent subsidies to the writers, of whom there are dozens in the many dailies and weeklies published in France. . . . It is a very dirty picture and as I see it, portends no very brilliant future for France. . . . Business here is rotten. . . . There is a surly attitude toward foreigners; one of injured innocence, strikingly apparent. There is an unwillingness to admit internal error and to seek to correct it. . . . [There] seems to me to be a fundamental misconception of a pernicious anemia that cannot be cured by applications of salves and other external medicaments. . . . The Chamber of Deputies with its 600 and odd members is a poor looking and bad acting national assembly. The members behave like a lot of naughty children in a nursery. . . . Many of the deputies hold four or five jobs, and I believe that each job . . . has some salary, honorarium or perquisite attached to it.

He concluded:

From all the above diatribe you may conclude that I am depressed. Not personally, but for France's future. . . . The atmosphere in Paris and in France is doleful. They look for a miracle man. . . . What does the future hold in store for France? It's anyone's guess. The French still proclaim their inventiveness, their integrity, their artistic sense . . . and their leadership in this, that and the other. . . . Something is bound to happen . . . unless they can, by the introduction of new blood, not only increase, but change the stature and character and mental make-up of the population.[29]

In his reply to Ambassador Straus, the president wrote that "in more pessimistic moments, I have of necessity come to believe, just as you do about France and the French future–yet I always say to myself that in previous parties France has always 'snapped out' of it. This optimism, I must confess, has little foundation because of several well-known incidents in the past one hundred and fifty years where revolution or its equivalent, and the emergence of some strong individual have proved the only salvation." Stressing that the crises of the past were much simpler than those the world faced in his own time, he added, "The armament race means bankruptcy or war–there is no possible way out from that statement."[30]

Straus countered that the French needed encouragement to stiffen their resolve, not unrealistic talk about disarmament. He urged "a new orientation of the United States policy regarding land disarmament in favor of the French thesis of need for actual security." He felt that a new approach

would create a most favorable impression on the French and perhaps make them more reasonable on other questions such as the debt and commercial matters. This question is vital above all others to the French and their public opinion deeply resents our constant pressure to get them to reduce their land armament. American policy has been too mystical and not realistic. It has been greatly influenced by pacifist opinion at home which does not understand the European political situation in the slightest.[31]

Straus had been very realistic in his assessment of France. He saw little chance of the country's "snapping out of it" unless radical changes (for which he saw no prospects) occurred. His implicit criticism of the president's policies was also to the point, for preaching disarmament and international trade would not encourage the democracies to stand up to the dictators. But perhaps by then France seemed beyond redemption.

The civil war that broke out in Spain in July 1936 was to cause new, more serious tensions in France. American attitudes before the conflict served to strengthen the positions of the many politicians in France ready to buy the dictators' goodwill through appeasement. Domestic considerations once more dictated far-from-honorable policies, as Eleanor Roosevelt was the first to recognize. The neutrality law invoked by Washington was intended to apply to hostilities between countries, not to an armed rebellion against a legitimate government; but Congress extended its provisions to include civil wars. The United States had a moral obligation to aid the government in Madrid, but the Roman Catholic hierarchy in the United States was solidly for Francisco Franco against his "godless opponents." The best the State Department could devise to uphold the rule of decency in international affairs was the policy of the "moral embargo." Roosevelt told Ickes that lifting such an embargo "would mean the loss of every Catholic vote next fall and that the Democratic members of Congress were jittery about it and didn't want it done." The cat was out of the bag, and, Ickes sadly concluded, it was the "mangiest, scabbiest cat ever." Roosevelt obviously assumed Roman Catholics always voted as a bloc. Diplomat Robert Murphy, himself a Catholic, commented that he could not "imagine any Roman Catholic president ever being as fascinated as was Roosevelt with the thought of the Church in world politics. . . . The President seemed to have exaggerated ideas of the bond existing between Catholics because of their religion."[32]

The consequence of these "exaggerated ideas" was disastrous. As Sumner Welles commented, "In the long history of the foreign policy of the Roosevelt administration there has been . . . no more cardinal error than the policy adopted during the civil war in Spain."[33] Too late did Roosevelt realize that appeasement was the road to war, not to peace. Years later, in 1940,

he volunteered the statement that he had made a great mistake in the manner of the Spanish embargo, that he was sorry that he had done this and that he would not do it again in similar circumstances. "But," he said, "not only England and France but the Low Countries and the Scandinavian countries urged us to take the position that we did on the embargo because they thought that it might prevent the spread of war."[34]

Shortly after writing his anguished letter to the president, Straus fell seriously ill and returned to the United States, where he died. On 25 August 1936 he was replaced by William C. Bullitt, whose contact with the French during the 1933 London Economic Conference had not been particularly friendly. Bullitt had spent a great deal of time in France, spoke the language well, and was a connoisseur of French wines.

From 1936 to 1940 Bullitt was the president's chief source of information on the situation in France. Roosevelt found him to be "mercurial." "The trouble with Bullitt," he stated, "is in the morning he will send me a telegram 'Everything is lovely,' and then he will go out to have lunch with some French official and I get a telegram that everything is going to hell." Yet Roosevelt kept Bullitt in Paris and Kennedy in London because he knew when to discount the information they cabled home. "The only thing that saves the information is I know my men."[35]

Bullitt's reports to the president contained some frequently recurring themes. He advocated a rapprochement between France and Germany as the only way to preserve peace. He urged that the United States not intervene if war broke out, for even if Germany were defeated, "the only gainers would be the Bolsheviks as there would be social revolution in every country in Europe and Communist regimes." Then, the United States would be in a position to "reconstruct whatever pieces may be left of European civilization." If the United States joined the conflict and Germany won, no one would be left to begin reconstruction. France, he kept telling French leaders, should not "base her security on an illusion of American support." On 8 June 1940 he asked Washington to send him twelve Thompson submachine guns to defend the embassy, for "there is every reason to expect that if the French Government should be forced to leave Paris, its place would be taken by a communist mob." As William Shirer commented, Bullitt had a tendency to believe all tall tales about communists.

During his tenure in Paris, Bullitt was very close to the French centers of power, conveying their thoughts and policies faithfully and at length (he also reported to Roosevelt on European developments in general). One looks in vain among his dispatches, however, for a realistic social analysis of the country; he failed to take the pulse and convey the mood of the people.

Bullitt's contact with the French political elite revealed their lack of self-confidence and their hope for U.S. intervention for France. Bullitt wrote the president, "It will be difficult for me to make you realize the degree in which the French Cabinet Ministers and representatives of all the countries of Europe in Paris talk as if they had within them the same phonograph record—playing the theme, 'War is inevitable, and Europe is doomed to destruction unless Roosevelt intervenes.' " Bullitt's standard response to this theme was that Roosevelt was not a *deus ex machina* who, as in Greek tragedy, miraculously appears to set everything right. "It became obvious that our money, ships and men are the things that they wanted. As the situation grows worse, you will hear much flattery about your moral prestige and your duty to Western civilization."[36]

Straus's hope that a leader would rise to divert France from the abyss into which it was headed emerged, or so the president hoped, with Léon Blum. Two days after the new premier had formed a government, Roosevelt expressed the hope that Blum would stay in power long enough to prove himself. He wrote, "These constant changes in Ministries in France are very disturbing, not only to France but also to her neighbors." Years later he would remind de Gaulle that in 1940 there had been eighteen political parties in France and that within one week he had had to deal with three different premiers.[37]

Bullitt apparently did not share the president's optimism concerning Blum. "The new premier," he wrote Roosevelt, "is not exactly a Rock of Gibraltar. The man the French need is a man who has both the intelligence and the character that people can respect. But such leader is utterly invisible at the present time."

François la Rocque? no brains; André Tardieu? utterly discredited; Georges Mandel? no character; Camille Chautemps? a jellyfish; Edouard Herriot? failing position; Edouard Daladier? completely distrusted. "Blum is strong because of the weakness of his opponents," Bullitt concluded.[38] The president had hoped that Blum might be able to set in motion a French version of his own New Deal and had instructed Bullitt to tell him so. The president's 1936 reelection offered Blum an occasion to manifest his admiration and respect. "Blum came personally to express his congratulations," Bullitt reported.

That is unheard of. If you could have seen the manner of his coming, it would have done you good. At least you would have laughed. He entered the front door, flunged his broad-brimmed hat to the butler, his coat to the footman, leaped three steps to the point where I was standing, seized me and kissed me violently! I staggered slightly; but having been kissed by Stalin, I am immune to any form of osculation, and I listened without batting an eye to as genuine an outpouring of enthusiasm as I have ever heard.

Bullitt felt the French admired Roosevelt because of their conviction that "you have genuine understanding of French civilization and a genuine liking for France, and that you will somehow manage to keep Europe from plunging into war."[39]

Sharing the premier's enthusiasm, without dissent the Chamber of Deputies passed a resolution of congratulations. "Henceforth democracy has its chief!" wrote *Paris-Soir.* "After his brilliant triumph President Roosevelt has become the statesman on whom every hope is to be pinned if the great liberal and democratic civilization of the West is one day threatened, either by Bolshevism or by autocracy."

Léon Blum could not survive a series of domestic tensions that the Spanish Civil War had raised to a dramatic pitch. He had been criticized for failing to assist the Spanish loyalists, but as he pointed out in a letter to Suzanne Blum in New York (9 July 1942), in the event of French intervention, "civil war in France would have preceded the foreign war."

The Spanish affair . . . is woven into the social crisis. We know today better than ever . . . what the military reaction would have been at the time and what would have occurred as soon as an opportunity arose of going into action. No sooner had the situation become dangerously tense than we would have had in France something similar to Franco's "coup de force." Even before the outbreak of a foreign war, France would have faced civil war with few chances of victory for the Republic. Thus Spain would not have been delivered while France would have probably turned fascist even before Spain. . . . It would have meant Hitler's conquest of the European continent without even a struggle.[40]

Roosevelt's sympathy for Blum continued through the years. On 31 January 1938 he wrote to him to say how distressed he had been to learn of Madame Blum's death. He expressed the hope that he might be allowed to "add a word of real sympathy in your grief." Roosevelt added: "My wife and I hope that you will find it possible to come to Washington and spend a night at the White House. It would be a pleasure to welcome you and to have time for an uninterrupted talk." Blum replied, "This direct contact you have offered me with such hospitable grace will be the most cherished compensation for my trip."[41]

Roosevelt's State of the Union message to Congress following his reelection was read in Paris as further proof of his determination to keep his country out of war. The United States therefore could not be relied on to stand by European democracies in the showdown with the dictators. De Laboulaye urged the French government not to jump to conclusions. In a note to Foreign Minister Pierre Laval, he recalled that during World War I – he had been in Washington as a young diplomat at the time, while Roosevelt was assistant secretary of the navy – Woodrow Wilson had tried for two years to keep the United States out of the conflict; but when he decided to ask Congress for a declaration of war, there had been unanimous, enthusiastic popular approval. "It cannot be excluded," he wrote, "that circumstances at present unforseeable will modify American attitudes now favorable to peace."[42]

After his reelection Roosevelt was intrigued to learn that to express their admiration, the French were electing him to the Académie Française. Actually, he had mistaken the occasion.

"In March 1937, I was offered membership in the French Academy – Rudyard Kipling's place," Roosevelt wrote. He asked his attorney general whether the offer could be properly accepted. The latter advised the president that "while the question is not free from doubt, there is enough question to make it advisable to decline."[43] The president did not know it at the time, but he had not actually been invited to membership in the Académie.

The Académie is made up exclusively of French citizens. The invitation, which must have been transmitted orally, for no trace of it was found in Paris, was evidently to the Académie de Sciences Morales et Politiques, to which Kipling *had* belonged, and which, together with the Académie Française, forms part of the Institut de France. Had he been correctly informed, the president could have accepted, for there had been precedents: Thomas Jefferson had been welcomed into the Académie on 26 December 1801 (5 Nivose, An X) and Theodore Roosevelt on 27 November 1909. After the liberation of Paris, Roosevelt and Winston Churchill were asked to join by unanimous vote. Since Marshal Pétain was still a member of the Académie, Ambassador Jefferson Caffery suggested that Roosevelt not reply to the invitation.[44] Disagreeing, Roosevelt personally signed an application. His election was confirmed by a presidential decree signed by Charles de Gaulle on 6 January 1945. A few weeks later Roosevelt died, and the Académie honored his memory in the course of a moving ceremony. "Yes," Académie president François Charles-Roux proclaimed, "we had hoped to provide both our society and along with it the entire studious house of the Mazarine Palace the honor of inscribing on its rolls the name of President Roosevelt."

With reelection behind him Roosevelt became sadly conscious of the narrowness of his field of action. In *The Prince* Machiavelli warned that *"profeti armati vinsero e i disarmati rovinarono"* (armed prophets prevailed, unarmed prophets failed). Roosevelt was at the time a "prophet unarmed," with hardly any military strength to back up his warnings. General Douglas MacArthur, then chief of staff, had ranked the United States Army sixteenth in the world, behind the armies of Romania and Spain–hardly enough to impress Hitler.

In April 1937, receiving newly appointed ambassador Georges Bonnet, the president told him: "I am very worried about the European situation. If there is no change, before two years we shall have a revolution in all countries or else a general war." Civil war was ravaging Spain, and Japanese aggression was becoming a serious issue. Roosevelt gave his foreign guest an impression of discouragement.

I would like to step in to stop the arms race, but I do not want to leave myself open to failure. . . . Let me use a household comparison here. It isn't enough to want to hang your hat on the rack: you need a hook to put it on. I don't see it. And what would people think of me if I boldly announced that I am going to hang my hat and I was forced to keep holding it in my hands. Everyone would laugh. And I would have contributed to diminishing an authority the world might need one day to settle its business.

Roosevelt insisted that stopping the arms race was the top priority because if every country rearmed, the United States would have to as well. When the ambassador insisted that despite the problems facing him, the president should use the prestige of his office to prevent war and strengthen the peace, Roosevelt admitted he lacked the means: "I want peace and I am glad the French government does too. I only want to help Europe avoid the dangers threatening it. But I can only act if I have every chance of succeeding. . . . I am truly looking for that hook to hang my hat on. Help me find it."[45]

"I know it would be desirable to act," the president added, "but I am advised to wait for the time nears when Germany will become more reasonable, finding it impossible to live in the autarchic system in which she has shut herself. I have been told this for the past two years just as in 1914 they were telling me that the war could not last more than three months."

Despite Washington's somber mood, the French were cheered when Congress modified the neutrality law by adding a cash-and-carry proviso obviously intended to favor England and France, which both had the cash and controlled the seas. Bonnet stressed the large extent to which France's liberal economic policies were dependent upon the free flow of international trade. Without the new law, countries like Germany, whose practice of autarchy made them far less reliant upon trade, would have been advantaged in case of war. The State Department cautioned Bonnet, however, that if hostilities broke out in Europe, neutrality could not be strictly applied for more than a few months; but even that much might prove decisive for France.

The French had hoped for a solution to a possible obstacle to U.S. assistance–

the unsettled issue of the debt – but the president was not optimistic: "That is a cloud that France's adversaries in the United States keep in being and that it will be necessary to dissipate. But at the present time, no matter what proposals you offer, I would be unable to have them accepted by Congress. We must await a more favorable moment." The French realized that if they hoped to receive the same wartime assistance from the United States as they had received in 1917, the debt issue must be resolved. The continued lack of a solution could delay or, worse, preclude U.S. intervention on the side of the European democracies.[46]

U.S. initiative under the prevailing political conditions must by that time have seemed a hopeless cause to the French. On 5 October 1937 the president had delivered his celebrated "quarantine speech" in Chicago, warning: "If lawlessness and violence rage unrestrained, let no one imagine that America will escape, that America may expect mercy, that this Western Hemisphere will not be attacked"; but Americans were not roused. The president told French visitor Jacques Stern that he had meant to "appeal to the country and clarify public opinion," but the French embassy interpreted the speech as conveying a feeling of impotence: "The Chicago declaration contains much of the sentimentalism typical of Roosevelt's political approach. While the country undoubtedly shares his desire to collaborate as widely as possible with those powers interested in preserving world order, and condemns all dictatorial and aggressive powers, public opinion is concerned lest this collaboration lead to dangerous consequences."[47]

A few weeks later, on 2 December, Chargé d'Affaires Jules Henry informed Paris that his pessimistic forecasts had been confirmed. "President Roosevelt's Chicago speech fell on deaf ears and in no way shattered public indifference. On the contrary, public opinion seems to become harsher if one is to judge by recent declarations and demonstrations, as well as the new bill proposed to strengthen the new legislation on neutrality." A major reason for the country's "absolute insensitivity" was that the United States had a new problem of its own: the economic crisis that the president, the administration, and the Congress were trying to bring under control.[48] Late in 1937 the New Deal was suffering under severe strains and the American mood was once again gloomy.

"Our Frontier Is on the Rhine"

The spring of 1938 found Roosevelt in a particularly somber mood. Efforts to reverse his Spanish policy and assist the Loyalists had come to naught. Franco was on his way to victory, and as a result Spain, Roosevelt told the French ambassador, would become a Nazi satellite. France had tried to come to terms with Germany, the ambassador assured him, but to no avail. The president was not surprised. He felt Hitler was a "visionary maniac who dreamed of continuing in the tradition of both Julius Caesar and Jesus Christ." Public opinion was 90 percent hostile to Germany, even more than during World War I. "If the German ambassador comes to me with tears in his eyes, complaining that his country is badly understood, I shall tell him he should know where he stands."[1]

Roosevelt was particularly frustrated by the British and the French. With the annexation of Austria in March, Hitlerism could no longer be considered an internal German affair, of no concern to the outside world. In April the United States followed the British and the French in recognizing Italy's Ethiopian conquest. It was a bitter pill for Roosevelt to swallow, however. He warned the French that a policy that consisted of trying to buy an accord with the Germans through colonial and other concessions could only have deplorable results. The Rome-Berlin axis was more solid than previously thought, and it would be a mistake to believe the Austrian question could compromise it. In July he alerted Daladier through Maurice de Rothschild: "Germany is stronger than you believe. Without the United States fully at your side, you and the British will be beaten. But the American people have gone back to isolationism. They refuse to get involved in the coming European conflict. They are only ready to make war against the Japanese. For the moment there is nothing that I can do."[2]

Roosevelt knew that whatever the mood of the country and the Congress, the United States was committed. At a White House luncheon he said, "If France founders, obviously we shall be swallowed up with her." The French ambassador observed that "these words were spoken with a profound conviction that left no room for doubt as to the personal feelings of the President, nor as to his attempts to influence American opinion in the event that France, backed by England, got caught up in the struggle against fascist powers for the defense of freedom and democracy."[3]

The president's words reflected his personal feelings. The country, however, was not with him. Americans had been horrified by the cruelty and destruction, the plight of civilians, and the mass executions during the Spanish Civil War. That was war at its ugliest, and Americans wanted no part of it. Was it possible that those born during World War I would come of age just to fight another war? The pacifist sentiment in the country was very strong; Americans opposed not only involvement in Europe's recurring problems, but also the absurdity of war itself as a means of solving those problems.

When the Czechoslovakian crisis broke out in September 1938, appeasement was the rule in Washington as well as in London and Paris. The French ambassador learned to his dismay that the State Department was more inclined to blame Czech leader Edouard Benes's "intransigence" in his efforts to elude the "necessary concessions" than Berlin. Some officials went so far as to admit the "legitimacy" of Nazi demands by claiming the right of self-determination–a right, incidentally, that has no legal standing in the United States, as the Civil War had demonstrated.[4] In Paris, Bullitt's attitude was similar. Daladier clearly hinted to Benes on several occasions that his own policy of appeasement had the support of the U.S. ambassador and therefore also of the United States. American talk of self-determination upset the French. What if, in the name of self-determination, Germany claimed Alsace-Lorraine?

Throughout the crisis the State Department attempted to keep the United States uninvolved. The European situation was evolving so rapidly, Cordell Hull said, that "the U.S. Government did not feel that it could exert any useful influence upon the development of events. Public demonstrations raised the risk of overexciting Hitler."[5] He took the same position following British prime minister Neville Chamberlain's visit to Hitler: "Given the whirlwind evolution of the situation in Europe, any diplomatic action would be useless and any public demonstrations untimely, especially for American public opinion."[6] These comments were duly transmitted to Paris. The French interpreted them as proof of the "violence of the emotions stirring up the country over the past three or four days. Any official word or gesture would immediately provoke very strong reactions."[7]

French hopes that Roosevelt would address a solemn warning to Hitler were disappointed. The president once more made it clear to them that given the near universal hostility to any form of U.S. intervention in Europe, his hands were tied. The French accepted this argument; what they resented was constant press criticism and references to the "so-called democracies." In some quarters it was felt that the French and the British were giving in much too easily to Hitler.

A typical British reaction was: "Why was Great Britain to be held morally bound to fight for justice in Czechoslovakia, while the United States was exempt?"[8]

The French were convinced that in Chamberlain's position, Roosevelt would have acted as the Briton had. At the height of the Munich crisis, Roosevelt urged a meeting of the involved leaders in a neutral capital, but without guaranteeing U.S. participation, adding that "the Government of the United States . . . will assume no obligations in the conduct of the present negotiations." In a message to European leaders on 25 September Roosevelt urged conciliation, but he made U.S. cooperation contingent upon a previous settlement of the difficulties among European countries. On the twenty-ninth, Chamberlain and Daladier went to Munich to confer with Adolf Hitler and Benito Mussolini. There the fate of Czechoslovakia was sealed. "Good man," Roosevelt wired Chamberlain.

After Munich the United States gave the impression of accommodating the new equilibrium established in Europe. As Europe stood paralyzed, like a hare before a serpent, the United States had no better suggestion than the "convening of international conferences, to which the United States would gladly lend their collaboration, dealing with the problem of disarmament and working toward a solution of world economic and financial problems." Nor were the French much relieved when told by Sumner Welles that Roosevelt believed a lasting equilibrium in Europe would enable its four major powers (Great Britain, France, Germany, and Italy), along with the United States, to control Japan. Welles also told the French ambassador that Americans knew that the only way for them to keep out of war was to prevent it and that the president wished to work toward the reestablishment of "order with justice."

During a trip to Paris Welles stressed to French ministers that the American press, particularly in New York, was often controlled by Jewish newspaper owners violently hostile to Germany. "He insisted, however, that this press does not express the country's deep feelings. Mr. Welles stated forcefully that 80 percent of American opinion was opposed to an American intervention in Europe."[9]

The impression the French had of American attitudes did not accurately reflect Roosevelt's deep feelings, however. He had been horrified by the violence of Hitler's speech at Nuremberg. He feared that Munich would lead to war. He was determined that the United States should never have to yield to intimidation, as England and France had done. He was resolved that not only the United States but the whole Western Hemisphere be protected from Axis aggression. As he did after the annexation of Austria, he asked Congress for military credit to ensure a decisive military superiority for the United States.

Roosevelt's determination to strengthen the United States was also in response to disconcerting news about French preparedness. General Requin, commander of the French army facing the strongly fortified Siegfried Line, viewed the prospect of a frontal attack against the German position with "absolute horror," Bullitt reported. The Germans could stop a French assault after it was launched, producing enough casualties to signify the "death of the race," in the general's own words. "German preponderance in the air would be such that

Paris would be destroyed by air raids."[10] General Maurice Gamelin, the French supreme commander, shared this opinion.

Lack of preparedness in the air was especially worrisome. French airplane production, Bullitt reported to the president, was 45 units per month, compared with 80 for the British and between 300 and 600 for the Germans.[11] As of late September, the Germans were believed to have at their disposal 6,500 planes of the latest model (two-thirds bombers, one-third pursuit craft) compared with 600 for the French. The ambassador urged that a way be found to bypass the neutrality law so planes for France could be produced in the United States. As documents released after the war show, the French had greatly exaggerated German production while underestimating that of France and Great Britain. In fact, production capacity was nearly equal on both sides.

Roosevelt shared Premier Daladier's conviction that Munich was but a pause on the way to further demands and that once set in motion, the Nazi war machine could be stopped only by superior force. He therefore aimed to facilitate French purchases[12] and develop a 20,000-plane reserve force for the United States to ensure overwhelming superiority over Germany and Italy. When a Douglas bomber with a French test pilot on board crashed, Americans drew the logical conclusion that Washington was providing assistance to the European democracies. To calm the resulting storm, the president invited the Senate Military Affairs Committee to the White House for an exchange of views. The president "began by painting the dark picture of Europe, describing the German ambitions in the most lively terms, stating that Hitler would not be thwarted, warning that war was imminent. War, he said . . . , would directly affect 'the peace and safety of the United States. The immediate struggle was for the domination of Europe, but as soon as a nation dominates Europe, that nation is able to turn to the world sphere.' "

After reviewing the German challenge to eastern and western Europe, the president added, "That is why the safety of the Rhine frontier does necessarily interest us." "Do you mean that our frontier is on the Rhine?" asked one of the senators. "No, not that. But practically speaking, if the Rhine frontier is threatened, the rest of the world is too. Once they have fallen before Hitler, the German sphere of action will be unlimited."[13]

Meeting the press on 3 February 1939, the president described as a "deliberate lie" a report attributing to him the statement that America's frontier is on the Rhine. "Some boob got that off," he said. The policy of the United States, he reiterated, shunned entangling alliances, encouraged trade among all the nations of the world, and sympathized with efforts to reduce armaments and with the maintenance of the political, economic, and social independence of all nations.

Roosevelt's denial did not completely convince the Vatican, however. Secretary of State Cardinal Pacelli, the future Pope Pius XII, asked French ambassador Charles-Roux for his opinion, which was that Roosevelt had "denied the form but confirmed the substance."[14]

Previously, in a conversation with Jacques Kayser, Roosevelt had declared that Hitler's recent speech did not represent an act of appeasement; to the contrary, he had warned, it contained justification for all sorts of initiatives. He considered the spring and summer of 1939 dangerous for peace and spoke repeatedly of the urgency of France's increasing its air armament.[15]

America's commitment to France had become evident by that time. Negotiations for American planes represented a turning point in Franco-American relations, proving that the president intended to do all in his power to aid France. Expressing his appreciation, Premier Daladier exclaimed, "President Roosevelt was for France a very great and noble friend."[16] Public opinion turned in favor of assisting France, provided that doing so did not involve the United States in a war.

The French read more into the president's words and actions than he intended. They urged him to make clear the American determination to resist aggression, for if he did so the Nazis would not dare to go to war. They also felt confident that if the Nazis forced war upon European democracies, the United States would feel it had no alternative but to intervene. As later events were to prove, both assumptions were correct; the president, however, could only move as fast as public opinion would allow.

Partly to force him to show his hand, the French ambassador Saint-Quentin enquired whether Roosevelt would seek the means "to oblige [the dictators] to make clear their intentions, assuming responsibility for them before public, especially American, opinion." The president replied that he was considering asking Hitler and Mussolini whether they intended to pursue their policy of domination by force, adding that England and France were not in a good position to undertake this initiative. The day before the interview, Foreign Minister Bonnet had told his ambassador, "You know to what extent the attitude of the U.S. is currently observed by the totalitarian states and the crucial influence the U.S. can exert over their determination."

Obliging the French, on 14 April 1939 Roosevelt wired Hitler and Mussolini, requesting them not to attack a specific list of countries. This initiative, which drew an insulting reaction from Hitler, was meant merely to gain time. As Roosevelt told Saint-Quentin, his message "put an end to the mortal uncertainty hovering over the world. It clearly establishes the dictators' responsibility before the American public."[17]

The situation was rapidly reaching its next tragic phase. Informed that Germany was preparing military aggression against Poland, in August Roosevelt sent personal messages to the king of Italy, the president of Poland, and Hitler urging them to abstain from hostile acts. This final effort failed, and World War II commenced.

We shall never know what the result would have been had the president been able to convince Congress and the public of the threat facing humanity—and acted accordingly. The president, and by extension the United States, had failed the European democracies. Roosevelt always believed war might have been averted by a more forceful U.S. posture. Perhaps the French were right in believing that Hitler would not have dared to go to war had the United States declared an intention to intervene.

Europeans had difficulty understanding Roosevelt's apparent lack of commitment to their cause. They did not realize that the Nazi threat was clearer to him than it was to most Western statesmen, but his hands were tied by public opinion; he could appear neither more belligerent than the Europeans nor indifferent to peace initiatives. It is unfortunate that by his words and deeds Roosevelt at times did more to confuse than to reassure: He irritated by sermonizing when he could put no muscle behind his initiatives, and his periodic insistence on disarmament and the virtues of international trade was irrelevant and destabilizing. But another facet to Roosevelt's activity remained largely hidden to Europeans: his patient efforts to convince his country that it could not be indifferent. By taking gradually stronger positions on world issues, step by step he adjusted Americans to the idea that the United States could not escape its responsibilities to the European democracies. The president's repeated appeals to the dictators were useless as diplomatic initiatives yet useful as a means of impressing on Americans the dictators' culpability for the situations. By the time Roosevelt could finally give full and open support to the anti-Nazi camp, the country was largely with him.

During the fall and winter of 1939–40 all was quiet on the front. Roosevelt appeared optimistic about the outcome. He told Ickes that "the French and English have more stamina than the Germans and that if the war goes its natural course, German morale will crack."[18] It was widely felt that the two sides would fight until exhausted and that in the end the United States would have to intervene to pick up the pieces and prevent the bolshevization of Europe.

Taking advantage of a lull in the fighting, the president undertook the controversial initiative of sending Sumner Welles to Europe to sound out the belligerents. Hull was not keen on the idea, feeling the trip would "hold out false hopes."[19] It is not clear what Roosevelt hoped to achieve by sending a personal envoy to talk not only to the British and the French but to Hitler and Mussolini as well. Whatever his reasons, the French and the British thought the initiative likely to backfire, strengthening the hands of those who advocated peace at any price.

Prior to his departure Welles assured Ambassador Saint-Quentin that "he would not be responsible for any proposal or suggestion of peace, that he would scrupulously refrain from being a messenger between the various capitals. It was strictly a fact finding mission, and he was in no way a negotiator." The president personally confirmed this, telling the ambassador that "he would never stoop to recommending a compromise peace with the dictators."[20]

Not in the least reassured, Premier Daladier instructed his ambassador to inform the White House and the State Department of "the exploitation being made abroad of these initiatives and the conclusions being drawn as to a so-called evolution of American policy favoring the partisans of a compromise peace." In a message to Bullitt, who was in Washington at the time, Daladier expressed his concern that the president either was sending Welles to Europe as a matter of domestic policy or else did not know as much about the European situation as the premier had hoped and believed. "Bill [Bullitt]," Ickes reported, "said that he had passed this message to the President."[21]

The Europeans probably saw more in the initiative than Roosevelt intended to convey. The French ambassador interpreted it as "a sweeping diplomatic gesture stemming from [Roosevelt's] temperament and the need for prestige." The British too were suspicious. The president's appointment the previous Christmas of Myron C. Taylor as his personal representative to the Vatican puzzled them. "Although with no intention of lending countenance to a compromise peace on Hitler's terms," the British ambassador wrote, "yet the President took a step . . . to keep open a channel of mediation between the Allies and Germany."[22] Despite their considerable reservations, the Allies were anxious that Welles not feel unwelcome. Saint-Quentin warned Paris against "any demonstration or comment that could cause Mr. Welles to lose face. He is very well inclined toward us, but he is extremely sensitive."[23]

Statements made by Cordell Hull at the time caused the French to question the realism of U.S. policies. A note by Daladier is revealing in this respect.

Mr. Cordell Hull's communiqué, recalling some conversations held with leaders to detect a possible basis for a just and lasting peace, hardly had the practical or instant reach that some have wanted to attribute to it. The very fact that it dealt with international economic organization and world arms reduction is sufficient proof that it is a general context very different from that of the problems raised by the current conflict. It in no way deals with finding a solution. It extends, in an academic rather than a practical fashion, the doctrinal action which has been undertaken for several years by the American Administration, in favor of international economic cooperation, which is presented as a panacea for all the evils which engender war. The concern of domestic policy and the need to reaffirm American diplomacy on the eve of a presidential campaign cannot be ruled out.[24]

The Ministry of Foreign Affairs, for its part, noted that "Mr. Roosevelt and his advisers are used to asserting the primacy of economics over politics and proclaiming that peace can only be found within a better world economic organization."[25] On the very day Welles arrived in Paris, 7 March 1940, Cordell Hull was assuring the French ambassador "how pleased he was to receive Mr. Rist and hear expressed [France's] adherence to the principles of economic liberalism. He expressed pleasure over the satisfactory solution found for the tobacco problem!" (Hull was from Tennessee, a tobacco state.)

In Berlin, Welles tried to convince a Hitler who made no mystery of his intention to crush France and England of U.S. eagerness to participate in the attempt to limit and reduce armaments as well as return all nations to a sane system of international trade relations. The Nazis could not have been less interested, for as Assistant Secretary of State Adolf A. Berle commented:

the Welles mission . . . has proved a theater for statements in public by the German Government as to real desires. These statements are nothing less than a demand for the domination both of the seas and of the continent of Europe, since they include a free hand in the East, the turning over of the Mediterranean strategic points – Gibraltar, Suez, etc. – either to Germany or to Italy; the relinquishment of the naval base of Singapore; the "freedom of the seas." This is called a "Monroe Doctrine" for Germany, clearing her of danger from foreign interference.[26]

In Rome Mussolini told Welles he had been informed by German foreign minister Joachim von Ribbentrop that Germany would undertake an immediate offensive, crushing France within three or four months (actually, it took the Germans three weeks) and that afterward Great Britain would be forced to its knees. Welles gave the Duce a personal letter from Roosevelt in which the president expressed the hope that the two leaders could meet somewhere in the mid-Atlantic. The president felt sure he could convince the Italian dictator to remain neutral. Welles considered it "not improbable" that had the two finally met, "the Italian people would have been spared the tragedy which they have since undergone."[27] Welles had totally misread Mussolini's intentions, as had so many politicians before him who had lauded the triumph of trains running on time. Italian foreign minister Galeazzo Ciano told him that even if Mussolini had been freely offered twice the territorial booty he was seeking, his decision to enter the conflict was irrevocable.

In France officials set aside their reservations and extended the president's envoy every courtesy. Welles met with ministers, army officers, and distinguished personalities, including Léon Blum. He then went on to a chilly reception in London. Sir Robert Vinsittart, chief diplomatic adviser to the government, wrote:

Mr. Sumner Welles emerges more and more clearly as an international danger. His idea of security via disarmament first is nonsense, and I am glad that the Prime Minister dealt with him so firmly on all grounds. . . . But Mr. Sumner Welles' chief crime against common sense and humanity is that he has now gone so far as to want to make peace with Hitler. That surely is lunacy for [which] both he and his chief, President Roosevelt, deserve the highest condemnation. It is now pretty clear, as the Prime Minister says . . . that President Roosevelt is ready to play a dirty trick on the world and risk the ultimate destruction of the Western Democracies in order to secure the re-election of a democratic candidate in the United States. It is not only the Prime Minister who has drawn this deduction; it is the general expectation of everybody that I know who also knows anything of the American situation.[28]

Upon his return to Paris, Welles found waiting almost 3,000 letters castigating him for having called on Blum, a Jew. Anti-Semitism was already rampant in France.

Welles left Paris disheartened. He found that to the recently appointed premier, Paul Reynaud, was "given neither the confidence of his fellow citizens, the support of the legislative branch of his government, nor, what was more essential in the shattering crisis with which France was faced, a country wholeheartedly determined to fight, to keep on resisting, and to triumph."[29] "While on the German side the morale of the forces had never been higher," he wrote, "it was already becoming notorious that the discipline of the French troops was giving their officers grave concern, and that the inefficiency and dubious loyalty of some of the French officers were giving equal concern to many of the patriots whom they were commanding."[30]

Bullitt, who considered himself mandated by the president to report on the European scene, deeply resented the Welles mission. A break resulted that was to have lasting consequences for both men. The ambassador was only too happy to inform the president of French reservations. According to him, "Welles 'eulogized' Mussolini and, in discussing Germany, produced the impression that Germany could not be beaten. . . . Daladier said the impression Welles produced was . . . that France and England ought to try to get a peace of compromise which would leave Germany in control of Eastern and Central Europe by using the good offices of a great man – Mussolini." Bullitt said he told his French critics of being "entirely certain that neither you nor Welles had the slightest intention of using Welles' visit to persuade the French and British to stop fighting and leave the fate of Europe to Mussolini as arbiter." He concluded: "There are, of course, a lot of defeatists in this country, including Bonnet, who attempt to make great use of Sumner's praise of Mussolini, but their campaign was cut short by Mussolini's approval of the German invasion of Denmark and Norway."[31]

Even though Bullitt had an axe to grind, his report undoubtedly reflected the real situation to some extent.

Roosevelt's 29 March statement to the press leaves little doubt that peace was the real object of the Welles mission. He spoke of a "clarification" of the relations between the United States and the countries visited that "will . . . assist in certain instances in the development of better understanding and more friendly relations" (with Hitler, too?). The president finally added, "Even though there may be scant immediate prospect for the establishment of any just, stable and lasting peace in Europe, the information made available to this government as a result of Mr. Welles' mission will undoubtedly be of the greatest value when the time comes for the establishment of such a peace." Even if not in the "immediate" future, a negotiated peace was, therefore, not to be excluded. "Even this statement was too optimistic, as events later proved," Hull would later comment.[32]

One may wonder what Roosevelt really knew of the French situation at the time: Did he genuinely believe the two sides would fight to mutual exhaustion, putting the United States in a position to impose a peace? Welles's contacts in France had been too superficial for him to be able to give the president details of the true state of affairs. He wrote about the conditions there long after his visit, when the true story had become generally known. Bullitt should have provided the president with full information on the state of France, but judging by his dispatches he did not. Although he reported the thinking and actions of the French government in great detail, he furnished no clues about the country itself. If anything, he conveyed the impression of a calm determination that, as events were soon to prove, was painfully lacking.

When the country mobilized in March 1939, Bullitt informed the president that the "spirit of the people is incomparably better than in 1914. . . . The quiet courage and serenity in France today is the only manifestation in a long time that has made me proud to be a member of the human race."[33] "The self-control and quiet courage have been so far beyond the usual standard of the human race that it has had a dream quality" (8 September). "The morale of the French army is superb" (1 November). "The fighting spirit of the French people is untouched and one defeat will not damage it greatly" (28 April 1940). "The morale of the French army and the civilian population is a credit to the human race" (30 May). "The French troops have held again magnificently. . . . Everyone is full of fighting spirit and hope. . . . The French soldiers and civilians are displaying a courage and character beyond praise" (6 June) – these are strange words, considering that by then France was practically beaten. It has been suggested that the president was supposed to read the opposite of what was contained in Bullitt's messages. However, it is difficult to see why this ruse should have been used in order to convey the true meaning of the situation. Roosevelt read the newspapers and wire reports just as everybody else did and thus knew the facts.

Indirect confirmation that Bullitt's dispatches might indeed have reflected his impressions was provided by Oswald Garrison Villard, who had visited with him in December 1939 and "found him to be most sanguine as a result of the war. Bullitt said that England and France together had greater and more efficient air forces than the Germans." Villard thought that Bullitt was "altogether too sanguine" and believed that the president "relies too much upon his opinion and advice." According to Villard, "Bullitt practically sleeps with the French Cabinet and there is no doubt that in many respects he is more French than the French themselves."[34]

What Bullitt failed to see, or at least to convey to Roosevelt, was that France was neither morally nor politically prepared to face its responsibilities as a great power. The French were weary, divided, bitter, tense, devoid of all sense of adventure, and reaching out for security and comfort. This depressing mood was reflected in the condition of the officers' corps and the army. A U.S. naval attaché noted "the complete ineptitude of General Gamelin and many other French commanders, the lack of fight in the French units, and the rapid spread of defeatism throughout the French government and nation."[35]

Ambassador Anthony Biddle, who accompanied the French government to Bordeaux while Bullitt stayed on in Paris, drew a more realistic picture: "A latent state of mind, prepared to accept defeatism ran . . . like an undercurrent through the minds of all France – not in government circles alone, but probably throughout the whole country at large. . . . It was like a rising tide that quietly permeated. Hence, few were surprised to learn that France was defeated, and not sufficiently endangered to react."

By 16 May the military in Washington had reached the conclusion that France was lost and so informed the president.[36] The French ambassador, Saint-Quentin, met with Roosevelt on 30 May and found him "in a poor frame of mind, defeatist and fanciful, speaking of German hegemony as if it were a fait accompli and already predicting the fall of Hitler's empire in twenty years. Saint-Quentin's attempts to obtain a realistic view failed against a wall of smoke and fatalism." Columnist Dorothy Thompson, who saw him the same day, confirmed the ambassador's impressions. Roosevelt was simply overcome by the very events he had forecast.[37]

Americans reacted to events in Europe with suggestions that the United States should abandon the Continent to its fate and instead concentrate on the defense of the Western Hemisphere. Many took the view that the United States, being destined to live on the same planet as Hitler, should come to terms with this reality, however unpleasant. At the time of the Welles mission, a Gallup poll indicated a 75 percent positive response to the question, "If Hitler offers peace, should Britain and France deal with Germany to end the war?"

Against this background, Premier Reynaud's desperate appeals to Roosevelt for help – a moving testimony to France's tragedy – could not evoke a positive response. Once again the French were pleading with the United States to save them, asking for "clouds" of planes. Although few were available, the Americans sent what they could. Of a total of 600 latest model pursuit planes capable of traveling 400 miles per hour, 500 were sent to the Allies; of a limited number of latest model bombers, all but one were also sent.[38] The president could only assure the French that if they continued to resist, if need be by moving to North Africa, help would be forthcoming in ever-increasing quantities.

News that France, its army crushed, had asked for an armistice caused consternation and disbelief. The ease with which the Nazis rolled through France produced the fearful impression that a new barbaric invasion had descended upon Europe. It was the end of an era and a leap into the unknown. France's collapse and surrender was a "stupefying disappointment," Harry Hopkins would later tell de Gaulle. The France Roosevelt knew had ceased to exist, and he "could not trust her to play one of the leading roles."[39] Winston Churchill commented, "France had been rotted from within before she was smitten from without."

Washington had expected the French to resist long enough for U.S. arms factories to go into full production. The French had sent reassuring messages about their military preparedness. Speaking in Lille in July 1939, General Maxime Weygand had proclaimed: "I think the French army has a greater value today than at any time in its history. It has equipment of the finest quality, first rate fortifications, an excellent morale and an outstanding high command. No one in my country wants war, but I do proclaim that if we are forced to win a victory, we shall win it."[40] Undersecretary of War de Gaulle had been equally optimistic.

He wrote Premier Paul Reynaud: "Obviously no one can assert that France is currently without aircraft, tanks or ships. Although we decided late in the day to manufacture the necessary equipment, production has begun. At the present hour, our country is in no way disarmed and the enemy who wishes to attack us will discover this at the earliest."[41]

De Gaulle had been accurate in his assessment, as data emerging after the war amply demonstrated. At Pétain's trial the former premier and war minister Edouard Daladier described the French weapons inventory as not in the least inferior to Germany's and commented: "If the 1939–40 troops saw few or no tanks and few or no aircraft to defend and support them, it is because this is the way the military command had wanted it to be."[42]

The president was aboard his yacht when he learned the French had given up the struggle. The French army had represented a barrier between the United States and Nazi Germany that had now collapsed, and the fate of the other barrier, the British fleet, hung in the balance. Churchill had warned that if the situation became desperate, another government might consider offering the Germans the fleet as the price of better conditions.

In a matter of weeks a United States that had felt secure between two oceans felt directly threatened. Without freedom of the seas for the Allies, Hitler would become the undisputed master of Europe, his sphere of action extending to Africa and from there to Latin America. Conversely, as long as the democracies controlled the oceans, the Germans and the Japanese did not stand a chance of winning a world war. In the months to come, help reached Great Britain and the Soviet Union across the Atlantic. When the United States entered the war, freedom of the seas enabled millions of young Americans to reach the war fronts.

Roosevelt's interest in the sea did not begin with his appointment as assistant secretary of the navy during World War I. Rather, the appointment was the consecration of a passion dating from Roosevelt's school years. At age sixteen he discovered the work of Admiral Alfred Thayer Mahan, the great theoretician of maritime power. From Mahan Roosevelt learned the role sea power could play in extending U.S. influence overseas and in transforming the country into a leading world power. Roosevelt countered advocacy of a fleet just strong enough to defend the U.S. coast with proposals for a fleet strong enough to meet all challenges. To Roosevelt, "an adequate navy is notice served by the United States upon the nations of the world that war shall never again be fought upon American soil." He viewed supreme sea power as the realization of Woodrow Wilson's vision of a dominant U.S. navy establishing world peace.[43]

"To study the role of the Navy in American development," Rexford Tugwell wrote,

was to understand the relationship of the nation to other nations. How independence was gained and kept was not a secret to be discovered by studying land campaigns or even the opening of the West; that secret lay off the coast, from Labrador to the West Indies. It lay in the approaches from the East and in the use of ships to take advantage of jealousy among potential enemies and favor among potential friends. The nice weighing of strength deployed over space and maneuver carried out in time was something Franklin came to as a scientist does to his laboratory or a litterateur to his books.[44]

Roosevelt never ceased trying to impress the importance of sea power upon the European democracies. "Naval power in world affairs still carries the lesson of history," he told Premier Reynaud (13 June 1940). And to Churchill he wrote, "As naval people, you and I fully appreciate the vital strength of the fleet, and command of the seas means in the long run the saving of democracy and the recovery of those suffering temporary reverses."[45]

Roosevelt had not waited for France to fall to be concerned about its fleet. In May 1940, as evidence mounted that France would soon be lost, the president had urged the French to send their fleet to the United States for internment. Ambassador Saint-Quentin countered by remarking that "the Allied fleets could only find asylum in the United States if America entered the war on our side."[46] The president returned so insistently to the subject that the ambassador warned Paris of the "damage beyond repair that the surrender of the fleet to the conqueror would create not only for the present government, but in the minds of the American people for many, many years."[47]

Once it became evident that the French army had lost, the president told the French ambassador the only chance for France to preserve its independence and integrity was to pursue the war in overseas territories and, if this proved impossible, to take the fleet over to the British side. Roosevelt recognized how very difficult it was under the circumstances even to try giving advice to France. Yet, in his opinion, the French would be better off allowing Germany to occupy the whole of their country while moving the government, part of the army, and the fleet across the sea, rather than asking for an armistice and coming to terms.[48]

Once the French did take the step of asking the Germans for conditions, Roosevelt warned the newly appointed Pétain government that unless the fleet were kept out of Axis control, France would forever forfeit the friendship of the United States. The president also insisted that the Germans should not be allowed to extend their control over North Africa. The British were, if possible, even more concerned. A French fleet in German hands could have starved Britain to death while also presenting an immediate threat to Egypt and the Suez. Churchill bombarded Roosevelt with messages stressing the immediacy of the danger, but the president did not need to be convinced.

A major concern for both Roosevelt and Churchill was that the Germans could have gained control of the fleet had they really wanted to. Sir Edward Spear emphasized this point when he wrote that "the Germans were completely ruthless and would stop at anything to gain their ends. They might well announce that the fleet must be surrendered by a given day, failing which they would burn down a great town for every day's delay, Bordeaux on Monday, Lyons on Tuesday, Nantes on Wednesday and finally Paris on Saturday."[49] Churchill made a similar point on 15 June. "Have you considered," he wrote the president, "what offers Hitler may choose to make to France? He may say, 'Surrender the fleet intact and I will leave you Alsace-Lorraine,' or alternatively, 'If you do not give me your ships I will destroy your towns." The Germans had shown in Warsaw the destruction they were capable of. United States Ambassador Anthony Biddle thought a last-minute safeguard consisting of sinking the ships in case of German treachery was "pitifully small." Churchill, too, mentioned in a 27 October letter to Roosevelt that "even if we accept assurances we can feel no security that they will in fact be able to maintain them."[50] As to French navy chief Admiral François-Xavier Darlan's "honor about her [the fleet's] never falling into German hands is rooted in dishonor." Churchill reminded Roosevelt, "How easy we found it to cop the French ships at Portsmouth and Plymouth."[51] De Gaulle was convinced that the Germans could intervene rapidly: "The Wehrmacht can cross in a few hours the short span from Moulins to the Mediterranean coast and render inactive our ships as soon as it is informed by its observers that they are preparing to leave. It takes 48 hours for ships to apparel for departure; German motorized units only need 12 hours to reach Toulon."[52]

Not trusting Vichy, and even less German assurances, the British resolved to seize and destroy French naval vessels within their reach. The units at Mers-el-Kebir and Alexandria were crippled or immobilized. The president approved. In a note to him, the British ambassador, Lord Lothian, wrote: "You will see that Winston Churchill has taken the action in regard to the French fleet which we discussed and you approved." "Even if there had been the remotest chance that your navy would have fallen into German hands, I would not have acted differently," Roosevelt told the French ambassador on 14 July. "I am a realist."

Washington and London agreed that Hitler could have taken possession of the French fleet had he been willing to pay the price. Evidently he was not sufficiently interested. "The Mediterranean is an Italian sea," Hitler told Mussolini. "Any future modifications of the Mediterranean balance of power must be in Italy's favor. Thus, since Germany must have liberty of action toward the East and the Baltic, by directing our respective energies in completely opposite directions, it will never be possible for there to be a clash of interests between Germany and Italy."[53] A high Nazi official further explained that Hitler considered the Baltic Germany's Mediterranean. Events later proved that Hitler had made a major strategic mistake. At the Nuremberg trials, Marshal Keitel stated that "history would have been different had we taken Gibraltar and the Fuehrer hadn't left France her navy, her colonial troops and her Empire." Shortly after France's surrender, however, Hitler saw the problem differently. On 28 October 1940 he told Mussolini:

It is in the interest of the Axis to see to it that the Vichy Government maintains control of the French Empire in North Africa. If Morocco were to come under the orders of de Gaulle, we should have to carry out a military operation in which success would be difficult, since it would have to be based entirely on the efforts of the air forces. The best way to keeping this territory is to see to it that it is the French themselves who defend it against the English. That is possible since the Air Force and the Navy are in the hands of anti-British commanders and the Army, too, if it feels that it can save something, will be faithful to Pétain.[54]

Hitler's main concern at the time was preventing the French fleet from joining up with the British; neutralization of the French fleet was his basic reason for granting France an armistice. Meeting Mussolini in Munich on 18 June, Hitler explained that should the fleet escape to England, in certain categories the actual power of the British fleet would practically be doubled, especially as concerned destroyers. Since a convoy protected by six destroyers would be immune from submarine attack, Britain would derive considerable advantage from utilizing French destroyers. Hitler would have preferred that the fleet scuttle itself and disappear, both as a threat to Germany and as a source of confrontation with Germany's allies.

A document presented at the Fuehrer's Conference on Naval Affairs early in 1941 is indicative of Hitler's policy toward France:

If France were to resume the struggle against Germany on her own initiative it would be impossible to prevent the remaining fleet from escaping from Toulon. Also the parts of the fleet at present in the British sphere would be active within a short time. This would have a detrimental affect on the conduct of the war in the Mediterranean; Italy would be entirely on the defensive; the employment of French forces to carry out escort duties and anti-submarine measures would render it more difficult to disrupt British and supply lines. . . . Italy's position in Tripoli would become untenable; she would be caught between British and French forces, since the enemy fleets would possess naval supremacy. Every bridgehead in Africa would be lost, so that Africa could not be attacked. This would be particularly grave if it later developed that Germany would have to gain her future colonies by military conquest. At a later date, a stronger center of power might be created in North Africa with American assistance. Germany would have to feed continental France as well as herself if she wished to benefit from French industry, as then all imports from Africa would cease. Deliveries of oils, ores, and rubber from French Colonies to Germany herself, which are being increased at present, would be stopped.

All anti-Axis forces in the world would be given fresh encouragement both politically and propagandistically. France would be missing when it comes time to rebuild Europe.

The document lists the advantages accruing to Germany if France were to agree to collaborate on "military tasks" provided it did so "without too great concessions on the part of Germany with regard to the future peace treaty." The French were not prepared to go that far. They conceived of collaboration in a limited sense, as when Darlan informed the German grand admiral Erich Raeder later that year of his readiness to provide information on the movements of the British fleet. "The Fuehrer," the document adds, "sanctions the exchange of intelligence on the British navy between Admiral Darlan and the German Naval Office."

It appears incontrovertible that the Germans could have taken possession of the French fleet had they so desired, but that their real interest was in seeing the fleet at best on the bottom of the sea and at worst neutralized under German-Italian control. The real question seems to be whether the French could have followed Roosevelt's advice, namely, not asked for an armistice, let the Germans occupy the entire country, and removed their government, what was left of the army, and their fleet overseas. They probably could not have.

Some military analysts believe France could have continued the struggle from North Africa. De Gaulle was one of them. As undersecretary of war he instructed Darlan to prepare a transport of 870,000 men, a project the admiral called *sugrenu* (preposterous). De Gaulle was sent to London by Premier Reynaud to obtain a loan of transport ships, but apparently the British had none to spare; besides, Churchill's only concern was the forthcoming battle of Britain: If Britain falls, so would Africa. French naval experts today maintain that through mid-May the transport of up to a half million men, minus their equipment, might have been possible. "It would have been a repeat performance of the Dunkerque evacuation when over 300,000 British and French soldiers made it to Great Britain but had to abandon their equipment," a War Department official said. "In June it was already too late."

North Africa lacked the means of warding off a German assault. General Weygand testified that four battle-trained divisions had been transferred from North Africa to the Alps region to fight the Italians; munitions reserve supplies were adequate for only one day of fighting; no anti-aircraft batteries, antitank cannon, or post–World War I tanks were available; some eight divisions, made up primarily of Africans and lacking modern equipment, were dispersed between North Africa and Syria; and French war planes were no match for the Luftwaffe. The British, despite Churchill's assurances to the French to the contrary, were in no position to help.

Vowing that England would never surrender, Churchill proclaimed that if the country were "subjugated and starving, then our Empire beyond the seas, armed and guarded by the British Fleet, would carry on the struggle"; but France had no "empire beyond the seas" to which to withdraw in safety. Unlike Great Britain, much of whose empire was out of reach of the Germans, French possessions were close to home. France's overseas possessions remained in French hands solely because the Germans did not perceive any immediate use for them.

The debate over France's continuing the war in North Africa is largely academic: The French had accepted defeat and, but for a small minority, were through fighting. The Germans had meant their victory to be total, and so it was. As the Berlin correspondent of the *Neue Zurcher Zeitung* wrote on 17 June, the Nazis intended France's military power on the Continent to be destroyed once and for all to ensure the Third Reich's dominance in the heart of Europe. "The entire new order which envisages the German conqueror can only rest upon the concept of total victory."[55]

As for the French fleet, it obviously had sufficient time to escape. But to where? Could it have found a new home in North Africa? French naval experts are doubtful. They argue that no logistical assistance was available, nor were provisions for resupplying ammunition or spare parts. The British would have been of no help because there lacked standardization between the two countries. In addition, the available naval bases were quite inadequate: Mers-el-Kebir was under construction; Casablanca, Oran, and Algiers could not provide adequate facilities; Bizerte was a good if old-fashioned base, but as it was located a few minutes' flight from Sicily it could easily be destroyed by the Luftwaffe, as Malta would be. To seek haven in British ports would have been no solution, as demonstrated by the grave difficulties encountered in maintaining French-built ships of the Free French navy. It took a year for the British to provide the submarine *Rubis* with mines adapted to the Free French navy's launching pads.[56]

The French fleet survived the collapse of France practically intact and could have contributed significantly to the war against the Axis. Excluding the rallying of British ports, which the fleet considered a form of subservience contrary to French honor, it at one time considered reaching Canada or the French possessions in the Caribbean. However, the French decided otherwise for fear of German reprisals. The Nazis periodically raised the specter of "polonization," that is, the threat of treating France as ruthlessly as they had Poland. Whether Darlan could have taken the fleet to the Allied side even had he wished to do so is thus open to question. Pétain's orders would have been obeyed, and Darlan's officers and men would not have followed him.

The French air force faced the same difficulties as the navy. During July 1940, some 1,200 planes of every type escaped the German advance and the Luftwaffe and landed in North Africa. They were, for the most part, incompletely equipped, and no spare parts were available in North African depots. Ammunitions were also defective and could not be replaced. Thus the French planes in North Africa could no longer be employed in the war against the Axis. They merely served to confirm France's feeling of impotence: North Africa was in no position to take up the fight.[57]

4

American Mistrust of Europe

During the French Revolution, Saint-Just had cried, *"Si Louis est innocent, la révo-lution est coupable."* In times of political upheaval, when references are not clearly established, one side can justify its existence only by denying any justification to the other. Once the armistice was signed, two authorities emerged to speak in France's name, Pétain and de Gaulle, each denying the authority of the other. To paraphrase Saint-Just, if de Gaulle was "innocent," that is, if the right was on his side, then Pétain *had* to be guilty. The proposition also worked in reverse, of course, with Vichy proclaiming Pétain "innocent" and de Gaulle "guilty." To be guilty, in such a context, simply meant to be a traitor. Neither side could accept attempts at justification by the other, for treason was the worst of crimes. Pétain had de Gaulle sentenced to death for "treason"; de Gaulle, after the liberation of France, had Pétain sentenced to death for the same alleged crime. Pierre Laval and other Frenchmen branded as Nazi collaborators were executed by firing squads not so much for their crimes but to wash away, in blood, their pretensions to innocence. In no other way could de Gaulle have established that he and only he was the innocent party. That innocence is today called legitimacy. The issue of legitimacy was at the heart of the French drama. It was also at the heart of a deep misunderstanding between Roosevelt and the French.

Wartime France occupied a position unique in Europe. In the case of the other European countries—whether friend, foe, or neutral—the United States had to deal with just one entity. In the case of France there were two, and dealing with one meant antagonizing the other. France was also unique among the belligerents for having accepted defeat (a situation with deep moral and political consequences, as Charles de Gaulle was the first to recognize).

In his passionate love of France, de Gaulle anguished over the shame of

France's surrender: "The worst drama in our history,"[1] which "had left – and for-ever! – a secret grief in the national conscience."[2] He felt France was honor-bound not to surrender:

I say honor, because France had been committed to laying down the arms only in agree-ment with the Allies. As long as the Allies continued the war, the government does not have the right to surrender to the enemy. Although the governments of Poland, Norway, Belgium, and Luxembourg were driven from their territory, they understood what their duty was. Not one government agreed to bear the yoke of the invader – not one, except, alas!, that one which claimed to be the government of France.[3]

Surrender had separated France from the other Allies. The armistice had led to the emergence of two political entities, each claiming to represent France to the exclusion of the other. The situation caused an issue to arise that Roosevelt was ill prepared to confront: that of legitimacy. This misunderstanding of a word to which both Pétain and de Gaulle attached major importance would prove to have the gravest of consequences. Much of the bitterness in wartime Franco-American relations was caused by America's failure to understand the significance of legitimacy in French tradition. In the United States the word *legitimacy* has a meaning quite different than that understood in France. The French view made little sense when Americans viewed it only in American terms.

In France legitimacy is of monarchical origin, and its justification is grounded in history. De Gaulle explained it in a historical sense when he declared:

No French government could be legitimate when it had ceased to be independent. We, the French, had in the course of time endured many disasters, lost provinces, paid in-demnities, but the state had never accepted the domination of a foreign power. . . . When France acknowledged herself as a power that submitted to the yoke, she was putting an end to her own future. A call of honor from the depth of history, as well as the instinct of the nation itself, led me to bear responsibility for the treasure in default of heirs: to assume French sovereignty.[4]

This passage is significant, for it shows de Gaulle drawing from French histor-ical experience his own claim to legitimacy and basing his denial of Pétain's claims on the same experience. The *Dictionnaire Larousse* defines legitimacy as "royal heredity by right of birth," that is, a historically based justification of the right to rule or govern. During the 170-year span from the French Revolution to the Fifth Republic, France changed regimes fourteen times, with each regime finding it needed to justify its legitimacy. The contrast with the U.S. experience is obvious: During that same period the United States had one constitution (the French a dozen!) and one form of government, finally accepted and supported by all political parties and the vast majority of its citizens.

Despite the numerous upheavals in their history, the French possess a strong sense of historical continuity. It is expressed in the word *patrie*, which for a

French citizen represents the summation of centuries of history, the present as a projection of the past. The philosopher Ernest Renan called France "a continuity of destinies founded upon a national history and a particular territory." The French give their country the attributes of a person, alive through the centuries. The historian Jules Michelet wrote that "England is an Empire, Germany is a Race, France is a Person." De Gaulle was wont to invoke "Notre Dame de France," Our Lady of France, and to identify with heroes of French history including Jeanne d'Arc and Georges Clemenceau. Jeanne d'Arc had redeemed France at a time of national agony; and so would he, de Gaulle, redeem the France that had capitulated. He would efface Vichy, Pétain, and collaboration with the Nazis; thanks to him that period would be uprooted from French history. In liberated Paris he proclaimed, "Vichy is null and void."

The American tradition lacks that strong sense of history. The closest English equivalent of *patrie* is "fatherland," a word practically alien to American usage. According to *Webster's* dictionary, it means "land of one's ancestors." American ancestors are European, Asian, African. Americans speak of "our country," "land of the free," "the American way of life"—expressions denoting not the past but the present and the future. The essential symbol of American unity is not a shared historical experience, but a flag to which allegiance is sworn. A "melting pot" of many various races, nationalities, and creeds, the United States built its unity around an idea and a set of symbols. Being an American means entering into a kind of contract between the individual and the Constitution, to believe in, protect, and abide by it. The U.S. contract is juridical, not historical.

As Michael Howard writes in *War and the Liberal Conscience* (1978), "the United States . . . virtually alone among nations, found and to some extent still finds its identity not so much in ethnic community of shared historical experience as in dedication to a value system; and the reiteration of these values, the repeated proclamation and dedication to the liberal creed, has always been a fundamental element of cohesion of American society."

Given the absence of historical perspective in the American tradition, legitimacy has quite a different meaning in the United States than in France. In the United States, legitimacy and legality are closely related. *Webster's* dictionary defines *legitimacy* as "the quality or state of being legitimate"; and *legitimate* as "lawful, allowed: as, a legitimate claim." Something that's legitimate is simply something that's permissible; the word has nothing to do with such abstract concepts as history and tradition.

Thus Americans tended to take a narrow, legalistic view of the issue; the battle over legitimacy that was tearing the French apart made little sense to Washington. Was not a legitimate government simply a legal government? And was not a legal government one that issued from an election? Hence the Pétain government's legitimacy could not be disputed. De Gaulle's pretension to legitimacy based on extralegal arguments was considered specious. In Morocco, during their first meeting, Roosevelt told de Gaulle he could not recognize him because his authority did not issue from an election. The general retorted that Jeanne d'Arc had not been elected either. The historical reference was very meaningful to de Gaulle, but it was completely lost to Roosevelt, who considered it a further example of French megalomania. The two protagonists simply did not speak the same language.

Roosevelt felt de Gaulle had little right to speak for France and even less right to behave as if he *were* France. It was laudable of him to want to free his country from German occupation; he, a general, should lead his followers in the war against the Nazis. Once liberated, France would freely elect its government; only then would legitimacy be reestablished. As fighter in the common cause, de Gaulle was accepted and materially assisted, but as politician he was rejected. The president's policy of supporting de Gaulle's military activities but refusing to recognize his political claims caused serious difficulties. For de Gaulle spoke as a man imbued with a sense of his country's history, whereas Roosevelt and the State Department responded as lawyers.

Unfortunately, Roosevelt was no better prepared than most politicians of his time to address the political and diplomatic problems arising from France's involvement in the war. The situation even defied categorization; it required a great deal of the kind of imaginative thinking that an isolated America simply did not possess. The United States was not yet a superpower compelled to assume worldwide responsibilities; nor had advanced communications yet broken down traditional barriers of time and distance between nations. International relations were simpler and more heavily based on tradition than today, and so were (or at least, so *seemed*) the answers to major challenges. We have seen how tenaciously Washington clung to the naive notion that disarmament and improved world trade represented a panacea for the world's ills.

On strictly legal grounds, there was no reason for Washington to have withdrawn recognition of the French government based in Vichy. The Pétain government had received a mandate from a freely elected national assembly and, at least in the beginning, was enjoying a high degree of popular support.[5] The Soviet Union, Canada, Switzerland, and several other countries, as well as the Vatican, were also represented at Vichy. Although ties had been broken with London, the British kept in touch with Vichy through the Canadians and the British embassy in Madrid. For nearly a year and a half following the fall of France, the United States was technically a neutral that maintained diplomatic relations with Nazi Germany and Fascist Italy. It was only natural that it should maintain relations with France as well.

By the time the United States entered the conflict, Vichy's claim to legitimacy had weakened. The country's independence, a prerequisite for sovereignty, was being gradually eroded by subservience to the Nazis. In addition, a number of French possessions around the world had opted for the Free French. Having been named to represent them, de Gaulle had a right to speak in their behalf that the United States could not ignore. Since Vichy's sovereign claims over territories that had rallied around de Gaulle had ceased to exist, Washington could now choose which representation to deal with: in territories faithful to Pétain,

Washington dealt with Vichy; in those faithful to the Free French, with de Gaulle.[6]

This policy implied, not recognition of the right to govern, but recognition of a *de facto* authority over a specific area. Both Vichy and de Gaulle strongly objected, each claiming the exclusive right to speak for France. The French found the U.S. position distasteful because, as de Gaulle explained to Admiral Harold Stark, it failed to recognize "the essential unity of France which is the product of French history and national life":

France is more than a total of all the parts of which she is composed. All French, whether in France or in the colonies, look to some symbolic authority. That is why France, since 1940, has looked either to Pétain or to de Gaulle. All local French officials were conscious of this national unity and felt the necessity of depending from some central authority symbolizing the centralized unity. . . . Americans, with their history of federal constitutional development, with their tradition of local autonomy and local leaders–chosen by and responsible to their constituency–might easily make the mistake of applying their own traditions to the French.[7]

By dealing with whoever was in power at a particular site, the United States was implying that neither Pétain nor de Gaulle embodied French legitimacy and that therefore neither had the right to speak for France. Prior to liberation, Roosevelt maintained that "France did not exist,"[8] an unfortunate expression that caused a great deal of resentment. Roosevelt actually meant that no one had the right to speak for France as long as the French, enslaved under foreign occupation, did not have a way of expressing their collective will. In Roosevelt's estimation, French legitimacy rested solely with the French people.

The contrast between a legalistic and a historical approach to the French question went beyond the issue of legitimacy, however. It carried clear ideological connotations whose importance Americans had difficulty grasping. Americans generally mistrust ideology, considering it alien by definition and a threat to the American way of life. Ideology involves revolution, that is, political and social upheaval as a means to its realization, and Americans have a traditional dread of revolutionary violence. As the historian Arthur M. Schlesinger, Jr., explained:

Qualitative differences remained between the American Revolution, which began in hope and concluded in democracy, and later modern revolutions, which began in bitterness and concluded in authoritarianism. The Americans were happy revolutionists, fighting as much to protect as to achieve a free and egalitarian society. Their purpose was national independence rather than social upheaval and reconstruction. . . . No one in the new nation, high or low, expressed a desire to repudiate the social, intellectual, cultural, and moral heritage.[9]

During the French Revolution the Terror caused a wave of collective hysteria in the United States for fear of contagion. The same occurred following the Bolshevik Revolution in Russia: Anti-alien laws were passed to "protect" the United States from subversive foreign influences. In terms of the American experience, the very word *revolution* was scary, and thus the notion of ideology was shunned.

The United States has undergone many changes throughout its history, but never an ideologically motivated social revolution. The New Deal was distinctive in its refusal to approach social problems in terms of ideology. Since its inception the United States has been free from the European heritage of feudalism and wars of religion. "It is the absence of the experience of social revolution which is at the heart of the whole American dilemma," Louis Hartz wrote. "Not only does this produce the quality of our absolute thinking . . . but in a whole series of specific ways it enters into our difficulty of communicating with the rest of the world."[10] By an ironic twist of fate, the United States emerged as a superpower when wars had become revolutions fought with the weapon of ideology.

Roosevelt shared to a great degree the average American's aversion to ideology. "Franklin Roosevelt," Joseph Alsop wrote, "was not an ideologist, or a theory monger, or a man with a gospel to peddle. If he dismissed an argument on the ground that 'It's all very theoretical,' that was a final dismissal. He disliked and distrusted ideologists, whether of the right or the left."[11] Roosevelt was a pragmatist; "being anti-ideological he did not suffer from that great enemy of statesmanship, the disease of rigid adherence to a theoretically developed plan of action."[12]

Roosevelt was not prepared to understand that nazism was not only evil in the moral sense that Kierkegaard had revealed to him, but an evil ideology that could be countered only by an ideology of liberation. The Four Freedoms were a noble, universal objective, but without a revolution to wipe away all that was rotten in France after years of Nazi occupation, they could not be implemented. Once again, Roosevelt's inability to view the French situation in terms of history was at the heart of his failure to understand what the French meant by revolution.

Roosevelt rejected ideological, or even political, debates as causing undue interference with the conduct of the war. Beating the dictators came first; everything else had to await the end of hostilities. That position suited the average American soldier, who but vaguely understood what he was fighting for and saw his task as finishing the job as soon as possible and then going home. For France, as for the other Nazi-occupied countries, however, peace would not entail simply a return to prewar conditions, in which life would resume its normal course. The French would have to rebuild upon the shambles of fascism, heal the physical wounds of war, and create a new political order. The differences between the United States and France were poignantly underscored by Eleanor Roosevelt.

I do not believe that, in our country, one realizes the time it will take to rebuild in the hearts of individuals all that the occupation, the prisoners' camps or service in obligatory work has destroyed. Most of us ignore what resembles a city in ruins. Most of us ignore the experience of having foreign armies within one's own borders possessing the right to order people around. Most of us have not seen our men taken to prison, shipped to other countries to execute forced labor. The true understanding of what Europe has endured from an occupation army is so far from our possibility of imagining that I often ask myself with despair if we shall ever be able to understand.[13]

Rejection of "alien ideologies" was accompanied by an almost universal conviction that the U.S. political system was the only one to have proven its validity. It had endured and matured while others had collapsed; accordingly, it represented an obvious example for other nations to follow. Europeans were invited to abandon their ways and to adopt the U.S. system of government; the world would then be at peace and American soldiers would not have to rush to Europe every twenty years to save what was left of its corrupt and decadent political structures. The sentiments were echoed in private conversations, political speeches, and newspaper editorials and columns. They catered to American idealism and sentimentalism, both of which Roosevelt shared as personal convictions and political instruments. The president seemed convinced that responsibility for making the world over rested mainly with the United States. He would draw up schemes and dispose of territories as if they belonged to him, to the considerable irritation of America's allies.

Roosevelt was merely projecting American hopes for a better world modeled on the American example. His was a time when Americans dreamed of One World, the American Century, the Century of the Common Man. The Good Neighbor policy toward Latin America and the absence of barriers between the United States and Canada were offered as examples for future relations among nations. In a speech about the common man, Vice President Henry Wallace proclaimed that the idea of liberty is derived from the Bible, with its insistence on the dignity and sanctity of the individual. Democracy was the only true political expression of Christianity; Hitler was the Antichrist; Satan had been set loose upon the world. Much of Wallace's rhetoric, which appealed to religious rather than political sensibilities, was forgotten, but the expression "Century of the Common Man" endured.

The idea of the United States as the wave of the future has deep roots in the country's political tradition. Woodrow Wilson proclaimed his belief that "God planted in us the vision of liberty; and, therefore, I cannot be deprived of the hope that we are chosen, and prominently chosen, to show the way to the nations of the world how they shall walk in the path of liberty." Years later, in 1942, Henry Luce noted in *Life* magazine that "because America alone among the nations of the earth was founded on ideas that transcend class and caste and racial and occupational differences, America alone can provide the pattern for the future. . . . American experience is the key to the future. . . . America must be the elder brother of the nations in the brotherhood of man."

As Robert Dallek explained:

The universalist impulse in America was an expression of strongly held feelings which no leader, however strong his grip on the public mind, could really change. Predictions of postwar international harmony and of vastly different peoples and systems imitating U.S. institutions were the product not of rational thought or close attention to the external world but of ingrained parochialism or blind conviction that everyone wanted to follow the American leader. For all the apparent danger of survival from World War II, Americans still could not see the world for what it was or substantially free themselves from thinking about the globe in domestic terms.[14]

The strong belief in the United States as the universal model made it easy for Americans to conclude that only the United States knew what was best for the rest of the world. This conviction led to plans for imposing American principles on the world order representing, not a projection of the past and its accumulated experience, but abstract schemes that were really no more than intellectual exercises. These futuristic visions combining idealism and national concerns were frequently viewed by Europeans as self-seeking. "United States policy is exaggeratedly moral, at least when non-American interests are concerned," Anthony Eden wryly noted.[15] This view was echoed by de Gaulle in his *Mémoires*.

To understand American wartime attitudes toward France, one must keep in mind their causes: One was America's failure to build upon the experience of the past and thus to understand the importance of legitimacy in the French historical tradition; the other, a failure to understand the meaning of ideology to Europeans, equating revolution with disorder, civil war, and anarchy. These failures were not Roosevelt's alone; they belonged to most of Washington's political class.

As George Kennan observed, Americans were not ready to "admit the validity and legitimacy of power realities and aspirations, to accept them without feeling the obligation of moral judgement, to take them as existing and unalterable human forces, neither good nor bad."[16] He lamented the "colossal conceit of thinking that you could suddenly make international life over into what you believed to be your own image; when you dismissed the past with contempt, rejected the relevance of the past to the future, and refuse to occupy yourself with the real problems that a study of the past would suggest."[17] Pointing to the pronounced tendency of Americans to transplant legal concepts from domestic to international affairs, Kennan recognized that "foreign statesmen were keenly aware of the inadequacy of these general propositions as definitions of any workable agreement or understanding on specific international issues."[18]

The Four Freedoms embodied a simple philosophy with a universal appeal. "President Roosevelt's proclamation of the four human freedoms was deeply felt in a France that is suffering and whom the enemy condemns to silence," de Gaulle told the Free French in New York.[19] Abstract principles invite unanimity, concrete plans controversy. Quite understandably, France objected to her future's being decided by outsiders.

In his scheme, Roosevelt did not include France among the great powers. The four powers already armed for war—the United States, the Soviet Union, Great

Britain, and China—would be sufficient to maintain peace in the postwar world. France was not needed for the task and should not be asked to bear the political and economic burden of armament. France would also be required to surrender a number of bases—in Indochina, Dakar, and elsewhere—from which the four major powers could move quickly with naval and air forces to deal with threats to the peace. At one point Roosevelt discussed with the British a plan of German origin called "Wallonia," to include the Wallon section of Belgium, Luxembourg, Alsace-Lorraine, and part of northern France. Anthony Eden, with whom he discussed the plan, "poured water," as he put it,[20] and the project was shelved. Vice President Henry Wallace appeared to be more generous toward France: He proposed to group around it Switzerland, Belgium, and Holland.

Anthony Eden, who did not think highly of U.S. interventionism, noted that Roosevelt's "academic yet sweeping opinions . . . were alarming in their cheerful fecklessness. He seemed to see himself disposing of the fate of many lands, allies no less than enemy. He did all this with so much grace that it was not easy to dissent. Yet it was too like a conjuror, skillfully juggling with balls of dynamite, whose nature he failed to understand."[21] When discussing the French situation with Americans, Eden found that "one of the troubles was that the Lafayette tradition was standing in our way. The Americans were convinced that they know better how to handle French affairs than we did."[22]

The president's ideas about the postwar world also failed to impress the Soviets. Churchill recalls Roosevelt's interview with Stalin and Molotov at the Teheran Conference, at which

many important matters were discussed, including particularly Mr. Roosevelt's plan for the government of the post-war world. This should be carried out by the "Four Policemen." . . . Stalin did not react favorably to this. He said the "Four policemen" would not be welcomed by the small nations of Europe. He did not believe that China would be very powerful when the war ended, and even if she were European States would resent having China as an enforcement authority for themselves. In this the Soviet leader certainly showed himself more prescient and possessed a truer sense of values than the President.[23]

Europeans were concerned that Americans—who "know nothing about Europe," as Eden put it—would insist on making all decisions concerning the continent's future, thus preventing them from organizing as they saw fit. That most faithful of America's allies, Winston Churchill, objected strenuously to Roosevelt's plans for France. Unlike the president, he called for a strong France, for "the prospect of having no strong country on the map between England and Russia was not attractive."

In the end Churchill's views prevailed. As the demise of Nazi Germany neared, the president modified his perception of the world and of America's role in it. There is no doubt that his brilliant, pragmatic mind would have contributed more to the shaping of a better future had he formed his plans on a more realistic basis.

5

De Gaulle and the French Exiles

Conditioning the president's policies toward France was the assumption that the end of the war would be the end of Pétain, but it could be just the beginning for de Gaulle. Pétain presented an immediate problem, de Gaulle a long-range one. Pétain's ideas were of no more than passing importance, but de Gaulle's appeared destined to have a great impact on the future of France and of Europe. This may explain why Roosevelt managed Pétain but confronted de Gaulle, whose ideas he found incompatible with his own.

De Gaulle had a condescending view of the United States that he shared with the social class into which he was born; at the same time, however, he knew that without the United States fully committed to the war, the chances of beating Hitler were nil. This ambivalence underscored his actions regarding the United States during the war years. Even after Roosevelt's death he distinguished between the power of the United States and the political wisdom of its rulers.

Following the collapse of France, de Gaulle sought to infuse his countrymen and women with courage by reminding them of America's decisive role in defeating the common enemy. In his regular broadcast from London, he invited his French listeners to look forward to the day when the "gigantic possibilities of American industry" would lead to the defeat of Germany (22 June 1940). "No sensible man conceives the victory of liberty possible without the contribution of the American continent" (1 August). "It becomes evident that America has undertaken, to help the Allies, an immense production of armaments" (12 August). "I say, because I know it, that an irresistible current carries the New World to the assistance of liberty" (22 August). The United States was the only ray of hope in France's dark night.

On hearing of the Japanese attack on Pearl Harbor, de Gaulle turned to Pierre Billotte, the aide who brought him the news, and said, "Well, this war is over."

Noting the aide's surprise, he added: "Of course, there will be more operations, battles and combats. But the war is over since the outcome is now known. In this industrial war, nothing can resist the might of American industry."[1] A week later, speaking from Radio London on 15 December, he told his listeners in France: "Indeed, in this mechanical war, America possesses, by herself, a potential equal to the total of all the other belligerents. Thanks to the assistance she has already begun to provide, next year Allied factories will produce three times more planes, two times more tanks, six times more ships than enemy factories."[2]

American industrial might was one thing; U.S. policies were another. Much as de Gaulle praised the former, he deplored the latter. When he was in an argumentative mood, as was often the case, he spoke as though the United States were the source and cause of all the ills that had befallen France and Europe. Typical in this respect was the lecture he gave presidential assistant Harry Hopkins, a friendly listener:

During World War I the United States intervened only after three years of combat in which we had exhausted ourselves repulsing German aggression.[3] America, however, had entered the conflict solely because of the damage to her commerce by German submarines and after attempting to affect a peace by compromise, according to the terms of which France would not even have recovered Alsace and Lorraine. Once the Reich was conquered, America had refused France the security pledges formally promised her, had exercised a stubborn pressure upon her to renounce the guarantees and the reparations due to her and lastly had furnished Germany all the aid necessary for a return to power. "The result . . . was Hitler." I recalled the immobility the United States had observed when the Third Reich attempted to dominate Europe; the neutrality she had clung to while France suffered the disaster of 1940; the rejection Franklin Roosevelt had offered Paul Reynaud's appeal, when a mere promise of aid,[4] even secret and long term, would have been enough to persuade our government to continue the war; the support granted for so long by Washington to those leaders who had subscribed to capitulation.[5]

Not only was de Gaulle's America – a country he considered "marginal" because lacking credibility – the cause of France's troubles, but her motives were also suspect. If Roosevelt had "done everything to enable his country to take part in the world conflict," it was because the United States "yielded . . . to that taste for intervention in which the instinct of domination cloaked itself. It was precisely this tendency that President Roosevelt espoused."[6] "This time the United States was less affected by our distress than the appeal of domination."[7] "Roosevelt expected that the crowd of small nations would . . . assure the United States an enormous political and economic clientele."[8] "Roosevelt had disclosed the American ambition, draped in idealism but actually quite practical."[9] "His will to power cloaked itself in idealism."[10] "Washington would affect as long as possible to consider France as a fallow field and de Gaulle's government as an inconvenient accident."[11] When Roosevelt tried to explain how strongly France's collapse had affected him, de Gaulle's only comment was, "It would have been easy but pointless to remind Roosevelt how much America's voluntary isolation had counted in our discouragement after the First World War, and again in our collapse at the beginning of the second."[12]

De Gaulle's accusations against the United States were as extreme as France's disaster and an obvious cover for it. They also reflected, however, views prevalent in certain other milieus at the time. The United States was viewed by them as a rich and powerful country, but not really a nation; a hodge-podge of races spanning a continent and producing a hybrid people; a materialistic country, ever looking for economic advantages, but naively and falsely idealistic à la Wilson. To de Gaulle Americans were hypocrites, proclaiming the loftiest of ideals while pursuing only the national interest, arrogant even in their show of humility.[13]

De Gaulle shared with political circles that had been very influential between the two world wars a prejudice against *américanisme*, considered a threat to France's traditional culture. Those circles were concerned lest French virtues be threatened by American materialism, lack of refinement, excessive love of money, and conformism. Americans were seen as a people anxious about the future despite their material comforts.

Under the impact of the Resistance and the realities of the French situation, de Gaulle would in time outgrow to a certain extent his conservative leanings. During the war, however, his values were made known through his writings and the company he kept upon his arrival in London. "The de Gaulle pre-war outlook was rightist, with semi-Fascist tendencies in its approach to internal politics, and traditional imperialist views of foreign policy," a State Department paper noted. "He was convinced of the instability of the political, social, and economic order of the Third Republic, and looked for a reaction in favor of a more disciplined and controlled society. . . . Like most French rightists, he placed no value on international organization and distrusted Britain."[14]

The people who first rallied to de Gaulle included far-rightist royalist dissidents from Action Française, Cagoulards or presumed such, and a sprinkling of leftists. Later, when some of the colonial territories joined de Gaulle, his followers included colonists and colonial officers. "Inevitably, any adventure (such as de Gaulle's) also attracted a certain proportion of thugs,"[15] according to the historian Henri Michel; "anti-parliamentary, myth of the chief, attracted by a unique party, to these permanent traits of Free France one must add in the beginning a dot of xenophobia and even anti-Semitism."[16]

De Gaulle directed his National Committee as Pétain did his Council of Ministers. Pétain: "There is no discussion in the Council. Everyone has a turn to give his opinion."

De Gaulle behaved like an autocrat, a prince, with the same disregard for democratic rules as the Marshal in Vichy. He alone appointed the commissioners. At the meeting of the Committee, there was an exchange of views expressed, but only the General made the decision. . . . On his arrival in London, the deputy Félix Gouin discovered a "sort of copy, in miniature, of the Pétain government." The slogan "Liberty, Equality, Fraternity" did not appear on any official document.[17]

De Gaulle "alone commands; in the Committee for the Defense of the Empire, as later in the Committee of National Liberation, there is no vote. Everyone expresses his opinion and General de Gaulle, as [King] Louis in State Council, selects and decides."[18] "The strong authoritarian tendencies which the movement developed, the idolatry and extravagant hero-worship which grew around the General, even the common hostility to the traditions and institutions of the Third Republic, constitute close parallels between Pétainism and Gaullism," wrote the British historian David Thomson.[19] Later the general looked back to this period with nostalgia: "That sort of monarchy which I once espoused . . ."[20]

This was the de Gaulle that the United States knew during the war years; not surprisingly, he gave the appearance of an apprentice dictator. American evidence was limited to his authoritarian demeanor and his somewhat contemptuous view of American society. That was not, of course, the way de Gaulle saw himself. His self-image, Robert Aron wrote, was that of "an incarnation of all the centuries, thus belonging to none, for whom 'la Grandeur, la Gloire, la Patrie' always took capital letters; evoking Clemenceau, Napoleon, Jeanne d'Arc. From the heights wherefrom he sees them, are they not his peers, almost his contemporaries? Contemporaries in the legend, contemporaries in the history of France where only heroes count; de Gaulle is the tradition incarnate."[21] He identified himself with France, "Je suis la France," and so to be against him was to be against la Patrie and hence a traitor. A slight to him was a slight to France.

Very few people in official Washington could understand the message de Gaulle was trying to convey. He had to counter Pétain's popularity by building a following of his own. He had to become an anti-Vichy symbol; he wished to be perceived as the antithesis, not so much of Pétain the person but of what he represented in popular imagery. He could only hope to succeed by proclaiming that he, not Pétain, incarnated France; that he, not Pétain, was the legitimate heir of French grandeur. According to David Thomson, "It became clear that de Gaulle could suffer no authority which was a potential rival to himself; and that to destroy any such authority he was prepared to sacrifice national unity and military efficiency to a jealous regard for selfish and partisan interests."[22]

De Gaulle's claim to legitimacy claimed a foundation in history. Washington feared that de Gaulle's appeal to history might be intended to justify violence and revolution, both endemic in France, as legitimate too, and eventually involving the United States. Statements about revolutionary justice raised the specter of civil war, a concern not laid to rest when a prominent member of the Resistance, Emmanuel d'Astier de la Vigerie, visited the United States under an assumed name. During an interview in June 1942 he listed thirty-eight French men and women accused of collaborating with the Germans, some of whom were to be executed, others imprisoned. The list included the actress Mistinguett, former pugilist Georges Carpentier, playwright Marcel Pagnol, Pétain, Count René de Chambrun, Darlan, Sacha Guitry, and even Maurice Chevalier.

Suspicion that de Gaulle harbored antidemocratic instincts was reinforced by periodic press reports of the torture of French citizens who were unwilling to join de Gaulle and of unspeakable repression inside the Gaullist movement. The following incident, which occurred late in 1944, is typical of the paranoia most probably fomented by French exiles then prevailing in some quarters of Washington.

The head of the Office of Strategic Services (OSS), William J. Donovan, had invited Colonel Andrew de Wavrin, alias Colonel André Passy, to Washington to meet with selected members of his staff for the purpose of forming plans for the penetration of Germany. Clearance for the trip had been obtained from the State Department and army intelligence. On 15 December the president found on his desk a memorandum from Attorney General Francis Biddle asking why the colonel had "been brought to America" and suggesting that "he should now be got out." Biddle enclosed a memorandum from J. Edgar Hoover, director of the Federal Bureau of Investigation (FBI), according to which the "real purpose" for de Wavrin's visit was the "organization of a secret foreign intelligence organization in this Hemisphere."

[De Wavrin's] background also would seem to direct particular attention to the probable character of the intelligence organization reportedly being planned by him. It appears that de Gaulle appointed de Wavrin, then using the alias Colonel André Passy, Chief of the French Secret Police in 1940. De Wavrin was said immediately to have proceeded to form a Gestapo-like organization and was said to have included in it many former members of the Cagoule. You may recall that that organization has been responsible for a number of bombings and assassinations in North Africa. . . . Colonel De Wavrin . . . is reported by reliable sources . . . to have become known as de Gaulle's Himmler and has been described as "a political hatchet man."[23]

Allegedly, de Wavrin added to his unsavory reputation by his "handling of various political purges" within the de Gaulle regime. The memorandum contains three single-spaced pages in the same vein.

Donovan countered with a fourteen-page rebuttal addressed to the president stressing the colonel's contribution to the Allied cause, for which he deserved medals, not slander.[24] The French colonel was allowed to proceed with his mission undisturbed.

Working against de Gaulle were not only the historical and political incompatibilities discussed earlier, not only a lordly personality that made no effort to please, but also, and perhaps most damaging, the attitude of his fellow French. In his "personal memoir,"[25] Raoul Aglion, de Gaulle's representative in New York, has provided a devastating picture. Of a resident French population of some 200,000, only 5,000 joined the organization "France Forever," created to support the Free French. An opinion poll among French residents and refugees showed that 85 percent of them did not approve of the general. The French-language press were divided on many issues, but they united in their antagonism to de Gaulle and the Free French. Aglion quoted Sumner Welles as saying that "Frenchmen of international status living in the United States–Alexis Leger,

Jacques Maritain, Jean Monnet, [Antoine de] Saint-Exupéry, Maurois – are keeping their distances" from de Gaulle. Most of the French and Franco-American associations registered in the United States remained under the influence of the Vichy embassy.

The atmosphere among the French in the United States was filled with hatred and mutual resentment, as de Gaulle's representatives were to discover to their astonishment and dismay. Aglion wrote that "politically, the quarrels and the hatred among the French were disastrous, their support for de Gaulle zero, and their influence usually negative."[26] Raoul Roussy de Sales, a French writer very much at home in American intellectual circles, wrote that the French in the United States "were not only divided, but full of hate, mistrustful, prepared to do any kind of informing or vile deeds. There are practically no exceptions."[27]

Jacques Soustelle, the distinguished anthropologist who represented de Gaulle in Mexico, was shocked at the "anti-Gaullist intrigues" he found among the French upon visiting the United States.

Some reproached us as being fascists, others for getting much too close to the Soviets. The resistance movements were nothing more, according to some, than a band of braggarts determined to establish the General's dictatorship; according to others, they were appendages of Vichy's intelligence service. The most absurd and hateful stories were broadcast and amplified by a number of French determined to ruin Fighting France in the already prejudiced minds of American officials. . . . The most contradictory accusations, the most evident inventions, everything went, provided that de Gaulle and his companions were defamed before the foreigner. It was a vile task a number of French were conducting. On the opposite, some Americans were speaking the language of reason.[28]

Hervé Alphand, who left a diplomatic post in the Vichy embassy in Washington[29] to join the Free French in London, has identified three distinct groups among the French. The first group, and the smallest, joined France Forever. The second, having accepted the armistice and convinced that Great Britain was finished, remained faithful to Vichy and supported American neutrality. The third, while accusing de Gaulle of dictatorial ambitions, refused to support Pétain; they felt that for the time being France did not exist and that French citizens living abroad had no alternative but to wait, while supporting, each according to his or her means, the Allied struggle. The latter were the French who exerted a strong influence upon the Department of State and the White House.[30]

Alphand was scornful as well of the French colony in the United States: "The tensions over the 'French issue' seem more serious in Washington than in London. The rifts, the fighting and the maligning among the French are horrible and degrading. What an explosion of hatred, personal ambition, confusion and sheer madness, publicly displayed in front of our friends and enemies. It is an atrocious sight."[31]

The situation in London to which Alphand referred was hardly different for de Gaulle, as the American press frequently reported. Sir Edward Spears, who knew the French community there intimately, wrote: "What must have been terribly wounding [for de Gaulle] was the bitter antagonism so often displayed by his own countrymen. . . . His critics were among the French, and the more individuals felt the lash his courage inflicted on their cowardice the more bitter they were, and the French are really experts at denigration."[32]

It was perhaps Jean-Paul Sartre, who, after visiting the United States as special envoy for *Le Figaro*, best depicted the impact the French residing in the United States had on U.S. public opinion. According to Americans, he wrote, the French

have not lost a battle but the war. As a consequence of their defeat, the French accepted without difficulty the Pétain government. At first, Vichy appeared to be adapted to the situation, speaking as it did of penance, effort, renewal. Americans were inclined to judge the French of France the way they judged the French immigrants who . . . were for the most part conservative petit bourgeois. They opted for Pétain as representing peace and social order. Americans had every excuse for recognizing a government our fellow citizens had accepted before them. At the same time, Americans were understandably inclined to conceive French society in the image of the reactionary small bourgeoisie represented by the French immigrants. They imagined France as a middle class country and the French as intelligent and hard working, loving order, lacking ambition and taste for risk taking, a bit old-fashioned, anxious to preserve their wealth. This France, accordingly, could not have been better represented than by an old Catholic marshal, who spoke of work and savings, of renewal and humility in a familiar language. . . . French Pétainists found the words that would convince Americans: that since France was wounded, the task was to heal her scars, and for so doing dissentions among Frenchmen were to be avoided. Pétain, they held, represented French unity. De Gaulle was synonymous with disorder and civil war. (3 March 1945)

The fact that some distinguished French exiles were against Vichy and were even supporters of the struggle of the Free French did not necessarily imply that they found merit in de Gaulle. The general's unquestioning supporters among the French elite were few, mainly some distinguished scholars at a French university established in New York. Their influence was limited to intellectual circles and could not match that of well-known personalities in politics and letters.

Among the former, the most influential official in Washington was Alexis Leger. As director general of the Ministry of Foreign Affairs, he had kept close ties with the State Department and upon reaching the United States had been warmly welcomed by the president, Cordell Hull, and Sumner Welles. Leger's prestige reached well beyond the political world, for he was also a distinguished poet who was awarded the Nobel Prize for Literature in 1960. Summarily dismissed from his post by Paul Reynaud, he developed a hatred for the former premier that spilled over to the latter's appointee for undersecretary of war, Charles de Gaulle. His legalistic approach to France's problems coincided with the president's, especially since he had become very close to the president's chief legal adviser, Attorney General Francis Biddle. Sumner Welles said that

Leger possessed "a great awareness and [was] an eminent and impartial man. The President feels that he has a wide knowledge of many problems. We listen to him with much interest."[33] He felt that Leger always "displayed magnificent clarity and logic in his thinking."[34] Aglion believes that Leger was largely responsible for Roosevelt's French policies, which is certainly an overstatement. The president might have appreciated that a distinguished and knowledgeable Frenchman felt the way he did about de Gaulle and for much the same reasons, but that's about as far as it went. Leger proved all the more convincing in that he had rejected Vichy and all it stood for. Vichy had deprived him of his citizenship, his legion of honor, and his ambassadorial rank. He lived modestly in Washington, having accepted a consulting position with the Library of Congress.

The United States was host to another giant of French letters, Antoine de Saint-Exupéry, whose *Night Flight* and *The Little Prince* had won him international fame. While in exile in New York, where he wrote some of his major works, Saint-Exupéry consistently refused to become involved in the French community's sordid politics. He rejected the Gaullist lure and maintained that the Vichy regime, which he "hated," had nevertheless saved France from "utter extermination" at the hands of the Third Reich. "A Frenchman abroad," he wrote, "should be his country's advocate rather than a witness for the prosecution." Of the Gaullists he said: "Because this group is taking part in the fight outside France and constitutes a normal 'foreign legion,' it claims the reward of ruling France of tomorrow. It's absurd. The essential characteristic of sacrifice is that it claims no rights." To de Gaulle's famous phrase, "France has lost a battle but has not lost the war," he retorted, "Speak the truth, General. France lost the war and her allies will win it."[35] In New York he met actress Marlene Dietrich and André Maurois, author of a number of best-selling biographies, who also disliked de Gaulle and found excuses for Pétain. Saint-Exupéry spent time in Hollywood, where two well-known directors, René Clair and Julien Duvivier, were pro-Pétain, while a third, Jean Renoir, refused to have anything to do with the Gaullists. Film actor Charles Boyer had the portraits of Marshal Lyautey, Pétain, and de Gaulle in his studio, a symbolic mixture. As the war progressed he showed his sympathy for the Free French and corresponded with de Gaulle.

Camille Chautemps, a three-time premier of France, arrived in the United States entrusted with a mission from the Pétain government and a salary, most comfortable at the time, of $1,300 per month. His task was to influence public opinion and report back to Vichy using the American code. The State Department and the Office of Strategic Services consulted him occasionally after he left that assignment, but his influence then was minimal. The Free French refused to have anything to do with him. In September 1941 de Gaulle wired his Washington representative René Pleven: "We don't want Chautemps at any price. He was positively disastrous in the Reynaud cabinet. He is the type of politician who is finished."[36]

Eve Curie supported the Free French while displaying great admiration for

Roosevelt. The two corresponded regularly, despite Curie's protestations that the president should not waste his time answering her letters and telegrams. Having been deprived of her French nationality, she toured the world with her only traveling document a personal letter from the president.

Geneviève Tabouis, a journalist who had gained a reputation for knowing what was going to happen before all the world's ministers did, had become very friendly with Eleanor Roosevelt. "She is a courageous woman whom I admire," the First Lady said of her. Mrs. Roosevelt addressed a moving message to the French in Tabouis's newspaper *Pour la Victoire*. She was unconditional in her affection for France and the French, regretting only the divisions within the French community. The spectacle of French divisions and hatreds, she complained, was pitiful to behold and did a great deal of damage to France's cause.

These examples will suffice to show the kind of atmosphere prevailing in the United States among French exiles and its negative impact upon the administration's French policies. Officials in Washington could not understand why French citizens resisting the Axis powers would not join together in a common effort instead of, to quote Sumner Welles, being split by "internecine feuds which had and which were increasingly having a disastrous effect upon public opinion in this country." "It seems unbelievable," Welles added, "in the present state of world affairs that French men and French women, who were supposedly determined to do their utmost to further the victory of the United Nations, should be spending ninety-five percent of their time in petty quarrels of the character which was only too evident among the Free French in the United States and England."[37]

French exiles were not the only ones fighting among themselves; de Gaulle's people were as well. De Gaulle had hoped that a distinguished personage such as Leger or the philosopher Jacques Maritain would agree to be his spokesperson in the United States, but in vain. After some trial and error, he settled on a socialist official of the International Labor Organization, Adrien Tixier. A Free French delegation was established in December 1941 composed of Tixier, Etienne Boegner, Raoul Roussy de Sales, and Raoul Aglion. Roussy de Sales accepted with reservations, Boegner got embroiled in a disagreement with de Gaulle and quit, and Aglion was highly critical of Tixier's leadership.

"Tixier was an ambitious, harsh and caustic man," Aglion wrote. "He never had a good relationship with official Washington because of his personality. With his compatriots he remained frenetically anti-American."[38] Being called "frenetically anti-American" was hardly the best introduction for de Gaulle's hand-picked representative; Tixier was also openly critical of de Gaulle and the cause he represented. "This personal attitude of Tixier's position was not easy, but it would have been better if he hadn't constantly presented de Gaulle's views with his own apologies and comments, openly disagreeing with his instructions."[39] As Robert Aron commented, Tixier "is the type of Frenchman who should serve domestically, but not in a foreign country. His character aggravates the French colony, split into rival clans. . . . He irritates his American partners who can't understand anything about our internal differences . . . , and who have more important matters to attend to."[40]

De Gaulle later recognized, in a conversation with General Dwight D. Eisenhower, the poor quality of his Washington representation, which he "deplored," and acknowledged that it "undoubtedly had done him much harm."[41]

Periodic irritation with the Free French did not prevent Washington from recognizing their representation and their passports, providing Lend-Lease aid, and appointing U.S. consuls in territories under de Gaulle. Washington simply wondered why anti-German French would not come together and join forces the way Americans did in times of crisis. Washington professed ignorance of the fact that the French, unlike the Americans, were not unified by one basic philosophy. Whenever it did admit to recognizing the ideological differences among the French, Washington argued that Vichy would collapse once Germany was defeated, so why not wait until then to settle disputes and meanwhile concentrate on beating the Germans. That scenario de Gaulle rejected. Aware that the Free French contribution to the common victory would be modest, his main concern was postwar France and the role he and his organization would play following Vichy's disappearance. Although he realized that his country was weaker than it had been for centuries, he wanted to restore France to great-power status and believed he could extract more concessions from the Allies while the war was on than after victory.[42] De Gaulle's ambitions were more political than military, a circumstance that Roosevelt could not accept. The general's power was not legitimate, as the president repeatedly made clear, and he could be accepted only in his military role. The president would not admit that de Gaulle was playing politics while Americans were preparing to fight and die for the liberation of France.

To a number of Americans the de Gaulle issue was not one of legitimacy or other abstract concerns. They simply saw in de Gaulle a leader who would compromise neither with Hitler nor with the French people resigned to Nazi domination of Europe. Any other consideration, as far as they were concerned, was irrelevant. Politicians close to the president made no mystery of their sympathy for and support of de Gaulle. Harold Ickes, the fiery secretary of the interior, was among the first to join France Forever and to let the Vichy ambassador know what he thought of Pétain. Secretary of the Treasury Morgenthau, always on intimate terms with the president, manifested support for de Gaulle and contempt for Vichy. Justice Felix Frankfurter, another close friend of the president's, intervened on behalf of the Free French. Harry Hopkins, the president's closest adviser and friend, was active in support of de Gaulle and played a considerable role on France's behalf. Eleanor Roosevelt accepted with thanks a Croix de Lorraine pin from the Free French, much to the dismay of the Vichy ambassador.[43]

The American press was on the whole very supportive of de Gaulle. The *New York Herald Tribune*, the *Baltimore Sun*, the *Christian Science Monitor*, and even, sometimes reluctantly, the *New York Times*, plus some mass-circulation periodicals such as *Life*, were unreservedly pro–Free French and anti-Vichy. Among politicians, New York mayor Fiorello La Guardia was an ardent supporter. Most important, however, most of the American people were for de Gaulle. They little understood the intricacies of French politics but admired the general as a fighter against the common enemy. They saluted in him the hero, not the politician, and greeted him enthusiastically during his visits to the United States.

Roosevelt saw the de Gaulle issue from an entirely different perspective. The hero could not contribute much to the common victory, and the politician could give him serious problems. At the heart of Roosevelt's hostility toward de Gaulle was their disagreement over the direction of the postwar world. As General Georges Catroux had correctly assumed, the antagonism between the two men concerning the French Empire "explain[s] . . . much better than the antagonism of their characters that Roosevelt had preferred the 'local authorities' to the President of the National Committee and, later, General Giraud to General de Gaulle."[44] The very idea of empire was repugnant to Roosevelt; he would not send Americans to war so that France could then reestablish the kind of world he was determined to see disappear. The world of the future, as he saw it, had no use for French *grandeur* and even less for a French Empire he considered, like all colonies and empires, a source of international disorder and war. He could not but feel hostile to a de Gaulle who wrote: "In the nation's fearful ordeal one element stands out as vital to her future and indispensable to her greatness. I refer to the Empire. . . . The French people are alive to their imperial achievements and the profound solidarity which unites them to the Empire. . . . Any attack on her sovereign rights in the Empire would indeed be odious to France."[45]

Roosevelt felt the great French people he had known and admired had nothing in common with de Gaulle. They were from a different generation and a different epoch – survivors, those who were still alive from a past that was gone forever. He admired men like Herriot and Blum, whose main concern was the welfare, rather than the glory, of France. They in turn admired in Roosevelt the man who had brought his country back from the brink of despair, advancing democracy and promoting social justice. They were not, like de Gaulle, men from the right, filled with all sorts of anti-American and, more broadly, anti–Anglo-Saxon prejudices. They could understand, as de Gaulle probably could not, the weight his immense responsibilities placed on Roosevelt and the pride he felt in having led the United States to a preeminent position among nations. Roosevelt's knowledge of France, in turn, was too sketchy and slanted for him to recognize in de Gaulle, as Churchill did, a leader who "seemed to express the personality of France – a great nation, with all its pride, authority and ambition."

Another aspect of the lack of understanding between Roosevelt and de Gaulle was the disparity in the images they wanted to project. A great American president projects the image of the average American. He does not place himself above other Americans, but displays qualities typical of millions of families. He is likable, smiling, unpretentious; he expresses the soul of the people. A great French leader is exactly the opposite: He is solitary, standing above the masses, representing the essence of what has made France great and powerful; he embodies France's *gloire* and *grandeur.* De Gaulle cultivated this image, and it came naturally to him to identify with French heroes such as Jeanne d'Arc and Clemenceau.[46] Roosevelt failed to understand this French mythmaking, while de Gaulle, in his ignorance of things American, viewed Roosevelt's bonhomie as a mask for hypocrisy and deceit.

De Gaulle was as austere and pompous as Roosevelt was relaxed and jovial. Like a typical American, Roosevelt liked to crack a joke. During an afternoon tea in 1944, Roosevelt served de Gaulle and then turned to his adviser and former ambassador to France, Admiral William Leahy, saying, "For you, Admiral, Vichy water would be indicated." Instead of joining in the laugh, de Gaulle got up, saying, "I find this pleasantry in the worst taste." Without taking leave of his host, he left the room. A Roosevelt aide had to run after him and offer profuse apologies. Roosevelt, head of state of the most powerful country on earth and commander in chief of the American forces fighting to liberate France, had never been addressed in such a manner–and he did not forget it.

The incompatibility between the two caused Roosevelt to develop an intense dislike for de Gaulle. The president did not realize that his hostility served de Gaulle well. It helped confirm in the eyes of the French the image of a leader who would not bow before "Anglo-Saxons" in defending French honor and independence. Ambassador Edwin Wilson, for a brief period U.S. representative to de Gaulle's National Committee in Algiers, warned Washington that "every effort on our part to thwart [de Gaulle], to diminish his prestige or seem to weaken the position of France, will have only the opposite effect and serve to strengthen his position in the eyes of the French people as the defender of French rights and sovereignty against foreign interference."[47] The last thing de Gaulle wanted was to be seen as an American stooge. By standing up to Roosevelt, de Gaulle soothed wounded French pride. The French would not admit the real reasons they lost the war. It was not their fault but someone else's– that of the Anglo-Saxons, in particular, who abandoned them in their distress. We have seen in his conversations with Harry Hopkins the extent to which de Gaulle twisted history to "prove" that the United States bore the responsibility for France's misfortunes. The xenophobia this attitude generated was most ably exploited by de Gaulle in furthering his political aims.

6

Pétain in Transition

The France that succumbed to the Nazis in a matter of weeks, with hardly a fight, did not deserve any better than Marshal Pétain: Without a doubt this sentiment entered into President Roosevelt's complex feelings about France. Pétain embodied a France that—in Roosevelt's unhappy expression—did not exist.

An asset for the old marshal was that unlike de Gaulle he, at least, was openly very fond of the United States. Even the Nazis were treated to his pro-American tirades. Americans like to be liked, and Roosevelt was no exception.

Du Moulin de la Barthete, who was very close to Pétain during the Vichy years, recalled that "the marshal exhibited more than friendship toward the United States: it was a real passion." He quoted Pétain as exclaiming: "A free people in a free country. A true democracy. Pershing, the most modest man in the world, one of our most brilliant leaders. My old friend Pershing. . . . If you could have seen the American troops taking Montfaucon there would have been tears in your eyes."[1]

One of Pétain's fondest memories was a trip to the United States in October 1931. The French government had appointed him to represent France at the one hundred fiftieth anniversary celebration of the battle of Yorktown, which had marked the young American army's decisive victory against the British. Two of the most prestigious units of the French navy, the *Dusquesne* and the *Suffren*, were dispatched to the scene. Pétain was accompanied by members of old noble families whose ancestors had taken part in the War of Independence: de Chambrun, a direct descendant of Lafayette, de Broglie, de Noailles, de Rochambeau, and the marquis de Grasse, to name a few.

During the two weeks of festivities there were enough banquets, receptions, speeches, balls, and solemn inaugurations to last, as one of his biographers noted, for a three-month period.[2] General John J. Pershing, who had com-

manded the U.S. expeditionary force during World War I, insisted on accompa-
nying his old friend during visits that took them from Virginia to Massachusetts.
Speaking at Yorktown, Pétain recalled that the 19 October 1781 British capitula-
tion was a memorable date not only in U.S. history but in world history as well.
The marshal was warmly received in Richmond and in Washington, where he
met Herbert Hoover and members of his cabinet. Pétain visited George Wash-
ington's home at Mount Vernon, was given a reception at the Naval Academy at
Annapolis, delivered a lecture before senior Army officers, thanked the Central
Committee of the American Red Cross for wartime assistance, and was taken to
Boston and then to New York and for a cruise on the Hudson River. New York
greeted him with a ticker tape parade. Speaking at City Hall he said that
Yorktown represented the past; New York, the future.

As the official visit came to a close, Pétain hosted a farewell party on board a
warship. Among his guests was the then-governor of New York, Franklin D.
Roosevelt. Years later he would reminisce with the German envoy Reuthe-Fink
about his American experience and his "warm memories" of the future president. "What a marvelous country," he is reported to have told the German. "One
breathes an air of camaraderie, of optimism totally unknown in Europe. America is a young nation that seems to have found a solution to the problem of
liberty and authority that we have such problems resolving."[3]

The two French warships departed without Pétain, who had decided to remain to visit New York, where he spent five days incognito. "As a civilian, the
marshal was as happy as a college student on vacation," recalled René de Chambrun, who accompanied him.

He visited Harlem, the Stock Exchange, and went to the stadium where he experienced
baseball, hot dogs and ice cream. His last evening was spent in congenial company. After
dining at the Côte Basque, we went to the night club at the Central Park Casino. The
party was in full swing at the stroke of midnight when [New York Mayor] Jimmy Walker
strode in with a woman on each side. For a moment he was taken aback–Pétain in this
night club? Hadn't he bid farewell from the deck of the *Suffren* almost a week earlier?
Then, as the marshal waved to him, he burst out laughing and sat down at our table.[4]

During his Vichy years Pétain often recalled his American experience. "He
had been deeply moved by the welcome he had received. He was fond of recalling the generosity of many Americans toward France, the acrobatic feats of Theodore Roosevelt, the accomplishments of the American flying unit Lafayette. . . .
In short, it was delirious."[5]

Pétain's pro-American sentiments dated back to World War I, when General
Pershing lent him his full support against bitter critics of his role as military
commander. The French people echoed his feelings. The marshal was close
enough to them to realize they would never pardon a policy that alienated the
United States from France. The French disliked the Germans and mistrusted the
British; they saw in the United States the only force capable of one day redeem-

ing them. "France-Amérique" committees were still active in a number of cities; they organized secret debates and published clandestine pamphlets. Several officials in the Pétain entourage firmly believed that only an Allied victory could save France and that only American intervention would make it possible.

Roosevelt was not indifferent to the "hero of Verdun," the epic battle he had described so movingly during his wartime visit to France. He respected the marshal's advanced age and was probably touched by his affection for the United States. The president was also convinced that Pétain represented the lesser evil. Unsavory characters such as Laval and Darlan might sell out to the Germans, but not Pétain. Accordingly, U.S. policy was aimed at strengthening the marshal's will to resist Nazi demands and go no further than the strict implementation of the conditions of the armistice.

The unquestioned loyalty of generals, admirals, and colonial administrators to Pétain could not fail to impress the president. Obedience to the marshal's orders were blind; disobedience was equated with treason and infamy. These considerations weighed heavily when the invasion of North and West Africa was planned. Nor could Roosevelt overlook the evident affection the French had for Pétain. During the tragic years that followed their country's defeat, the French people felt for Pétain the same sentiments they would later display for de Gaulle. They turned to these leaders for reassurance and protection. As France's second postwar president, Georges Pompidou, wrote:

France cannot and must not deny the fact that during 1940–44 she was to a large extent favorable to Marshal Pétain. . . . The crowds that applauded de Gaulle beginning in the summer of 1944 were the same that had applauded Pétain the preceding spring. I remember a remark General de Gaulle made upon his return from Nancy, where he had been enthusiastically greeted on the Place Stanislas. He showed me a photo of the Marshal on the balcony of the same place before an enthusiastic crowd. He said to me: "Make no mistake, the people are the same." The truth is that in both cases the people demonstrated the same sentiment: hostility before the enemy and confidence in the leader who protected them.[6]

Not everyone in Washington was taken with the Pétain legend. Secretary of the Interior Harold Ickes told the French ambassador Henry-Haye that he "did not think much of Marshal Pétain and referred to critical comments made about Pétain in books written by such men as Foch, Clemenceau, and others just after the last world war."[7] Similar sentiments were voiced by those who appreciated de Gaulle's efforts to bring France back into the war. But this group was in the minority and, apart from Morgenthau, not particularly influential in foreign affairs.

Most of those who counted in Washington followed Roosevelt, who had for Pétain an "old and deep affection."[8] The French ambassador reported on a long conversation with Secretary of War Henry Stimson, who "bade me to transmit a personal message to Marshal Pétain. In it he stated that he had a very vivid

memory of his meeting with the head of the French State in 1931 [at the time
Stimson was Secretary of State], and expressed his admiration for the work the
Marshal was accomplishing daily."[9] The president's personal representative to
the Vatican, Myron Taylor, reportedly told Ambassador Léon Berard of "the admiration the Marshal inspired."[10] Bullitt, too, had a "high personal regard" for
Pétain.[11] Admiral Leahy professed to hold Pétain "in the highest regard as a patriot completely devoted to the welfare of his people."

Americans involved with foreign relations or the war effort – diplomats, industrial managers, bankers, businessmen – were as a rule deeply conservative,
viscerally anti-Communist, and fearful of violence and revolution. Quite understandably, they felt at home in Vichy's strongly conservative atmosphere, where
the military and the navy were highly influential, high-ranking civil servants
leaned to the right, and for the first time members of the privileged classes
headed municipalities and departements.[12] Cardinals and bishops sang Pétain's
praises. The very wealthy felt reassured that the specter of social revolution they
had feared in 1936, when the socialist Léon Blum was in power, had vanished
forever. "Vichy was more the creation of experts and professionals than of any
other social group," Robert O. Paxton wrote, "and to judge Vichy is to judge the
French elite."[13] Roosevelt shared his privileged class's dread of mob violence and
revolution, and he worried that one day American soldiers would be fighting the
Germans on French soil. Would they also be called upon to fight anarchy in the
rear to prevent threats to U.S. lines of communication? Roosevelt was deeply
concerned about this possibility, and this concern certainly colored his politics
regarding the French.

As ambassador to Vichy the president selected an old friend, Admiral William
Leahy, whose judgment he trusted completely. The appointment was warmly
welcomed by Pétain: "The Marshal is delighted that the choice of the U.S. Government is a personality that combines distinguished service with the privilege
of being close to the President and personally approved by him. He is furthermore very sensitive to the mark of sympathy toward his person that the choice
represents."[14]

Leahy kept a diary (now in the Library of Congress) in which he listed all his
appointments. In addition to government officials, his contacts included diplomatic colleagues, French aristocrats, and people who counted in Vichy's unreal
world. He was once scolded by Darlan for "constantly" receiving "people like
Louis Marin and Edouard Herriot whose hostility to the Marshal and his government is well known." Leahy considered the accusation a "direct reflection on
my loyalty to the Marshal," adding that he had never met Louis Marin and had
only once met Herriot, when he called at the embassy to pay his respects, at
which time no political matters were discussed. He maintained that he had "not
discussed political questions with any other individuals than the Marshal and
the Minister of Foreign Affairs." While Pétain was "gracious and agreeable,"
Darlan mentioned "reports from his secret police and his telephone intercepts
that many individuals antagonistic to the Marshal's Government have visited

the American Embassy, that some of them claim to have access to the Ambassador and have the backing of the American Government, and that there are reports that these individuals do have contacts with subordinates in the Embassy." Leahy objected that "the only information of any value received by the Embassy comes from officials of the Marshal's Government who are not, or have not heretofore been, satisfied with the prospect of collaboration with the Germans" (4 June 1941). On one occasion the ambassador did list the names of officials who fell into the latter category. It seems obvious that due to police surveillance, telephone tapping, and official rebukes, the ambassador's view was limited to Pétain and his official circles. On 28 July Leahy wrote the president, "All of us in the Embassy are under constant police surveillance, all our telephone conversations are reported, and at least some officials in the Government have been warned not to become too friendly with any of us."

In the same letter (now in the National Archives), Leahy reported:

The de Gaulle movement has not the following or the strength that is indicated in British radio news and in the American press. The Frenchmen *with whom I can talk* [emphasis added] have little regard for M. de Gaulle, even those who are completely desirous of a British victory and whose hopes have been stimulated by the slow progress of Germany in Russia. I have conclusive evidence that there does exist in the occupied zone an organization of the Gaullists which is devoting itself with some small success in sabotaging methods and annoying the invaders, and to propagandizing the inhabitants. The radical de Gaullists with whom I have met do not seem to have the stability, intelligence, and popular standing in their communities that should be necessary to success in their announced purpose. One of them recently told me that all the Ministers of the Vichy Government are under sentence of death which can be carried out when it suits the purpose of the organization.

In other words, the organization was nothing but a band of terrorists! Vichy's officials would not have phrased it differently.

Fear of disorders, civil war, and violence leading to communism were constantly recurring themes, to which Roosevelt was sensitive. "The Government is very concerned about the present and prospective Communist activities, particularly in the occupied area. The Communist 'Party' seems to be the only organized self-styled political party and the only group with sufficient courage to act against the invaders."[15] "It is generally believed now that even if the marshal should remain until a peace is made a withdrawal of the German forces of occupation will be immediately followed by revolutionary activity instigated by professional politicians who are now out of office."[16] The marshal hoped that Germany would defeat the Soviet Union, to avert a Communist uprising, and that the United States would in turn defeat the Germans. "I am convinced from personal conversations with the Marshal," Leahy wrote, "that he and his Ministers are very much afraid of communism in France and that he looks to America for aid in preservation of so much of France as can be saved." "Laval fears a

Communist revolution in France when Germany withdraws its army of occupation," he added.

From time to time members of the underground would slip into the Embassy. Sometimes they practically forced themselves on me and told what they were doing. These undergrounders (maquis) generally seemed to be erratic. They did not seem to be organized or well directed. They had strange ideas about what they were accomplishing by throwing a bomb here and there. Such information as they gave was not particularly valuable. . . . I would have to say to them that although I had a great deal of sympathy for them, I was accredited to the Government of France as represented by Marshal Pétain and he was the only person with whom I would do business.[17]

As for de Gaulle, "like Laval and Darlan, he thirsted for power. . . . His political philosophy appears to be little different from that of the Government of Pétain."[18] At the time of the Syrian affair, "there was still no indication in occupied France that the self-styled 'leader of French resistance' had any important numerical following." At another time he had to admit that "the de Gaulle movement is much stronger in France than is indicated by the attitude of officials of the Marshal's Government."

The shooting of hostages by the Nazis was mentioned in passing. All Leahy had to say about the Jews' tragic fate was that "there had been discrimination against the Jews at Vichy, aimed principally at getting hold of their money. Many Jewish families feared their homes would be searched or even confiscated. . . . So far as I know, however, no Jewish homes were searched."[19]

It took several months at his post for Leahy to reach the conclusion that Vichy was at the mercy of the Germans; that Pétain was a spineless "jellyfish"; that Darlan was ready to throw himself on the winner's side; that he had no positive results to show for his efforts; and that it would perhaps be best for the president to show his displeasure by recalling him to Washington for "consultation."

In March 1942, in reply to a further request for action, Roosevelt said that

the timing of such step has now become of paramount military importance. In fact, the joint Staff missions have very definitely urged that we postpone as long as possible any evidence of change in our relations with France and they consider that to hold the fort as you are concerned is as important a military task as any other in these days. . . . Not only is our presence in France and North Africa the last bridgehead to Europe but it likewise helps to hold the Iberian Peninsula in line.

The president referred to the "impending Mediterranean drive [which] will be one of the most important of the war," an obvious reference to the planned invasion of North Africa.

France had proclaimed her neutrality in the struggle between the United States and the Axis powers; good relations with both were a condition for its respect. At Vichy, sentiment varied from one belligerent to the other and according to the fortunes of war. Whatever the final outcome, Vichy intended to be on the winning side. "When you have three thousand tanks, six thousand planes and five hundred thousand men to bring to Marseilles, let me know. Then we shall welcome you," Darlan told Leahy.[20] At the same time Vichy offered to adhere to the Tripartite Pact – joining Germany, Italy, and Japan – and to assume all necessary obligations. Later that same year, on 25 December 1941, Vichy proposed that France and Germany join in defending Africa. Two weeks later, on 11 January 1942, it offered to join the Reich in a military alliance, and in September it made a request to participate actively in the defense of the French coast. Thus, four times did Vichy propose to throw itself into Hitler's arms in exchange for political concessions that were contemptuously rejected.

Despite Germany's repeated rebuffs, the two most powerful men in Vichy after the marshal, Pierre Laval and Jean Darlan, believed the French would outsmart the Germans in the end.

Laval at a dinner in presence of a "highly placed American": You will see, we will be the gainers in the end. We shall become the Number One ally of Germany in the new order for Europe. Italy? The Germans have only contempt for the Italians. Nothing can stop the Germans. They will have the English on their backs in a few weeks. America is fat, rich, lazy, and ignorant. They will not resist. The Russians even now are shivering in their boots. We must pretend to collaborate in good faith with the Germans but the French are a much cleverer race. Within ten years it will be us, not them, who shall be ruling Europe. We shall accomplish this with the formidable German army. True it is not a French army, but what of that? Any army will do, as long as it serves our purposes. Our loins have failed us, not our wits. As for France, she needed this lesson. She needed a strong fist to restore discipline and order. But now we must begin to repair our losses with guile.[21]

Darlan has a more moderate view of the future, but he too was optimistic. His son Alain has quoted him as saying, "The more time passes the more the difference between France's feebleness and Germany's power will be reduced, because, on the one hand, Germany will keep burning up more and more of her energies in the war, while, on the other hand, if we maneuver with ability, France will be in a position to more and more recover her strength."[22]

As Mussolini's foreign minister, Galeazzo Ciano, caustically noted: "The Laval Government is formed. It is a government of under-secretaries and unknowns. It practically remains a Pétain-Darlan government. Thus France prepares for all three eventualities: a British victory, de Gaulle; a Germany victory, Laval; a compromise, Pétain."[23]

In their vanity, the Vichy French feigned ignorance of the contempt in which the Germans held them. Joseph Goebbels noted in his diary on 2 April 1942 that

we must not hold any great hopes in respect of the French situation. I consider the French people to be sick and rotten. Something worthwhile in the way of positive contributions to the resurrection of Europe is hardly to be expected from them. This proves that the Fuehrer's policy toward France has been absolutely correct. The French must be put on ice. As soon as they are flattered, they treat it as pseudo-revenge. The more they are left in suspense, the quicker they will be inclined to stay in their place.

Hitler told his Paris ambassador Otto Abetz that he had no respect for a people who threw themselves into the arms of the victor against their former allies.

In August 1942 Goebbels explained to Nazis senior officials what the Germans meant by "collaboration": "If they hand over until they can't hand over any more and if they do it of their own free will, then I'll say that I am collaborating, and that must be made clear to the French."[24] The Germans, agreeing with the Americans in this respect, considered Darlan shifty and unreliable. He was not trusted to collaborate in the way Hitler wanted France to collaborate. The only person the Germans did trust for the task was Laval, and they insisted on his return to power. Roosevelt warned that Laval's recall would lead to a break in relations. The Germans considered the American ultimatum sufficient reason for imposing him on France.

In a telegram to French ambassador Henry-Haye marked "ultra-secret," which found its way to Roosevelt's desk, Laval reported on his interview with the departing Admiral Leahy:

I told him that in spite of the abuses lavished on France and especially on me by the press and radio of the United States, I would do nothing, I would not perform a single act, I would not make a gesture, I would not say a single word which might be interpreted as being hostile, or even impolite, toward the United States. . . . France will do nothing to break diplomatic relations with the United States. France will not take any initiative. Besides it should be noted that Wilhelmstrasse, although representing a victorious nation, never asked France to engage in any act hostile toward the United States.

Laval then explained the reasons for his actions:

My policy is based on collaboration with Germany, for without collaboration I see no possibility for peace, neither for Europe, nor for France, nor for the world. I am certain that Germany will be victorious [underlined by Roosevelt]. But even if it should be conquered, my policy in regard to it would remain the same, for it is the only country in favor of a definite peace. . . . I am now convinced that France will be the necessary intermediary between the United States and Europe.[25]

Documents that came to light during the Pétain trial show the ambiguity of the marshal's position on international affairs. On 21 June 1941, the very day on which the Germans invaded the Soviet Union, he received a paper, based on conversations at the highest level, from a nonidentified "witness to U.S. war preparations," detailing the enormous scale of military buildup in which that country was engaged. The writer offered numerous documented examples of America's gradual shift from a peacetime to a wartime economy, stressing the irreversible nature of the process, and concluded:

French policy must adapt itself to a double exigency: to conduct a policy of survival until the country has recovered its sovereignty; to account for the U.S. joining the war and its determination to emerge victorious. The first exigency can only be implemented in accord with the occupying power. The second must consider the need of managing the future. . . . We no longer need to ask ourselves what will happen to the British, but what the Americans have decided."

This document was one of the few the marshal took along when, following the total occupation of France, Hitler exiled him to Germany. Another document Pétain preserved was Sumner Welles's statement explaining why the United States, despite its loathing of bolshevism, had decided to assist Soviet resistance. Pétain marked in the margin a reference to Americans' rejecting both nazism and bolshevism and appended to the text a "personal note":

We are, Americans and French, confronted with two doctrines whose implementation we consider undesirable: Nazism and bolshevism. Bolshevism is for Europe the greater danger. There is no reason why we Europeans should regret the blows it receives. The rule of Nazism is also not to be desired for it would impose on the people under its control constraints very heavy to bear. One can foresee that due to these constraints and the enormity of the enterprise, cracks will soon appear that will cause the edifice to collapse.[26]

This note could comfort the thesis, stressed at the Pétain trial by his attorneys, of a *double jeu*, the necessity of managing the Nazis while awaiting a hoped-for Anglo-American victory. He even told Chargé d'Affaires Freeman Matthews that an Anglo-American victory would be in France's interest. Vichy's policy was in fact based on the assumption that neither the West nor Germany could win the war and that its continuation would only mean exhausting Europe and opening the way to bolshevism. Only a compromise peace could avert the danger and at the same time save France from once again becoming a battlefield. Both the United States and France being neutral, should they not join in promoting the peace to which Germany aspired?

Pétain kept hoping that Roosevelt would see the light even after the United States had joined the war. He shared Laval's conviction that the future reserved a major mediatory role for France. Nothing will ever stop the French from dreaming of *grandeur*. The November 1942 invasion of North Africa, however, put an end to Vichy and its hopes for the future.

Vichy failed to understand that Hitler's plans never included a federated Europe in which France, as Laval had thought, could occupy an honorable place. His objective was the creation of a Greater Germany surrounded by satellite states, each serving, according to its means, the master race. Hitler's policy for France was to compromise collaborators so severely, to cause them to be so hated, that they could have no choice but to serve him to the end. Collaborators were to be made aware that the Reich's defeat would mean their own deaths. Indeed, a number of them supported Hitler to the end before facing French firing squads. If Hitler and von Ribbentrop agreed to receive Laval and Darlan at regular intervals, it was not so much to discuss mutual concessions as to remind them that if the German army were compelled to abandon France, they would no longer be able to contain the French masses. "This communion in malediction," wrote the German historian Eberhard Jäckel, "was the only basis Hitler could conceive for a collaboration."[27]

Washington misread the motives behind Hitler's Vichy policies. The president believed his own policy on Vichy had been dictated by military necessity and had paid off. The U.S. embassy was in close touch with French military intelligence (the Deuxieme Bureau), which provided useful information; meanwhile, U.S. consulates at Lyons, Marseilles, and Nice kept discreet contact with the Resistance, and intelligence agents disguised as vice consuls had been placed at strategic North African centers. These presences were also a way of letting the French know they had not been forgotten.

Roosevelt seemed convinced his policy had strengthened Vichy's determination to prevent German encroachments on the fleet and North Africa, though it is now clear he overestimated Pétain's ability to stand up to Hitler. Hitler was not interested in the French fleet and was quite happy to let the Italians have it. As to the eastern Mediterranean, after Franco's refusal to allow the Wehrmacht to cross Spain on the way to subduing Gibraltar, it was for Hitler a secondary theater of operations.

Hitler's strategy was focused on the East, to the plains of the Soviet Union, where he planned to settle his own people. Once the Soviets were defeated, he thought, the British would realize the futility of continuing the war and would come to terms. At that time, and only at that time, would he settle accounts with the West as a whole. Great Britain would be requested to hand back former German colonies in Africa and undertake never again to meddle in European affairs; France would become an amusement park for the benefit of the Greater Reich. The fate of the colonies would be decided as part of a general settlement; meanwhile, the French could preserve their overseas possessions on condition they succeeded in preventing their seizure by the British or the Gaullists. Vichy was to give proof of compliance.

While awaiting a final settlement, Vichy served Hitler's strategy. The Germans did as they pleased in France, and they considered illusory any thought that Washington could strengthen Vichy's will to resist. It could be argued (even though the argument is risky) that for Washington to prop up Vichy was to do the Germans a favor. Berlin found merit in U.S.–Vichy ties and never asked for a break, but obviously not because Vichy might one day mediate between the United States and Germany. With the Paris Protocols of August 1941 Vichy was ready for military concessions in Tunisia and Dakar in exchange for political concessions that Hitler was under no circumstances willing to make.

For a year and a half following the fall of France, the United States was technically a neutral, maintaining diplomatic ties with Hitler's Germany, Mussolini's Italy, Franco's Spain, and Salazar's Portugal. There was therefore no reason not to maintain an embassy in Vichy as well. After all, the British continued to accept Vichy's consuls in Great Britain until 1943. There was a U.S. ambassador in Vichy, but also one with the Free French in Algiers, and one was to be appointed in Paris upon the establishment of a government in the French capital. No such split of authority had been necessary with the governments representing the other countries at war with Germany. All were recognized by the United States as legitimate. Unlike France, they never ceased to "exist."

This highly legalistic approach might have satisfied official Washington, but not the countries at war with Germany, which, unlike France, had not come to terms with the Nazis. They took offense at the aura of respectability the U.S. presence conferred on the Vichy regime. By dealing with Vichy, the United States was, in the words of British historian Sir Llewellyn Woodward, attempting "to buy the last-minute support of collaborationists and quislings." This policy "would offend not only French feelings but the feelings of other European peoples who had suffered from German methods of warfare and occupation, and yet, unlike Vichy, had refused to come to profitable terms with them." Leahy obviously had not realized "why the British and other European allies felt so deeply about the moral offense of French collaborationism."[28] Upon his return to the United States, he told the press that except for the Franco-Japanese agreement on Indochina, the Pétain government had done nothing to provide the enemies of the United States with any form of assistance!

Pétain's benign countenance had seduced many American *bien-pensants* while offending French citizens who loathed what they saw behind the mask. Roussy de Sales, the French exile, poignantly stressed the contrast:

I do not pretend that the French are not responsible for the Vichy regime, the armistice, the passive submission of the collaborators and everything else. They might not have wanted it, but they accepted it. Pétain corresponds to a real state of mind. He was the symbol of a defeated France, ready to try anything so long as no effort was asked of her. This was a France strangely masochistic, denying its own history, its allies, everything that was honorable. Pétain was an anachronism who pleased bourgeois and peasant France, as well as the working classes with their middle class outlook, seeking an impossible refuge against reality in a return to the past. Pétain was the France of priests and generals, egoistic peasants and penny pinching penpushers. Pétain was the France of the worldly set, the "right" women sleeping with the "wrong" ministers, ambassadors and bankers, who said, "The true blood of France is its gold." This was the France of the discouraged intellectual, the sad academic and shady journalist. Pétain was the France that only believed in the dead and in money.[29]

7

No Recognition for de Gaulle

The United States entered the war against the Axis without a clear definition of its aims. During the preceding six years Roosevelt had striven to influence events while lacking the means to take action on his policies. Clear in his mind was the conviction that fascism and democracy could not coexist; not so clear was his vision of the world that would emerge from the destruction of fascism. He was capable of compromising his principles to attain his ends and was often impatient with "star-gazing idealists." He considered himself a realist, but his realism seldom took into account the lessons of history. The issue of France, as he saw it, fell within a framework in which historical references had no place. He could not be expected to agree with Anthony Eden that the full restoration of France as a great power was a "practical necessity, if post-war reconstruction is to be undertaken within *the framework of that traditional civilization* which is our common heritage" (emphasis added).[1]

Roosevelt's project was mainly an intellectual exercise based on abstract notions that found little credit with men like Churchill and Stalin, who possessed a far greater understanding of the impact of the past upon the present. By suggesting that concern with French politics awaited the liberation of France, what he was in fact proposing was a nonpolicy, for it ignored the fact that people fight in pursuit of an ideal that finds its concrete realization in politics. This deliberate disregard of politics preceded the invasion of North Africa and paved the way for the problems that followed. Anthony Eden finally reached the conclusion that Americans "know very little of Europe and it would be unfortunate for the future of the world if the U.S. uninstructed views were to decide the future of the European continent."[2]

The invasion of North Africa had been agreed on in principle late in 1941, and the decision to carry it out was made the following spring. Since the area to be invaded comprised a French departement (Algeria), two French protectorates (Tunisia and Morocco), and a colony (West Africa), a review of U.S. French policies became imperative.

In the months preceding Pearl Harbor, Washington had shown a marked increase in sympathy for the Free French. They began to receive Lend-Lease assistance, defense of Free French–controlled territories being deemed "vital to the defense of the United States." They were also allowed representation in Washington, and Free French passports became valid. "No divergence of interests existed at the time between Washington and the French Committee; relations were a dream," Pierre Billotte wrote.[3] Upon being notified of the constitution of a French National Committee in London, the State Department stated that U.S. policy toward France "is based upon the maintenance of the integrity of France and of the French Empire and of the eventual restoration of the complete independence of all French territories," adding that "in its relations with the local French authorities, the United States will be governed by the manifest effectiveness with which those authorities endeavor to protect these territories from domination and control by those powers which are seeking to extend their rule by force and conquest, or by the threat thereof." The rule was evidently general: Whoever was in a position to prevent the Germans from extending their domination over French territories, whether Vichy or the Free French, would be entitled to U.S. assistance. This policy was dictated by military, not political, considerations.

A May 1942 Gallup poll confirmed American sympathy for the Free French: Of those interviewed, 58 percent believed that Vichy favored the Axis and 65 percent disapproved of Vichy's policies, but 49 percent advocated continued recognition of Vichy. When asked who represented French opinion best, de Gaulle or Pétain, the response was de Gaulle, 75 percent, and Pétain, 13 percent; 74 percent also favored extending Lend-Lease assistance to de Gaulle, with only 16 percent against it.[4]

The atmosphere soured following the Free French occupation of two small islands off the Canadian coast, St. Pierre and Miquelon.[5] Americans applauded the deed that followed Pearl Harbor by just a few days, but Cordell Hull considered it an act of defiance toward the United States and a violation of the Monroe Doctrine. His "so-called Free French" epithet became notorious and brought forth an outpouring of protests to the "so-called State Department." The president was deeply embarrassed by what he termed a tempest in a teapot and suggested charging Sumner Welles with handling the situation. He disapproved of Hull's turning the incident into a personal affair because it betrayed in Hull a lack of the objectivity required of a high government official.[6] For a time he considered replacing Hull and desisted only because of the secretary's influence with the Senate.

There is no evidence that at that time the president shared Hull's visceral hostility toward de Gaulle. What turned him against the French general was the fiasco of the British–Free French expedition to capture Dakar. He had never liked the initiative, for it seemed to him that de Gaulle was out to provoke a civil war merely to satisfy his personal ambitions, without consideration for French and Allied interests. Robert Murphy, who was to play a key role in North Africa as the president's personal representative, believed that "Roosevelt never lost the distrust of de Gaulle's judgement and discretion which he formed then, and this distrust was a major factor in French-American relations right up to the President's death in 1945."[7] The fiasco was also the result of loose talk by the Free French, strengthening Roosevelt's conviction that de Gaulle's headquarters in London was a "leaky sieve," not to be trusted with military secrets. Washington was concerned that had the expedition succeeded, the Germans might have countered by occupying North Africa. De Gaulle was considered irresponsible for overlooking the disastrous effect that a Nazi countermove would have had on the Allied military efforts. A Nazi-controlled Dakar would have presented a direct threat to Brazil and hence to the entire Western Hemisphere.

The differences in character and political judgment between Roosevelt and de Gaulle, examined earlier, might well have influenced the president's attitude. The question remains whether his French policies might have been different had he felt for de Gaulle as warmly as he did for Churchill. Most probably not.

Washington's relations with the Free French in the months preceding the invasion of North Africa had their ups and downs. All was serene when on 9 July 1942 the United States recognized in the National Committee a "symbol of French resistance to the Axis powers," with de Gaulle expressing his appreciation to the president the next day; relations grew stormy when the president supported the British in their conflict with the Free French over the Middle East and when the British took over the island of Madagascar. Roosevelt approved the move. When the weather was fair, U.S. recognition represented, in de Gaulle's words, "a powerful moral encouragement for the French people in their heroic will of resistance to the oppressor"; when not, de Gaulle gave vent to denunciation of America's "expanding imperialism." Relations could on occasion become stormy enough that so staid a person as General Catroux could argue in a "strictly personal" message to de Gaulle: "American policy continues to be the result of the most various factors: starry-eyed romanticism, brutal materialism, economic imperialism, machiavellism and puerility, the whole merging into a sort of messianism, both unconscionable and arrogant (*sur de lui*)."[8]

The Free French were particularly anxious to convince Washington that the Resistance was fully on their side. During the second half of 1942 they undertook a campaign for American opinion highlighted by the visit of a distinguished Resistance leader, Emmanuel d'Astier de la Vigerie. He provided figures on Resistance activity that attested to the cooperation between the two groups. (Both the American and the British secret services considered the figures blown out of proportion.) Events, however, spoke louder than figures. Following the heroic stand by the Free French at Bir Hakeim, Laval's statement favoring a German victory, and the increasing impatience of the American press with a pro-Vichy policy, American sympathies began to shift to de Gaulle's followers. Tixier reported that "the atmosphere is much improved . . . and a détente is evident. Our demarches are better received throughout the administration. It seems evident that new directives have been issued indicative of a wish to be favorable toward us." But when in November Tixier pleaded for admission of the Free French to the United Nations, Welles retorted that they had not received legal authority from the French people to represent them. The legitimacy issue thus again reared its head.[9]

The year 1942 marked the beginning of an evolution in U.S. policy toward France due primarily to the emergence of the U.S. military as a determining factor in the war. Secretary of War Henry Stimson gradually assumed many of the policy functions normally delegated to the State Department, to the point that the latter often became subordinated to the former. George Kennan remarked that during the war the State Department regarded its role "as nothing more than that of a messenger boy for the Pentagon" and became accustomed to "sneezing whenever the Pentagon got cold."[10] The president decided the large strategic issues facing the United States, but unlike Winston Churchill, who intervened in every military decision, he left a very wide berth to his generals. His primary concern was to get to Berlin by the shortest possible route at the minimum cost in American lives.

With an army of some 20,000 men, it was felt de Gaulle could afford to speak "morality"; the Americans were in the process of putting 15 million men in uniform and had other priorities. Neither de Gaulle nor, to a lesser degree, the British, fully appreciated the complexity of the president's task. Due to the tremendous responsibilities the United States was assuming, the president's policies became steadily more militarily oriented. Roosevelt relied increasingly on his brilliant army chief of staff, General George Marshall, "the noblest Roman of them all," as Churchill called him.[11] Lacking Roosevelt's emotional involvement in French politics, his generals in time came to appreciate the role de Gaulle could play, and that, as we shall see, represented a major turning point.

Admiral Harold Raynsford Stark played a significant role in changing the direction of U.S. policy regarding France. Chief of naval operations prior to the Pearl Harbor disaster, he had been assigned to London as commander of U.S. naval forces in Europe.[12] Cordell Hull had asked him to consult with de Gaulle and get permission for the United States to use the territories under Free French control for a variety of purposes. He acquitted himself so well that he soon became the *de facto* U.S. ambassador to de Gaulle. An admiring Anthony Eden half jokingly asked him if he would handle British relations with the temperamental general as well.

A few pages from the admiral's diary are revealing:

Thursday, May 7, 1942. Had most interesting call on General de Gaulle today. I had been told that the ego stuck out all over him and he was dominating, and I gathered pompous and rather difficult. I found him just the opposite – calm, easy-going and very pleasant. I had, what I was afraid might be, a delicate mission. I was delighted to accomplish it with so much ease. . . . From my own standpoint the meeting was most satisfactory in every respect.

May 9. . . . found dispatch from COMINCH [commander in chief, U.S. Navy] requiring that I again visit de Gaulle to obtain his consent for action in New Caledonia. . . . Upon reaching his Headquarters, found de Gaulle somewhat upset and in a truculent mood but after about a twenty minute talk, his Aides and our manner had calmed him to such a point that we obtained practically all that we desired.

May 11. . . . after lunch . . . , we went to de Gaulle's headquarters and found him in the most evil temper that I have ever seen him so far. However, our own calm, I believe, made him feel somewhat ashamed of his actions and upon leaving after a short visit, he was well on the road of being reasonable once more. . . . [Sent] the last results of our conference with de Gaulle to Washington.

May 12. . . . made a final review of the de Gaulle situation.

June 3. . . . [Long interview with Admiral Musilier, who explained his problems with de Gaulle.] In the course of the conversation, Admiral Musilier explained that from a political point of view, the de Gaulle Movement should absolutely cease to be dictatorial in his policies because after victory was achieved if General de Gaulle should return to France with this dictatorial type of Government, the result would be civil war. . . . Admiral Musilier concluded by offering his services to us.

June 16. [Visit by de Gaulle.] General de Gaulle remarked that the Coral Sea and Midway battles had appeared to be definitive setbacks to the Japs, to which I agreed.

June 20. . . . designated as Representative for the United States Government for military consultations with General de Gaulle and the French National Committee in all matters concerned with the conditions of the war.[13]

The actual date of the appointment was 9 July; Vichy issued a protest on 13 July. Brigadier General Charles L. Bolte had been appointed at the same time to represent the army. Also on 9 July, the United States issued a declaration recognizing the contributions of de Gaulle and the French National Committee to keeping France's traditional spirit and institutions alive; it added that the U.S. military objective would be aided by lending all military assistance and all possible support to the French National Committee as a symbol of French resistance, in general, to the Axis powers. Once again recognition of de Gaulle and his National Committee was military and in no way political. That condition remained unchanged until the liberation of France.

Bolte having been transferred to other duties, Stark was left as sole U.S. representative to de Gaulle. Even though Cordell Hull had been responsible for the designation, the admiral reported to Secretary of the Navy Frank Knox, who in turn made the information available to the Pentagon and, on rare occasions, to the State Department. Stark was fortunate in having been seconded by Lieutenant Commander Tracy B. Kittredge, who was born in Paris, spoke fluent French, and was ever the diplomat. His sympathies for the Free French soon became evident.

De Gaulle was aware that the cross-Channel invasion had been decided upon, with only the date to be set, and he resented being excluded from the planning sessions. Profiting from the arrival in London of George Marshall and Ernest J. King, he asked for an interview; a meeting was arranged on 23 July 1942. The conference that followed was described by Marshall's biographer, Forrest C. Pogue, as "one of the stuffier confrontations of the war" due to a British request that details of future initiatives not be revealed to the French leader.[14] De Gaulle was in an argumentative mood, and King noted that his approach was "scarcely calculated to make friends"; he merely succeeded in making a terrible impression on Marshall, thus losing the backing of "one of the few officials who might have been able to soften the president's antagonism."[15] It was particularly unfortunate for the Free French and the United States that Marshall's impressions confirmed the anti-Gaullist attitude already prevalent in Washington precisely when the decision to invade North Africa was being finalized.

Roosevelt realized that the invasion would inevitably lead to a break with Vichy. He believed contacts with de Gaulle might prove more useful if the National Committee became more democratic. A more representative image might also induce distinguished French personalities to lend their support, something they had so far refused to do.[16] The general realized the absence of well-respected names had been detrimental to Free France's image. He had persistently tried to induce Leger and Maritain to join him in London, and their refusal had not exactly inspired other personalities to join de Gaulle. No significant political figures were among his followers; not one diplomat (the French embassy in London had returned en masse to France), no high officials, no captains of industry.

Washington consulted London on ways to induce de Gaulle to improve the image of his Committee by accepting majority rule and tempering his autocratic demeanor, but publication in the New York Times of 26 May of a summary of the conversations between Sumner Welles and Ambassador Lord Halifax infuriated de Gaulle. He reacted testily to the Anglo-Saxons' intrusion into his domain. British suggestions that de Gaulle might be satisfied with recognition as head of resistance in occupied France were turned down in Washington in the name of legitimacy.

The British were soon to modify their relationship with the Free French, who had changed their name to Fighting France. On 14 July La France Combattante was recognized as the symbol of French resistance worldwide, the French National Committee (no longer de Gaulle personally) representing its unity. The Committee was not considered competent, however, to represent internationally the French citizens not belonging to the organization.[17]

René Cassin, future Nobel Peace Prize winner and among the first to rally to Free France, lamented that de Gaulle had "too long neglected by an excess of confidence" to contact Washington. Late in October, probably aware that the Americans were preparing to land in North Africa, de Gaulle finally addressed a letter to the president. Official Washington wondered why it had taken two years for the French general to "discover" the United States. Ray Atherton, head of the European Desk at the State Department, commented that had the letter "been written at the outset of the de Gaulle movement it would have been a great asset in our relations with them, but it was two years too late." He regretted that de Gaulle in his "blindness" failed to understand that U.S. relations with Vichy were "based on the best hopes for preserving the French Empire."[18]

The letter, beautifully written and at times quite moving, proposed to allay the impression that Free France was intent on acting as a government and to dispose of the charge that the writer had dictatorial ambitions. Its central thesis, however, was at odds with the U.S. position that France would begin to exist only after liberation and that in the meantime Washington would deal with whoever was in charge locally. "We deem it necessary," de Gaulle wrote, "to be approached each time the issue concerns France's general interests, French participation in the war, the administration of French territories that the evolution of the war gradually places in a position to resume the combat and which had not spontaneously rallied to us." De Gaulle's ambitions to take charge of French interests everywhere could only encounter American refusal, as events in North Africa were soon to demonstrate.

Roosevelt had been focusing his attention on North and West Africa for quite some time. For over a year before the actual landing he had been determined to secure at least West Africa and Dakar. The president informed Lord Halifax that he had told Stimson and Marshall to make a study of the possibility of sending a U.S. expeditionary force to West Africa. This request, Lord Halifax wrote, "greatly excited" the war secretary and the army chief of staff, who thought the president "was going off the deep end and embarking on a dispersal of efforts that they thought unwise."[19] The president was not contemplating immediate action, but if Pétain were to die and Weygand were to feel himself released from his personal pledge of loyalty, affairs might heat up quickly. All Roosevelt wanted for the time being was to have the question studied. Knox had talked to Halifax about landing 150,000 U.S. troops in Morocco. "We must be ready if possible with a simultaneous offer, or anyhow a British offer, to General Weygand," Churchill wrote to General Ismay.

Roosevelt had already spoken to Lord Halifax in October 1940, more than a year before Pearl Harbor. In May 1941, again long before the United States entered the war, Ickes was writing in his diary: "More and more people are coming to believe that if we do not occupy Dakar before the infiltrating Germans take it over, we will have lost a major battle in the greatest war in history."[20]

The deadline for the invasion of North Africa was approaching, and soon the military would have to deal with the French directly. Of immediate interest to them was whether recognition of de Gaulle would favorably affect the impending operations. In September the Joint Chiefs of Staff directed a Joint Intelligence Committee to prepare, as a matter of urgency, "an estimate of the military effects of a policy of political recognition, or non-recognition, of General de Gaulle."[21] Note that it was the "military effects," not the political consequences, that were addressed.

The Department of War Military Intelligence Service opined that immediate recognition would have a negative effect, but it added, "The policy of non-recognition had its drawbacks more from a political than a military standpoint." It continued, "On balance, it would seem that if consideration of the official recognition could be further deferred the military effect of such a policy would be beneficial even though the long range political aspects of the situation might suffer thereunder."

An estimate of the total strength of the Free French army accompanied the memorandum:

	Whites	Natives	Total
French Equatorial Africa	1,500	12,500	14,000
Syria (Syrian and Lebanese special troops, including guards, police, etc.)	1,000	12,770	13,770
Egypt (colonial infantry)	1,500	6,340	7,840
New Caledonia	600	600	1,200
Tahiti	300	–	300
Great Britain	1,000	–	1,000
St. Pierre and Miquelon	300	–	300
	6,200	32,210	38,410

The Syrians and the Lebanese proved to be unreliable; de Gaulle's army was rated at slightly over 25,000 men.[22]

The State Department's Division of Near Eastern Affairs, while admitting that recognition would increase the general's "presumption," realized that "the advantages of recognition of de Gaulle outweigh the disadvantages. We can deal with the presumption and we need his utmost contribution." The U.S. Navy assumed the Free French had no option but to cooperate, while North Africa, under Vichy control, could prove receptive to U.S. occupation. "In a military way, Fighting France is not in a position to be of great service." The State Department's Division of European Affairs recognized that "the policy of maintaining diplomatic relations with the Vichy Government is unpopular with the American people and the latter's reaction to a diplomatic break combined with recognition of General de Gaulle would undoubtedly be overwhelmingly favorable"—a most revealing admission! "At the right time we should throw our full weight behind a leader of French resistance . . . ; but no figure exists to challenge de Gaulle in this role at this time." The conclusion was that the time had not come.

The Office of Strategic Services (OSS), considered best placed for an impartial judgment because of its intelligence-gathering function, was categorical: "Neither military nor psychological considerations would justify the United Nations' recognition of de Gaulle's National Committee as the *de jure* government of France. The advantages of such recognition fall far short of the disadvantages.

The OSS was concerned "de Gaulle might feel that through his increased influence in France he could make or destroy the success of a second front in Europe and hence might seek to control [Allied] strategy." Furthermore, "in view of de Gaulle's unwillingness to admit advice or counsel, or his questionable political philosophy, of the presence of Fascists among his advisers, it seems probable that by recognition the United States would place in power a group of men hostile to its institutions and traditions." The OSS agreed with the estimate that recognition would antagonize both the military and the administration in North Africa, which it described as anti-British, anti-German, and anti–de Gaulle.

The Joint Intelligence Committee concluded that "there are no important military advantages to be derived from political recognition of de Gaulle, but serious disadvantages would result therefrom. Military considerations clearly favor a continuation of existing policies." The committee therefore advised the Joint Chiefs of Staff as follows: "The recognition or non-recognition of de Gaulle is primarily a political question. In view of the serious military disadvantages that would probably result from such recognition, however, the Joint Intelligence Committee suggests that, unless compelling political reasons exist, military considerations should govern and recognition should be withheld."

This document had an important bearing on the situation. In his capacity as commander-in-chief, the president was bound by the opinion of the Joint Chiefs of Staff. He felt he could not overrule the military on military matters even had he wished to do so, which was clearly not the case.

Another major concern to the Pentagon was the French fleet. When it left the war, the French fleet was still a powerful fighting force, but following the British attack its importance waned. In 1940 it totaled 580,000 tons, reduced by the end of the year by 175,000 tons lost in battle, destroyed or captured by the British, or immobilized at Alexandria or in the Caribbean. Following the evacuation of Brest and Cherbourg, many units sought refuge in Great Britain; among these were 12,000 sailors, most of whom asked to be repatriated. The ships under construction or repair in both ports – including the battleship *Clemenceau*, the aircraft carrier *Joffre*, and the cruiser *De Grasse* – were scuttled. Two of the most powerful modern ships, *Jean Barthe* and *Richelieu*, were crippled at Dakar, though their firepower had remained intact, as de Gaulle discovered during his unsuccessful attempt to capture the base and as the Americans would discover during the 1942 invasion of North Africa.

With the passing of time the fleet gradually lost its political value. Admiral Darlan was given to boast that while the strength of the Allied navies was being eroded in combat, his own fleet remained intact. Nothing could have been farther from the truth. Darlan did not take into account the enormous expansion of the U.S. Navy. In fact, in 1939 the French fleet comprised 24 percent of the Anglo-Saxon navies; by 1944 it was but 6 percent.

The Vichy government had an obvious interest in keeping the legend of a powerful fleet alive in the hope of strengthening its political stance toward both the United States and Germany. Sumner Welles wrote that the future of the fleet "was to be the dominant issue in deciding United States policy toward the French people throughout the succeeding three years."[23] Was a fleet so reduced in tonnage and strength worth being called *the* dominant issue in policy regarding France? The question of the fleet's political worth arose at the same time the United States was planning the invasion of North Africa.

A June 1942 report by the Joint Chiefs of Staff stated that "the battle efficiency and material condition of most units are believed to be poor due to the stringent terms of the German armistice, the inability of France to provide appropriations for upkeep, and unavailability of repair facilities outside of metropolitan France." The Joint Intelligence Committee which prepared the report concluded that "the active participation of the French Fleet in the Axis Naval effort would compel further dispersion of United Nations' sea power. The capabilities of the Fleet, while limited, are significant as affecting the balance of naval forces. It is unlikely, however, that French intervention would increase intrinsic military strength and there is reason to believe that the economic position of the Axis would be weakened."[24] By implication, then, the Germans would have nothing to gain by capturing the French fleet.

French naval sources agree that by summer 1942 the French fleet had no value to the Germans. They believe that in occupying Toulon, where what remained of the fleet was at anchor, the Germans intended to sink the ships rather than to seize them. The Toulon units totaled 250,000 tons, or 45 percent of the 1939 tonnage. Half the ships were either disarmed or superannuated and in need of repair. The other half consisted of the high seas fleet, whose tonnage was one-fifth of the 1940 total. Its manpower was reduced by 6,000 to 7,000 sailors, and munitions were dangerously deficient. In a 25 January 1942 note to Darlan, Admiral Auphan wrote: "For material and other reasons, one cannot ask of the navy anything more than a brief defensive action against a non-provoked attack at our coasts or maritime traffic. All offensive action in the center of the Mediterranean is beyond our capabilities."[25]

Contrary to a belief widely held at the time, the French fleet was in no position to contribute more than symbolically to the Allied war effort. "By the end of 1942," the French naval historian Philippe Masson wrote, "the Allies disposed of considerable naval forces, modern and perfectly trained. . . . A rallying of the Toulon fleet to the Allied side would have had a considerable psychological effect, but no strategic value. By the end of 1942, the French Navy was but a shadow of what it had been at the start of the conflict."[26] Before they could fight again, numerous French ships had to be sent to shipyards in Brooklyn, Boston, Bermuda, and Canada for refitting. Even after modernization, the French navy could play no more than a secondary role, its size and firepower being vastly inferior to those of the American and British navies. At the end of the war the French disposed of a 400,000-ton fleet, compared with 4.3 million tons plus 2 million tons of amphibian units for the Americans and 2.5 million tons for the British.

North Africa: Walking with the Devil

On 7 November 1942 President Roosevelt addressed a radio message to the French:

I have held all my life the deepest friendship for the French people – for the entire French people. I retain and cherish the friendship of hundreds of French people in France and outside France. I know your farms, your villages and your cities. I know your soldiers, professors and workmen. I know what a precious heritage of the French people are your homes, your culture and the principles of democracy in France. I salute again and reinstate my faith in liberty, equality, and fraternity. No two nations exist which are more united by historic and mutual friendly ties than the people of France and the United States.

Vive la France éternelle.

The following day, a U.S. expeditionary force began landing in North Africa, encountering an opposition serious in Morocco, sporadic elsewhere. Never before had an amphibious operation been projected across the ocean. "Ninety-five percent of Frenchmen exult at the American success in North Africa," wrote an observer close to Laval.[1] Darlan, who chanced to be on the scene, took charge in the name of Marshal Pétain and agreed to a cease-fire. The American commander, General Dwight D. Eisenhower, accepted the admiral's offer and the continuation of Vichy's rule it implied. This acceptance raised questions of morality and tactics, and it opened one of the most controversial chapters of World War II.

Darlan was one of the most baffling personalities of the period, whose aim, according to a perhaps hypercritical assessment, was to emerge on the side of the winner. As long as a German victory appeared certain, he was both anti-British and anti-American. He considered Americans "military larvae" whose lack of military preparation meant "it would be several years before a single U.S. soldier will land in Europe." "Social conditions are such that the United States will be unable to sustain a war. The country is in a state of decomposition more advanced perhaps than in which we found ourselves in 1939." He feared that in case of a peace advantageous to the United States, "Morocco and Dakar will become Anglo-Saxon" and France's northern provinces, including Cherbourg and Brest, would be either occupied by the Anglo-Saxons or integrated into a state vassal to the Americans. To Darlan, American politics were a continuing source of irritation.[2]

As Soviet resistance dimmed the prospect of a swift German victory, Darlan became less insulting toward the "Anglo-Saxons," the Americans especially. On 21 July a certain Senator Bardoux told Leahy that "collaborationist members of the Government, including Admiral Darlan, are losing faith in a German victory and are inclining toward the side of the democracies." In a conversation with Leahy in August, as we know, he had offered to welcome the Americans if they arrived with overwhelming strength.[3]

When the United States entered the war, Robert Murphy informed Washington that he had been approached by French officers willing and anxious to join the Allies in fighting the Germans and requested instructions on how to respond. One of them might have mentioned that Darlan too was ready to join, for on 12 January, at a meeting in Washington with Churchill, Roosevelt stated that "Admiral Darlan had asked if he would be accepted into a conference; that the answer had been – not under present circumstances. That if he brought the French Fleet over to the Allies, the situation would change."[4] On 26 January, this "ambitious crook," as Churchill called him,[5] wrote to General Weygand: "The struggle that has lasted for eighteen [months] will end with victory of the stars and stripes."

Of perhaps decisive importance in Darlan's change of heart toward the United States was the American victory in the battle for the Pacific at Midway (June 1942), which he was said to consider the turning point of the war. In thanking Chargé d'Affaires S. Pinkey Tuck, who had sent him a translation of the Navy Department communiqué on the battle, he "rendered the homage which is due to the tenacity and the brilliant courage of the American aviators."[6] As a navy man he realized "this war will be won by whoever dominates the Mediterranean and the Atlantic."

Darlan had not expected an American move on North Africa before 1943; in October, however, having learned from German and Japanese sources that an invasion was in the making, he informed Murphy that he was ready to join the Allies, bringing the fleet with him, provided he was made commander-in-chief of the French armed forces in North Africa.[7] Some three weeks before the invasion, Darlan upped the ante by asking for the supreme command of any U.S. expedition to North Africa, claiming that he would be able to rally the troops there to the Allied cause. The same offer and similar claims were made by General Giraud, living in retirement in unoccupied France.[8] They both found themselves in North Africa when the American troops landed, but having realized the military would not listen to him, Giraud yielded to Darlan. Darlan became the immediate problem; Giraud, a future one.

Accepting Darlan meant excluding de Gaulle, a decision in which the military concurred. The element of surprise was essential to the success of the operation, and the Free French had the reputation of being unable to keep a secret. U.S. intelligence was convinced that somewhere in their ranks a mole was passing information on to Vichy. On occasion the Free French had been furnished false information on the chance that it would find its way to Berlin via Vichy.[9] It was almost certainly Free French loose talk that had alerted Vichy to the ill-fated British–Free French attempt to take Dakar. De Gaulle would have been kept in the dark even if there had been no Darlan. The problem was that the operation was not really a secret one. The Germans and the Japanese suspected a U.S. move, and so did the Fighting French. In a 16 August note from London, Maurice Dejean alerted de Gaulle, then in Beirut, that the Americans planned to rally the North African chiefs with assurances that they would be treated as the "new local authorities of the French Empire."[10]

American intelligence possessed ample evidence that military and naval commanders and civil administrators in North Africa were strongly pro-Vichy and anti–de Gaulle. To a British public wondering why this should be so, Winston Churchill explained that "the Almighty in His infinite wisdom did not see fit to create Frenchmen in the image of Englishmen." The answer must be sought in French, not British, traditions. Unlike the British, the French had experienced many political upheavals; this led to a highly legalistic habit of mind in officers and officials, a subconscious sense of the need for national self-preservation against the dangers of anarchy. "For instance, any officer who obeys the orders of his lawful superior is absolutely immune from subsequent punishment. Much therefore turns in the minds of French officers upon whether there is a direct, unbroken chain of lawful command, and this is held to be more important by many Frenchmen than moral, national or international considerations." They believed the authority of the French state to be vested not in de Gaulle, who rebelled against it, but in the person who was, in Churchill's words, "the antique defeatist who to them is illustrious and venerable Marshal Pétain, the hero of Verdun and the sole hope of France."[11]

The Americans, who like the British have had little experience of social upheaval and revolution, based their policy on the simple evidence that in the name of their divided loyalties French soldiers were fighting French soldiers. In June 1941 the French army battled the Gaullists in Syria, convinced, as General Catroux discovered, "that they had done their duty by obeying Marshal Pétain, to whom they had sworn fidelity. . . . Truth was with Pétain and error was called de Gaulle."[12] The French army did not like the Germans any more than the Gaullists did and were convinced the marshal was only biding his time before taking France back into the war against Germany. The fleet's devotion to Pétain was complete, however, and discipline, Admiral de Laborde said, is the supreme virtue of him who wears a navy uniform.[13] Army units who had fought the Gaullists in Syria had been transferred to North Africa and could be expected to welcome the Gaullists with bullets. Many French officers, while averse to the British and de Gaulle, were itching to fight the Germans again, waiting only for the "legitimate" authority to give the order.

The Free French were understandably torn, for although resenting the U.S. policy of excluding them, they were also fully conscious of North African fidelity to Pétain. "The density of believers in [Vichy's] National Revolution," Colonel Passy wrote, "was qualitatively and quantitatively much higher in North Africa than in France. That proved sufficient for giving to the African Army and the colons in their vast majority a tonality very much pro Pétain."[14] "The army's blind fidelity to the Marshal," commented Catroux, "and the certainty that the order to resist would be followed were uncontested."[15] It was the same in West Africa, according to Catroux: The French were "totally attached to Pétain and the National Revolution."[16] As General Bethouart exclaimed, *"La mystique de Pétain est épouvantable."*

A few weeks before the landing, on 24 September, Admiral Stark hosted a luncheon for Free French leaders at which the conversation turned quite naturally to North Africa. His guests told the admiral that "the officers of the Vichy armed forces were . . . blindly loyal to Marshal Pétain. . . . The officers of the Navy, and to a lesser extent the Army and Air Force, will obey the Marshal's orders to maintain the unity of France and its Empire against all attacks, even to the point of resisting by force any American or Anglo-American operation in North Africa." Colonel Billotte felt confident that opposition to an American operation would be "symbolical," especially if such an operation "were announced as intended to carry out the basic policy of Marshal Pétain of resisting the Axis and of contributing to a German defeat, which he, as virtual prisoner of the Germans, could not personally make effective."

Once the operation got under way, the Free French were very indignant because the Americans used the tactics they themselves had suggested would meet no more than a "symbolical" resistance. As Harry Hopkins wrote:

The basis of legitimacy which permitted Darlan to effectively bring North Africa alongside the Allies, is due to the fact that he represented what was then the existing constituted authority of Vichy. . . . Men entrusted with authority in an orderly society are not revolutionaries, and it is to be revolutionary to act contrary to the orders of the central accepted authority. Admiral Darlan gave the order that was wished for—but the order had to be given. He alone could give it.[17]

Hopkins warned, however, that it was "important to prevent the use which Darlan made of Pétain's authority from being developed into a legitimacy recognized or fostered by the Allies." The issue of legitimacy as understood in Washington had been clearly defined by Hopkins: Darlan acted in the name of a legitimate authority, but his own authority was not therefore legitimate. The total occupation of France marked the end of Vichy and of the source of Darlan's "legitimacy." The resulting political vacuum cleared the way for de Gaulle, who knew how to take full advantage of the situation.

Shortly after the invasion of North Africa, Laval went on the air insisting he had never done anything to antagonize the United States or cause problems between the two countries, adding that Germany had never asked France to break diplomatic ties with the United States.[18] That was only partially true. In a May 1942 letter to Laval and Darlan, Fernand de Brinon wrote: "It is absolutely false to believe that Germany is anxious to avoid a break between France and the U.S. The truth is that for military reasons Germany does not wish the break to occur now, lest it provokes an aggression against North Africa."[19] De Brinon was well informed, for in his position as Vichy's ambassador to Nazi-occupied Paris, he was very close to the Germans.[20] Hitler, however, could not shake off his mistrust of the French and did not for a moment believe they would declare war on the British and the Americans. Toward the French the attitude would no longer be one of collaboration, but one of *diktat*.[21]

As Hitler had expected, the Vichy government preferred to stick to its pretense of neutrality. While French collaborationists had not given up hope that the secret weapons Germany was boasting about would reverse the slide toward defeat, they did so without real conviction. Laval's declaration is revealing of those illusory hopes:

I'm acting as though the Germans must win the war. Will the Germans win the war? I haven't a clue; I am no fortune teller. The longer it lasts, the less I believe it, but I think that a two-faced policy is worthless. There are two men who can render service to their country: General de Gaulle and myself. If the Germans win the war or manage to arrive at a compromise peace, let us practice a policy of loyalty with them and not one of haggling. Perhaps I can still be of service to my country and discuss an honorable peace treaty with the Germans. If the Germans are beaten, General de Gaulle will return. He will be supported, and I have no illusions about this, by 80 or 90 percent of the French people and I shall be hanged. So what? There are two men who can save our country at the present time, and if I weren't Laval, I would like to be General de Gaulle.[22]

Laval had astutely pointed out the "advantage" for France of having a foot in both camps: Whatever the outcome of the war, France would find itself on the victor's side.

Following the North African landing, the Wehrmacht occupied the whole of French territory. "The movement took place on 12 November according to plan and without the slightest incident. The French army, loyally, assisted our troops. The French police is zealous and full of goodwill," General Rundstedt reported.[23] Darlan invited—but did not order—the fleet at Toulon to join him. The admiral had hoped the invitation, calculated to please the Americans, would be rebuffed. He knew how frightfully Hitler would have taken revenge against France had it been otherwise. The base commander, the pro-German Admiral de Laborde, who despised Darlan, replied with a typical French expletive. He prepared to engage the fleet in fighting the British, but not in supporting the Allies. German archives show that Hitler was relieved the French had scuttled the fleet at Toulon. "I fear that the fleet might fall intact into our hands," he had written to Mussolini before the event; should that happen, the ships would be turned over to the Italians.

The bulk of the fleet could have left Toulon had the decision been made to rally to the Allies. The fuel tanks were full, and the time needed for taking to the sea was relatively short, three to four hours. The German air force might have caused considerable damage, but the bulk of the fleet would have gotten away. Hermann Göring once told Mussolini that the air force could not play a decisive role against an enemy fleet. "It must be remembered," Göring is quoted as saying, "that an air force can tire and wear down naval forces by continually chasing them out of port. Aerial forces could not, however, destroy a naval fleet."[24] The Luftwaffe was at that time not even close enough to intervene. The situation changed shortly afterward when eight submarines surrounded Toulon harbor. Admiral de Laborde had been waiting for instructions from Pétain, which never came.

With Vichy out of the way and Pétain a German prisoner, Washington insisted the time had come for the French to bury their disputes and concentrate on waging the war. In a proclamation on 3 December 1942 Eisenhower stated that "all Frenchmen worthy of their country's great past had forgotten their small differences of ideas." The administration and the military viewed quarreling among the French – while a war was being fought and Americans were preparing to fight to free France – as almost treasonous.

Since de Gaulle would not speak to Darlan nor Darlan to de Gaulle, to achieve the necessary unity it was hoped that a personality acceptable to all parties – Edouard Herriot or a similar prominent figure – would emerge and bring de Gaulle, Jean François Darlan, René Godfroy, Henri Giraud, Georges Catroux, August Nogues, Jean Pierre Esteva, and the rest together. To the military, a national committee composed of these military figures was "obviously desirable." Neither they nor Roosevelt was prepared to understand that World War II was also a civil war, fought in the name of certain principles and ideals, in which the enemy was not only Germany but also a certain group of French citizens. The French Resistance symbolized that ideological engagement.

The U.S. military evolved considerably when put in contact with the realities of the French situation, but immediately after the North Africa invasion the U.S. command felt it owed an obligation to those generals faithful to Pétain who had opened the gates to the U.S. forces – a point of view the president shared. The legitimacy Pétain incarnated having disappeared, Roosevelt was strengthened in his conviction that France "did not exist." Were he to recognize any other person as the representative of France, he would be contributing to imposing a new leader on the French, and that he was unwilling to do.

While hoping for the unlikely emergence of a miracle worker, the United

States was stuck with the problem of Darlan. Was it militarily necessary to come to terms with him? And even if it were, could association with so dubious a character ever be justified?

By the time Darlan ordered a cease-fire, military operations had progressed to the point at which the whole area could be occupied and held. When defeated Republican presidential candidate Wendell Wilkie visited North Africa as part of a world tour, he "never accepted without discount stories of the probable losses we would have sustained at the hands of the French if we had gone in directly as Americans without dealing with Darlan." He had reached this conclusion after talking with French soldiers and sailors in North Africa. To what extent Eisenhower was influenced by his political advisers is not clear; what is clear, however, is that he opted for the Darlan deal for the sole purpose of saving American lives. Robert Murphy and the vice consuls had spent time in North Africa in an effort to influence the local authorities on the assumption they were needed to open the way.

The issue was less North Africa's military occupation by the Anglo-Americans than the aftermath of the occupation. Had the occupants been faced with the task of administering the territory and assuming the responsibility for maintaining law and order, it would have meant an enormous dispersion of forces urgently needed to chase the Nazis from Tunisia and the consequent risk of facing serious disorders. The province of Algeria was administered by the Ministry of the Interior, the protectorates of Tunisia and Morocco by the Ministry of Foreign Affairs, and West Africa by the Ministry of the Colonies. An immediate task was blending three administrations into one, recognized and obeyed by all inhabitants, European and Moslem. Only a Frenchman acceptable to a majority of the population could have done the job—and Darlan proved to be such a man. Eisenhower had no choice, therefore, but to deal with him.

Eisenhower had been caught in a dilemma, for while needing Darlan in the immediate, dealing with him was politically and morally reprehensible. Would it imply that every Quisling in Europe could hope to stay in power as long as he or she cooperated with the Allied forces? Although there is no proof that he actually spoke the words, Roosevelt had been quoted as saying he would deal with Laval if he opened the gates of Paris to the Americans. The French, in particular, were concerned that Americans would duplicate in France the North African experience. Were that to happen, Catroux commented, "the soil of France would be freed, not her soul."[25] Darlanesque solutions for Europe were unacceptable not only to a majority of Americans—"The number and quality of those who disagreed was astonishing," Stimson wrote—but also to U.S. allies who resented what Churchill called "the filthy race of Quislings." Stalin was the lone dissenter. On 14 December he wrote to the president that he considered Eisenhower's policy absolutely sound: "I consider it an important achievement that you have succeeded in winning Darlan and others to the Allied side against Hitler." And to Churchill he wrote, "The military diplomacy must be able to use for military purposes not only Darlan but 'even the Devil himself and his grandma.' "[26] Did not Stalin deal with "the devil himself" when he joined with Hitler in a nonaggression pact?

Despite widespread condemnation in Great Britain, Churchill stood by the president: "I gave strong support to the State Department over Darlan. They seem rueful about the episode now. Looking back upon it, I consider it was right. Several thousand British and American soldiers were alive today because of it, and it got us Dakar at a time when we could ill have spared the large forces needed for its capture."[27] But on 9 December 1942 he warned Roosevelt of efforts by the "local French authorities" to preserve a Vichy-like regime in North Africa.[28] The president forwarded the message to Eisenhower, who in his reply stressed he was dealing with problems "as they arise and will continue to do so."[29] A few days earlier the president had received a message from Ambassador John Winant warning that Darlan did not see himself as a "temporary expedient." "Today's papers," he wrote, "carried a statement from [Darlan] that he had assumed 'the rights and responsibilities of government,' and had established under his authority a high commissariat and a French imperial council which together would 'represent France in the world.' "[30]

The Fighting French were understandably outraged that a man with Darlan's record could presume to speak for France. To an attempt by Stark to explain the situation, de Gaulle replied on 15 November:

Admiral,

I acknowledge receipt of your letter of 14 November.

I understand that the United States pay the treason of traitors if they find it profitable, but that must not be paid with France's honor.

Instructed to return the letter, Kittredge was to ask de Gaulle if perhaps there had been a mistake and the letter was not meant for the admiral. If it had been meant for Stark, it indicated de Gaulle wished to put a stop to any further discussion or cooperation regarding the Free French question. Gaston Palewski, a personal assistant of de Gaulle's, called on Stark the next day to apologize and thank him for returning the letter without taking further action. Although the letter had been withdrawn and apologies extended, it was leaked to the press and included in the general's collected papers. Thus the general had his cake and ate it too.

Stark had learned to play along with de Gaulle's fits of temper and wait, often along with embarrassed Free French officials, until he cooled off. He sincerely sympathized with de Gaulle and had come to appreciate what he stood for, but he could not understand why the Free French had made such a fuss over the Darlan affairs. He reflected on this, the prevailing view of the military, for whom any political expedient was justified if it helped the war effort at the cost of the fewest American lives. The battle for control of North Africa had resulted in American losses of 500 dead, 900 wounded, and 300 missing—not considered too high a price for so great a gain.

In a letter to Stark (part of the Navy Archives), Knox wrote:

Harry Stimson told me that General Patton, in Morocco, was greatly alarmed over the situation he found when he reached there and had advised his superiors that if resistance continued as it started out, and a threatened uprising of the tribes followed, he would need at least 60,000 reinforcements in that area alone. The effect of Darlan's action was instantaneous in Morocco and all along the African coast. It undoubtedly saved thousands of lives and gave to the expedition a measure of success which was of first importance (18 November).

In his reply to Knox, Stark commented: "If we stop to think what might have happened if there had been no Darlan – well, we may be fighting yet, and would, in all probability, have to undertake the complete military occupation of North Africa. I recall when I was home that we figured to take Dakar would cost us many, many thousands of men" (24 November).[31] Stark told de Gaulle that confronted with the same problem, he (de Gaulle) would have acted as Eisenhower did.

Faced with furor from every side, the president sought to set the record straight. On 16 November he asked Eisenhower to "have in mind the following policies . . . : 1. That we do not trust Darlan. 2. That it is impossible to keep a collaborator of Hitler and one whom we believe to be a Fascist in civil power any longer than is absolutely necessary. 3. His movements should be watched carefully and his communications supervised." The following day Roosevelt announced at a press conference: "I have accepted General Eisenhower's political arrangements for the time being in Northern and Western Africa. . . . The present temporary arrangement . . . is only a temporary expedient, justified solely by the stress of battle."[32] How temporary was "temporary" the president did not specify. Darlan understood it to mean until the liberation of France; meanwhile, he could go on running things in the name of the marshal.

Roosevelt went into greater detail at a meeting of the Pacific War Council:

Yesterday . . . I told the newspapers, off the record, of an old Bulgarian proverb, approved by the Church, which runs something like this: "My children, in case of imminent danger it is permitted to walk with the devil until you are safely across the bridge." Here we are, walking with the devil. We dislike him very much but it is just one of those things. Eisenhower admittedly took many chances, but apparently it has worked. In any event, Eisenhower's action has hastened the hour of our attack on Tunis. Darlan has played fair so far but if he doesn't continue to do so we will lock him up.[33]

The Darlan deal was presented as a military decision made by the military in the field. The commander-in-chief supported his generals, covering them with his authority. "It was in his warmhearted and unhesitating support of his soldiers on such trying issues . . . that Mr. Roosevelt earned the particular affection of the Secretary of War," Stimson wrote.[34]

De Gaulle had found comfort in the storm of protests the "expedient" deal had aroused in the United States and showed Stark clippings from the American press to strengthen his case. The president's statement had changed the atmosphere; "they are delighted over here," Stark reported, referring to the Gaullists. The general cancelled a press conference scheduled for 18 November in which he had intended to denounce U.S. policies. Presumably speaking for the National Committee, Palewski suggested to Stark that Giraud be appointed Fighting France's high commissioner in North Africa. The query, the admiral commented, "does indicate the [National Committee's] complete reversal of attitude within the last 24 hours (that is, since the President's broadcast), and their willingness to start playing ball again." The way was now open for de Gaulle to go to North Africa. Stark urged Churchill to intervene with the president to facilitate a trip by de Gaulle's delegates.[35]

Shortly before the president's statement, the French National Committee, "extremely desirous of obtaining a direct contact with the White House," as Stark informed Ambassador Winant, enquired whether the president would receive André Philip, who was visiting Canada at the time. "I take pleasure to inform you," Stark wrote de Gaulle on 19 November, "that Secretary Knox has cabled that President Roosevelt could see Mr. Philip today or tomorrow if he could arrange his immediate return to Washington. . . . If Mr. Philip returned to Washington, he should inform the Secretary of the Navy of his time of arrival so that a definite appointment at the White House can be arranged."

The visit to which de Gaulle attached such importance took place – and was a disaster. The Free French did not hesitate to acknowledge that the interview had done more harm than good. Colonel Passy, chief of the Free French intelligence service, wrote:

André Philip, who thought he was persona gratissima in the United States went there on a mission. . . . He asked to see President Roosevelt. He arrived for his appointment very late. The president, rightly angry at this violation of protocol, agreed to grant him another audience. This time Philip, accompanied by Tixier . . . , arrived on time. Tixier, who was anything but a diplomat himself, told me that his hair stood on an end as he heard how our national commissioner of the interior addressed the President. It was a long monologue: FDR was unable to get a word in. Holding nothing back, Philip violently condemned U.S. attitudes. He screamed and practically threatened the President, who was rather taken aback by this outpouring of eloquence. . . . The visit, as we were soon to find out, did not enhance Free France's prestige with the President of the United States.[36]

Pierre Bloch, also of the de Gaulle entourage, recalled: "Tixier had warned Philip not to smoke in front of the President, who was already ailing. In the midst of the conversation, Philip took out his pipe and constantly blew smoke in Roosevelt's face."[37] Finally, Jacques Soustelle, another champion of Gaullism, wrote: "The audience was a disaster. Philip did not show the slightest decent admiration for the military effort. . . . No one was more sensitive toward this matter than Roosevelt, Commander in Chief of the Armed Forces. It is only right to say that the American army deserve this recognition."[38] According to Sumner Welles's account, Roosevelt did not make things easier by stressing that "if at any moment [he] had reason to believe that Admiral Darlan was not satisfactory . . . he would at once remove him." The president added that "this applies equally to all other authorities in Northern Africa. . . . So long as the United States was the occupying power in North Africa, the final decision would be reached solely" by Washington. He further "expressed it as his policy that until all France was liberated, the sole decision as to what, if any, Frenchmen would administer the liberated territory was a matter solely for the Government to determine." Quite understandably, the president's views did not go down well with his visitors, who asserted the Free French would never "permit" any liberated town, village, or farmhouse to be administered by foreign powers, their decision in this regard being final.[39]

Concerned about the misunderstanding between Washington and the Free French, on 26 November de Gaulle urgently requested a meeting with Admiral Stark.

France [said General de Gaulle] has passed through many reverses and trials in its long history but never one of more tragic significance than the present disastrous situation. This necessarily leads the French to attach particular importance to questions of morals. They may occasionally overemphasize (like he himself) such considerations and express themselves in a manner that may irritate or offend their American friends.[40]

The general stressed that "more than a military decision and a military victory must be sought in this total war. . . . The United Nations must seek a total victory to maintain the most precious values and open the way for a new period of political and moral as well as material progress." He warned against turning to leaders of the past, "survivors of another age [who] no longer have any real contact with the France being born of the humiliation and suffering experienced since 1940." The new France would be more democratic and liberal than the old, and this was the reason for "the particular importance that the French must attach to moral, political and social consequences or repercussions of the United Nations war program and policy." De Gaulle had a certain idea of what the new France would be and a single objective, France herself. He was anxious for plans for the postwar period to be in tune with his hopes and objectives. Had he been part of a coalition that included among other countries the Soviet Union, each member having different, often contrasting ideas as to what represented the war's "moral character," he would have had no choice but to propound generalities, such as the Four Freedoms and the Atlantic Charter. Roosevelt was determined not to anticipate postwar decisions while the war was on, precisely in order not to compromise the unity of purpose of the different parties constituting the United Nations, and to keep them united until victory was achieved. A world vision and a national vision could hardly be reconciled. De Gaulle's main concern was not the war, in which the French could only play a minor part, but to make sure that France's future corresponded to his plans. He could explain his moves and position only in political terms, attributing to them a "moral character." Along that road there could only be a parting of the ways. Roosevelt refused to accept the French general as the exclusive arbiter of morality. If each member of the United Nations insisted on his or her own interpretation of the subject, the prospects for unity would disintegrate. Roosevelt also rejected the civil war among the French factions; to the Free French and the Resistance, however, that war was a basic issue in the war at large.

The day after receiving de Gaulle, Stark had a conversation with Catroux, who, evidently having assuaged his anti-American fury, took a moderate line on Darlan (whom he knew, his wife being a cousin of the admiral's). Catroux agreed with Stark that "General Eisenhower had taken the only action possible in the situation encountered in North Africa by making provisional arrangements with Admiral Darlan." He insisted, however, that for a number of reasons the arrangement should not be maintained longer than was absolutely necessary. Darlan was a fence-sitter who might sabotage Allied efforts if he felt Germany was gaining the upper hand. Furthermore, Catroux said, Darlan had not announced the active reentry of French North Africa into the war. Liberty of military action and security of their rear and of their supply lines could be guaranteed the Allied forces only by replacing Vichy officials with Frenchmen wholeheartedly devoted to French participation in an offensive war against the Axis. Having been commander-in-chief of all French forces in North Africa prior to 1939, Catroux said he knew the region and the situation intimately. Catroux was a man after Stark's own heart who spoke in terms of military advantages, not ideology. Stark would have liked him to meet the president, who, he was sure, would be impressed.

The Pentagon was aware that the arrangements with Darlan could not last indefinitely and began looking for an alternative. The immediate problem was what to do with Darlan. Knox passed on a suggestion from Cordell Hull that

we take whatever French fleet there was in Dakar and whatever was left in North African ports we seized and that in Alexandria and make them all into a squadron or task force and give Darlan command of it within the highest rank the French Navy possesses. This would do two things. It might satisfy Darlan taking him out of the political picture and, incidentally, it might give him a springboard for some real recognition in France after the war. I think the suggestion is filled with subtle possibilities. . . . Stimson was present when Hull made this suggestion so it may easily be possible that action will be taken by the War Department to try this out.[41]

Knox, incidentally, thought the scuttling of the French fleet at Toulon was good news: "I think I would rather have them on the bottom of the harbor of Toulon than to undertake to overhaul them and put them in commission."[42]

A projected visit to Washington by de Gaulle furnished Stark the occasion for an exchange of views prior to the trip. They met on 17 December. De Gaulle said he hoped to have an opportunity for a free and frank talk with the president, whether or not agreement followed. He would place himself completely at the president's disposal to furnish whatever information or to discuss whatever question his host chose. According to the confidential minutes taken, de Gaulle

agreed fully with the immediate decisions and arrangements in North Africa made by General Eisenhower for military reasons to permit his expeditionary force to establish itself as quickly as possible, with a minimum of local resistance and a maximum of local support in launching an immediate attack on Axis positions in Tunisia and in Tripoli. De Gaulle himself, as a soldier, could easily understand and agree with Eisenhower's decisions.[43]

But that was the past, and he was concerned about the present and the future. With Pétain a prisoner, the fiction of a power deriving from a central authority had vanished. Keeping Darlan in power meant

preventing a natural and inevitable evolution of opinion toward the real image of France – a fighting France to which the majority of the population of North Africa have always looked for inspiration. . . . Were it not for American support, [Darlan] would soon disappear. The Fighting French are only reflecting national opinion and resolution in refusing to deal with him or other leaders depending exclusively on him.

He made it clear that although he was ready to cooperate with generals like Giraud, Juin, Bethouart, and Barre, he would not work with men like Darlan, "who were seeking to capitalize in their own interest on the calamities and misfortunes of France, for which they had so long a great share of responsibility."
De Gaulle, Stark wrote, believed

his role was to give expression to the opinions and resolves of all true patriots and to preserve the unity of the historic tradition of the true France. . . . France's tragedy of 1940 had made it necessary for other people to deal with France's problems and to make decisions that are in reality French decisions. President Roosevelt thus had a singular responsibility at the present time. . . . Upon his decisions and upon the policies inspiring the use of American power the destinies of the world today depend – and particularly the destinies of France. . . . Only by giving expression to the spirit of an eternal France can current problems be wisely solved. The General hopes he might help the President better to understand the difficulties and complexities surrounding France and the French in their present tragic hour of destiny.[44]

These conversations, duly reported to Washington, proved extremely important as a reflection of Free French hopes and aspirations. Both de Gaulle and Catroux had been wise enough to show an understanding of Eisenhower's decision to deal with Darlan – an understanding most fruitful in the months to come–and to concentrate on the future. Thanks to these reports the military were able to gain a more balanced view of the North African situation and, as events were soon to prove, were quicker than the president in drawing the necessary conclusions. In this respect, Stark's role as conveyor of Free French ideals to the Pentagon proved to be of major importance.

The president had said he would see de Gaulle some time in December. On 27 November Stark put de Gaulle on twenty-four-hour notice for sailing, ideally on one of the Queen ships. On 29 November, however, the Joint Chiefs of Staff raised a serious objection to the general's visit. They advised the president that "if he [Roosevelt] should confer with General de Gaulle at the present time, it might have a serious adverse effect on our campaign in Africa."[45] Following Darlan's assassination, de Gaulle was requested to postpone his visit until the situation was stabilized.

"The beginnings of the achievement of French unity were thereby delayed for five months," Sherwood wrote, "during which some animosities deepened to an almost irreparable extent. It was a deplorable mischance."[46]

9

Giraud or de Gaulle?

Roosevelt's decisions to reject wartime discussion of future political projects had far-reaching consequences for U.S. relations with France. All European countries at war with Germany, France excepted, were represented by governments whose legitimacy was uncontested. In France's case, legitimacy was claimed by two opposing political entities between which Roosevelt refused to choose.

"As to the future of France," Roosevelt told the press, "I think that everybody is agreed that we must not influence by any act or deed today – by recognizing this, that or the other individual as to what the future has got to be."[1]

Since political dialogue regarding France was out of the question, only military arrangements remained to be dealt with. Subsequently, a supreme commander would be entrusted with the conduct of the war and would assume all powers, including political, over the zone of operations. The supreme commander would in turn be responsible to the commander-in-chief, that is, the president. Thus the final authority rested with Roosevelt.

North Africa would become the first testing ground for this policy.

North Africa was not liberated, since the French military and civil apparatus was kept in place, but occupied militarily. No one group or committee was recognized as the representative of the French Empire or the French government. The French people would settle their affairs when the war ended in victory for the Allies. "Until that time," a directive given on 2 January stated, "whenever our armies are in occupation of former French territory we will deal on a local basis with local Frenchmen, and if these local officials will not cooperate, they will have to be replaced."[2]

These instructions were further expanded on 8 January in a message from the Joint Chiefs of Staff to Eisenhower:

The President's view is that sovereignty of France rests in the people of France and that the United States cannot recognize any French Government that does not spring from the will of the people. He therefore desires that you should avoid discussing of these matters with the French before consulting us. He further believes that any government set up must of necessity be a de facto government established by you as Military Commander of an occupied territory and should be subject to change by you when change appears to be necessary.[3]

If the same standards were to be applied eventually to France, occupation would imply that all Vichy structures would be kept in place and that it would be the responsibility of the Allied military commander to "establish" a French government and dismiss it at will. A solution of this sort was absurd and impracticable, and no self-respecting French citizen would accept it. But that was the result of Roosevelt's policy of refusing to take sides in French politics by applying a strict American interpretation of "legitimacy."

The extent of U.S. involvement in local decisions became apparent at Dakar. When the question of naming a new governor for West Africa arose, the president insisted on being given "an opportunity to comment upon the acceptability of the candidate." "Once more I must make it clear," he instructed Eisenhower, "that the full control of Dakar is so vital to the United Nations in this war that I shall otherwise have to direct that several regiments and ships be sent there unless I am convinced beyond a doubt that the French leaders there are with us and will take our orders without question."[4] When Pierre Cournarie was selected to replace Boisson, the president concurred, but added:

Due to the unusual military importance of Dakar to the defense of the American Hemisphere and the control of the South Atlantic . . . the following point should be made absolutely clear to the French Committee: if at any time during the rest of the war the United States requested a change in Cournarie's command, such a change will be effected by putting in his place a man totally agreeable to the United States. The fact that this proposed measure is for military reasons in the conduct of the war should be emphasized.[5]

The president intended Dakar to be a postwar controlled base "where we shall have sufficient air, and sufficient Navy, and sufficient airfields . . . to prevent any aggressor nation in the future to reestablish a threat against this continent."[6]

Roosevelt's firm intention of having the last word on decisions affecting France predated his 22 January meeting with de Gaulle at Anfa, Morocco, during the Casablanca Conference. The press had a great time reporting the little melodrama preceding the meeting: de Gaulle's fits of temper for having to meet Giraud under "Anglo-Saxon" auspices; Churchill's threat to repudiate him; the two French leaders' handshake under the complaisant eyes of their patrons—the atmosphere was one of a shotgun wedding, around which many tales of the "bride" and the "groom" were woven.

The Anfa meeting proved to be a failure not because Roosevelt and de Gaulle had failed to understand one another but, rather, because each was convinced he had been understood by the other. This misconception was to have the gravest of consequences for Franco-American relations.

"The President persuaded himself that he had 'managed' de Gaulle – Roosevelt's own words – and could continue to manage him. The illusion that a French solution had been found was one of the most unfortunate consequences of the conference. The President held to this mistaken view for several months."[7] Churchill believed ("to my relief") that the two "got on unexpectedly well. . . . The President was attracted by 'the spiritual look in his [de Gaulle's] eyes.' "[8] Equally pleased, de Gaulle told his aide Boislambert: "You see, I met today a great statesman. I believe we have well understood each other." According to Boislambert, "the General evidently had the hope that all misunderstandings will dissipate." "Roosevelt is a patrician," de Gaulle told Gaston Palewski, who was with him during the interview.[9] "My conversation with Roosevelt was good. I think he understood what is Fighting France. That will be important for the future," he assured his followers in London.[10] On 13 February de Gaulle wrote Tixier that he still hoped to visit the United States: "You may so inform Mr. Sumner Welles and add, which is the truth, that I had been greatly impressed by the conversations I had at Casablanca with the President and that I am personally convinced of their usefulness."[11] The following day he wired Cordell Hull:

I would be grateful if you would transmit to the President of the United States an expression of the great pleasure I have had in making a first contact with him. His sentiments of ardent sympathy toward France could not fail to deeply touch a Frenchman. May I renew the assurance of the National Committee's determination to consecrate all its moral forces to the unification of the French Empire for the war of liberation.[12]

Previously, on the occasion of his birthday, he begged President Roosevelt to "accept the expression of my admiration for the effort undertaken under your high impulsion by the army and people of the United States of America, whose friendship forms a part of the patrimony of France."[13]

Even though each side believed it had convinced the other, it was obvious they had been speaking different languages. The general spoke in terms of history; the president, of law. De Gaulle could not be recognized, the president told him, because not having been elected, he lacked legitimacy.[14] Once again, contradictory interpretations of legitimacy were at the root of the problem.

A record of the conversation between the two leaders is not available. De Gaulle might have compared himself to Jeanne d'Arc to make the point that a patriot did not have to be elected to lead the French against an oppressor. Only through historical reference could de Gaulle justify his actions and presume to speak for France. Roosevelt obviously missed the point completely, whereas de Gaulle did not realize that his arguments were not of the nature necessary to have the desired impact.

Roosevelt's version of the conversation has been recounted by Felix Frankfurter:

The President told in some detail of his session with Giraud and de Gaulle so that at first hand I heard the story of de Gaulle's replying to the President when asked to take the field in France that he was no longer a military man but had become the leader of a great national movement, like Jeanne d'Arc – "I am the Jeanne d'Arc of today" de Gaulle told the President. The President said he received that with a serious grace and did not smile, but when on the following day he said to de Gaulle: "After all, our first job is to win the war. France can be liberated only if we win this war. So let's work out a practical program between you and General Giraud," General de Gaulle replied, "That is easy. The last war furnished the answer: General Giraud is the Foch of today and I am the Georges Clemenceau." The President said, "I then had to laugh and said 'Now, see here, General de Gaulle, I knew Georges Clemenceau and I don't think I ever knew anybody who was less spiritual than Clemenceau. You can't be both Jeanne d'Arc and Clemenceau.'" To which de Gaulle replied, "It is not difficult. That's just what I am." The President commented on his two interviews with de Gaulle by saying "I think he is a little touched here" – tapping his right temple.[15]

This version, obviously romanticized, showed clearly how the misunderstanding began. Clemenceau had not been "spiritual," implying that de Gaulle was, and to be spiritual meant (to Roosevelt, at least) to be a bit crazy.

In his *Mémoires* de Gaulle made no mention of historical references, but he did restate his conviction that the United States yielded "to that taste for intervention in which the instinct of domination cloaked itself."[16] "Beneath his patrician mask of courtesy," he wrote, "Roosevelt regarded me without benevolence."[17] These judgments were expressed and these words written several years after the event, when his unforgiving nature caused him to give vent to his hostility toward the president for what had simply been a mutual misunderstanding. At the time of the Casablanca Conference his mood and his reactions had been quite different; the gap between the conference and the *Mémoires* dramatizes the bitterness he must have felt at having assumed there had been a meeting of minds when in fact there had not.

In the months following the Anfa meeting de Gaulle easily won his contest with Giraud – a man of limited vision and limited perspicacity – and the need for a U.S. decision concerning the French National Committee became urgent. Stark had warned Washington that a delay in recognition would merely serve to strengthen de Gaulle's position and generate anti-American feeling. With the same ease with which de Gaulle had managed to push Giraud into a corner, he outwitted Catroux and civilian members of the National Committee not totally with him. Army officers were lured with offers of better pay and conditions, with the result that Roosevelt's 17 June instructions to Eisenhower – "We will not permit at this time de Gaulle to control through his partisans on any Committee or direct himself the French Army in Africa, either in the field of operations or training or supplies" – could not be implemented. De Gaulle having filled the National Committee with his protegés, Roosevelt wired Churchill:

"This augmented Committee claims full authority over all the war efforts of the French and French territory. We cannot accept, and I am sure you agree, that our Allied military position in North Africa can be jeopardized by an antagonistic element in such control."[18]

With North Africa under U.S. occupation, Roosevelt's wish to isolate and then sidestep de Gaulle could have easily been implemented. But the U.S. military, who had become totally disenchanted with Giraud, discovered in de Gaulle a general knowledgeable about modern methods of warfare, and a general who could deliver. If de Gaulle succeeded in directing the French military effort, it was largely because he proved acceptable to the U.S. military, who in a sense adopted him. Assistant Secretary of War John McCloy, in charge of civil affairs, recognized de Gaulle as a symbol of the Resistance and the choice of the French people. He believed the reemergence of a powerful and stable France to be in the American national interest. Stressing that "Europe is not Anglo-Saxon by a long shot," McCloy wrote Eisenhower, "We gain . . . by incorporating the French more closely into our effort." He was of the opinion, he told Stimson, that "General Eisenhower should be authorized to turn over to the de Gaulle group the civil government of areas in continental France that the Germans might be forced to evacuate," and he proposed that the National Committee receive general recognition as the *de facto* government of the whole of France as soon as part of France was liberated.[19] McCloy's strong support for de Gaulle irritated the president. "One more crack from McCloy to the Boss about de Gaulle and McCloy leaves town," Harry Hopkins warned. The last thing the military wanted was the chore of "handling" the French; they would gladly leave that to de Gaulle, who was clearly up to it. Without the support and the sympathy of the U.S. military, it is doubtful that de Gaulle could have gone, as he did, practically unchallenged.

At that time Eisenhower was planning the invasion of Sicily and the beginning of the Italian campaign; he refused to get involved in France's internal affairs unless they interfered with his military mission. De Gaulle had shown he could take charge of the situation competently, and the composition of the French National Committee was reassuring in its moderation. In a 19 June note to George Marshall, Eisenhower stressed that

the balance of power is held by a group of 6 or 7 moderate independents including men like Catroux and Monnet and this feeling of independent thought will grow as the individual members begin to find themselves on firm ground. . . . I hope you will inform the President that he need have no fear as to my firmness in dealing with the matter of military command in North Africa or in preserving a situation entirely acceptable to him in the West African area. . . . I am sure we understand his concern and his desires and there will be no deviation from his instructions.

At the same time he added that "some latitude in negotiation should be advantageous in maintaining our position and in keeping the vast majority of local Frenchmen as our firm friends."[20]

The North African atmosphere was charged with emotion, but as Stark warned his superiors in Washington,

the French would surely never forgive any ungrateful handling of General de Gaulle. . . . It is perhaps unfair to say de Gaulle dislikes the British and Americans, but better to say that he feels France's defeat so deeply and her humiliation so personally that almost anyone who has not gone through the same experience is open to some resentment . . . hence the high-handed attitude of approach. . . . Gaullists can have little physical part in the liberation of France which must be accomplished by forces from the outside. They are fundamentally interested in what is going to happen to France after she is freed and what is going to happen to themselves and to the cause they support.[21]

An understanding of what troubled the French was important to Eisenhower too. He wrote Marshall that friendship is "important to us, particularly as the enemy is trying to sabotage important installations by means of paratroopers. We cannot spare our own troops to guard all vital points."[22] Roosevelt's negative attitude toward the French National Committee had become an embarrassment not only to the American military but to the British as well. As an Allied commander, Eisenhower was responsible to London no less than to Washington. Eden complained about the president's "special brand of obstinacy," while admitting that "de Gaulle has not done much to shake all confidence in him."[23]

Roosevelt's problem was not just "obstinacy,"[24] for he had concerns beyond the immediate military necessity. He was hostile less to de Gaulle personally than to his projects for the future. For Roosevelt, the idea of empire that de Gaulle espoused and that had provoked unsavory episodes in Syria and Lebanon, where the French had suppressed aspiration to independence, was a threat to peace. He found de Gaulle's attempts to speak of France as if it were still the France of Clemenceau ludicrous. Equally ludicrous was de Gaulle's expectation of sitting as an equal among the victors despite the country's modest role in the war. In Roosevelt's scheme for the future, France was to play but a secondary role. In addition, the issues of self-determination and legitimacy needed to be considered.

Legitimacy was precisely what de Gaulle believed he was in the process of acquiring in line with historical tradition. The total occupation of France by Germany following the North African landing produced major realignments within that country. The old marshal, received enthusiastically in the localities he visited, still retained popular affection, but the Vichy regime was finished. With liberation on the horizon Nazi brutality and repression increased, and efforts to recruit youths for forced labor in Germany only caused swelling of the ranks of the Resistance and the emergence of well-organized Maquis. The Resistance had a number of leaders, none of whom could be accepted by the others as overall authority. A unifier and a symbol had to be sought outside the country; since only de Gaulle qualified, he became the Resistance's uncontested leader. This recognition was all de Gaulle needed to make him feel entitled to speak in the name of France.

The day after the North Africa invasion, the major Resistance organizations – Combat, France-Tireur, Libération, Mouvement Ouvrier Français, Comité d'Action Socialiste – and a number of political parties addressed a message to the Allied governments heartily congratulating the British and the Americans for liberating North Africa, expressing their thanks to Giraud, and saluting all French citizens who freely rallied to de Gaulle, "uncontested head of the Resistance," also urgently requesting that the destiny of the newly freed North Africa be placed in the hands of General de Gaulle.

There were good reasons why a France that had not suffered much during the war, and that had remained for the most part passive during the occupation, should so readily identify with de Gaulle. One of the most distinguished Resistance leaders, Claude Bourdet, explained:

De Gaulle has brought to millions of French a major psychological prop. One cannot identify with a government without being part of it. But one can identify with an exceptional personality. . . . The redeemer's attraction through the ages derives from such identification. If de Gaulle was the redeemer, if he absorbed in himself the whole Resistance, then it would be possible to be rescued through him of past mistakes and "saved." Identification with a redeemer is a supernatural phenomenon, defying reason. In other words, one can say: "De Gaulle was for all of us in London, for all of us at Bir Hakeim, for all of us in the maquis." . . . A redeemer only requires faith, not deeds.[25]

In other words, a French citizen could reason thus: "De Gaulle resisted; de Gaulle is France; ergo France resisted." This identification of a people with its leader would serve the French well in the years to come. By becoming one with France (de Gaulle was heard to say, *"Je suis la France"*), the other France – Vichy, collaboration, the Milice, Jewish persecutions, denunciations to the Gestapo – was simply swept under the rug. The near-mystical aspect of the de Gaulle phenomenon was not only incomprehensible to Roosevelt but, interpreted within the framework of American traditions, considered dangerous because irrational and as such potentially leading to excess. The president was convinced such "irrationality" would invite revolution and disorder, seriously affecting the war effort.

The ghost of revolution haunted official Washington, raising the prospect of bloodshed and civil war. Once more cultural differences were the root of the problem. The United States had fought a civil war, with traumatic consequences, and there was a tendency to transpose the experience to the European continent. But the American Civil War was really a war of secession, not a revolution. Americans reject revolution as an attempt on their way of life; no party, except for fringe groups, has ever advocated revolutionary change, and the New Dealers certainly did not. The word *revolution* is therefore suspect generally and a cause of grave apprehension in official Washington. Such was certainly the case in World War II. To the Europeans in revolt against Nazi domination, revolution meant renewal, a new beginning. De Gaulle caused a scandal in Washington when he declared in April 1942, "One thing dominates the whole French question today – the face of revolution. For France, betrayed by her ruling and privileged classes, has embarked in the greatest revolution in all her history. . . . In the secret of her suffering, an entirely new France is rising, and she will be guided by new men."[26]

Washington's suspicion of de Gaulle was deepened not only by the general's references to revolution, which the administration failed to understand, but also by his overtures to Moscow. De Gaulle's references to the "continental" tie of France and the Soviet Union, which made them natural allies, were seen in Washington as an effort to eliminate Anglo-Saxon, especially American, influence on the political future of France and Europe. Roger Garreau, the Free French representative in Moscow, never ceased complaining about the British and the Americans. The Soviets, however, were not taken with de Gaulle and viewed his efforts to drive a wedge between the Soviets and the Anglo-Saxons as rather naive. The Soviet ambassador to London, Ivan Maisky, reported in January 1942 that de Gaulle's program was tinged with "a good many Italian-Fascist elements." "What he said pretty well confirmed what I had already heard about him before. On the whole his political attitude savors of a modernized kind of Bonapartism, though, in fact, he lacks any firm political views."[27] This view did not depart much from the one held in Washington, except that now de Gaulle was supported by French Socialists and Communists, which could imply a switch on his part. De Gaulle had been identified previously with the far right, but a shift from the right to the left was not unusual. At Vichy, former Communists had become Nazi collaborators; an anti-Vichy swing could lead to a reverse reaction. In American terms, de Gaulle was a puzzle, seesawing from right to left, which proved him unstable and hence dangerous. The few in Washington who used French rather than American frames of reference in figuring out de Gaulle reached different, far more realistic conclusions.

Fear of communism was much too deeply ingrained in the American outlook for a possible Communist future for France to be regarded with equanimity. Roosevelt made repeated references to his concern about this. OSS chief William Donovan, himself a staunchly conservative Republican, tried to present the president with a more realistic picture. In a May 1942 memorandum he explained that people in France retained their prewar political allegiances and that the Communist party, despite the persecutions it had suffered and despite Soviet successes, had scarcely won any ground.

The Communists have the prestige of a very active group, which gives the impression of being very numerous; they profit from a martyr's crown; and finally as the German successes created a kind of trance responsible in no small degree for the defeat, so the present successes of the Soviet armies put many people in an hypnotic sleep, from which they would not awake for fear of falling. . . . An inferiority complex motivates some; for it is surprising how easily the Soviet victories become "our victories." These are satisfactions which are difficult to deny to those who stand in need of them.[28]

The Resistance press was often both idealistic and unrealistic, promoting at one time the United States of the World and at another time a European Federation. It argued for justice, liberty, and the avoidance of past mistakes through the emergence of a new elite. Interestingly, it did not implicate the German people in its denunciation of nazism. The Germans needed to be saved no less than the rest of Europe.[29] The French Revolution, more than Marx or Lenin, inspired the ideals of the Resistance.

Roosevelt's attitude toward the French Resistance was ambiguous precisely because its primary concern was to reach political objectives through revolutionary means. Its aim was not only to chase the Germans from France but to change the face of France. Roosevelt would not admit that legitimacy might be acquired simply because those fighting for liberation and change identified with their leader. He clung to the idea that France was the only country at war with Germany whose legitimacy was suspended until after liberation. Since no legitimate authority existed to represent France, the country would be occupied territory wherein U.S. military commanders dictated the law. According to Roosevelt's plan, an Allied military government (AMGOT) would take charge of administration, its officers having been trained in American universities for the purpose. Neither de Gaulle nor most of the Allies, for that matter, agreed with Roosevelt's notion that "France did not exist" and would continue not to exist until free elections gave birth to a legitimate government. De Gaulle believed his leadership of the Resistance conferred upon him all the legitimacy that was required for assuming the administration of territories progressively liberated. According to a strict application of Roosevelt's dictum that legitimacy derives only from free elections, the French would not have had a legitimate government in 150 years, since most of its regimes, whether monarchy, empire, or republic, had come to power through revolutions, coups d'état, or war. Had de Gaulle not existed, AMGOT might have proved necessary; but he did exist, and "revolutionary" France was wholeheartedly with him. In the end, U.S. military commanders were grateful it was de Gaulle, not AMGOT, who took charge.

Washington's ambiguous attitude toward the French Resistance was not shared by the American people, who supported the Free French enthusiastically. The Resistance was hailed in articles, motion pictures, and books, while prominent Europeans extolled in lectures and newspaper interviews the heroic deeds of the anti-Nazi underground fighters. Indeed, Americans were largely indifferent to the administration's concerns.

In April 1943 the Bern (Switzerland) office of the OSS offered an envoy from the United Resistance Movement (MUR) substantial financial assistance and use of the organization's communication facilities. The French, who had made clear their sentiments regarding de Gaulle, were told the OSS was interested only in their military role. The controversy between Giraud and de Gaulle, the OSS explained, was for the French to resolve; if the Resistance was for de Gaulle, that would be supported without hesitation. Fearful of American interference in the

Resistance and determined to exert his authority by strictly controlling the allo-
cation of funds, de Gaulle disapproved of the initiative. Henri Frenay, the leg-
endary leader of the Resistance group Combat, tried to dismiss de Gaulle's
objections by arguing that contact with the Americans could not only provide
the funds the Resistance needed but also serve to influence Allied attitudes.
"The Resistance's delegation has consistently found on the part of our American
friends a total understanding and the greatest tact. To speak of an American
attempt at manipulation represents a grave mistake that could turn to calumny
if persisted in," Frenay stated. As new Maquis were organized and new resistance
movements emerged, the financial needs of the Resistance increased and London could not provide funds in sufficient quantities. But because of de Gaulle's
objections the Resistance was forced to terminate its contact with the Americans. The real reason for de Gaulle's insensitivity to Frenay's arguments, Claude
Bourdet explained, was that the general and his followers

> could absolutely not admit the evidence . . . that the Resistance, born independently of
> de Gaulle, and adhering to him of its own independent will, supported him the way free
> citizens support a government of their choice, not like soldiers obeying their unit's com-
> mander. . . . Receiving money from the Allies would have contributed to strengthening
> our spirit of autonomy, to transform us in a sort of second power with Free France. That
> was what de Gaulle and his aides feared, far more than our falling under an impossible
> American or Giraudist subjection, incompatible with the very spirit of the French Resis-
> tance.[30]

It should be added that William Donovan, the OSS head, had been consistently
favorable to the Free French, and it was unfair of de Gaulle to state that he had
"always played against us."[31]

In March 1943 Jean Moulin,[32] de Gaulle's representative in France who was
later captured and tortured to death by the Gestapo, met Admiral Stark during a
brief visit to London. Colonel Billotte, who arranged the interview, wrote: "We
gave our interlocutors measured and realistic information on the actions the
Resistance could undertake mainly against road and railroad networks along the
axis where an Allied landing in France could take place."[33] Stark prepared a very
detailed record of the conversation, in which three other Resistance leaders had
taken part. The visitors made it clear that "all resistance organizations in France
now accept de Gaulle's direction and leadership"; groups had sprung up spontaneously that "consider themselves 'gaullist,' a term that has become synonymous in France with resistance to Germany and Vichy 'collaborationists.' They
all accept the direction of de Gaulle and his staff and look upon de Gaulle as
their representative for assuring collaboration with the United States and British
governments and forces." The report dealt extensively with the organization of
the secret army, present sabotage operations, the planning and conduct of the
battle of the interior, and the role of Fighting France.[34] The document was destined, through the Navy Department, for the Pentagon.

On 15 May Stark sent another confidential report to Washington on the formation of a French Resistance Council comprising all the main resistance organizations. A message by the council read thus: "All the resistance parties of the Northern and Southern zones renew their assurance to you and to the National Committee of their absolute devotion to the principles for which you stand and from which you can never waver without clashing with French opinion."

A number of memorandums from Donovan to the president stressed the growing importance of Gaullism in France:

De Gaulle's prestige has risen to an extraordinary degree in recent months. He is backed by a strong popular current which favors a democratic France with pronounced socialist leanings. The French resistance movements find America's attitude to the Committee of National Liberation incomprehensible. This attitude is leading to a strengthening of pro-Russian sentiment among the French. (August 1943)

De Gaulle and his followers . . . are a symbol of the spirit which resisted the Nazis from the darkest days of 1940. This symbol is more important than the man himself who, regardless of his virtues, is admittedly difficult. (October 1943)

The majority of the French people consider de Gaulle the personification of all French resistance. . . . Because he is a symbol of the utter rejection of capitulation and collaboration . . . his stature within France far transcends that of the usual political leader. (December 1943)

Donovan stressed more than once that Washington's hostility to de Gaulle was counterproductive.

When dealing with de Gaulle, Washington was wont to consider appearances more than substance. Even though he spoke of revolution and vengeance, de Gaulle was still very much a conservative. He received his legitimacy from the Resistance while at the same time fearing the consequences for France if the movement were to get out of control and thereby compromise the authority of the state he was determined to reestablish. The military in him advocated authority, not disorder; this sentiment was shared by the middle class, ever fearful of revolution, and a number of Gaullists as well.

While preparing to govern France, de Gaulle had to contend with the immediate problem of North Africa. The Allied military command found both reassurance and a clear evolution toward the democratic process in the moderation of the French administration. The formation of the Consultative Assembly was a step in the right direction; the support of distinguished personalities like Léon Blum and Edouard Herriot strengthened de Gaulle's prestige by showing that traditional groups such as the Socialists and the radicals were behind him. Let us recall that Blum and Herriot were particular favorites of Roosevelt's. Their attitude should have been reassuring to the president, but it evidently was not. Even more important, an inner cabinet formed early in June included personalities that added prestige and a measure of moderation to balance the more excitable Free French. These personalities favorably impressed the Americans and the British, contributing to a more relaxed atmosphere.

Particularly important to French-Allied relations was the appointment of René

Massigli as commissioner of foreign affairs. He brought to the organization a degree of seriousness and professionalism sorely missing in the past. A career diplomat of distinction and moderation, Massigli had served for some years as director of political affairs at the Ministry of Foreign Affairs. Following the armistice, he resigned his post as ambassador to Turkey and retired to France. On 15 September 1942 he called on Chargé d'Affaires S. Pinkney Tuck at Vichy to inform him that he had been asked by de Gaulle to join him and take over the direction of foreign affairs for the National Committee. "Massigli," Tuck informed Washington,

is today convinced that de Gaulle enjoys such prestige in the country that he constitutes an essential element in the future restoration of France. He is, therefore, ready and willing to collaborate with de Gaulle and Edouard Herriot, whom he has seen, encourages him to do so. He does not, however, wish to do so unless he is certain of being persona grata with Washington and unless he is sure that his arrival would be viewed with pleasure and that a confidential collaboration in the common interest could be established.[35]

Massigli found his way to London, where Assistant Secretary of State James Dunn conveyed to him his warm recollection of their meeting at the disarmament conference and assured him that the State Department greatly admired his professional qualities, integrity, and patriotism. Dunn told Massigli he regretted that some members of the National Committee failed to understand the United States and the complexities of the U.S. political scene.[36] Cordell Hull took the view that "any strengthening of the French National Committee in London would be of friendly interest to this government, since it is our hope for greater and more extended collaboration for the ultimate defeat of the common enemy."[37]

In conversations with Stark and Winant, Massigli said his only objective was the union of all French activities in the war against the Axis, adding that he would not remain in his present post if opposition within Free French circles made complete agreement and union with Giraud and the French in North Africa impossible. At the time, military leaders of Free France such as Catroux, d'Astier, d'Argenlieu, and Auboyneau had urged de Gaulle to reach an agreement with Giraud without demanding prior guarantees. Most civilian commissioners instead favored subordinating both the administration and the military to de Gaulle and the National Committee. Massigli's task was facilitated by the January 1944 appointment of Anthony Biddle as Eisenhower's liaison officer to the Gaullists. Biddle was warmly welcomed in Algiers, for he had been the only U.S. diplomat to maintain friendly relations with de Gaulle and oppose State Department policy toward France. Another welcome appointment was that of Ambassador Edwin Wilson as U.S. representative to the French National Committee. He got along famously with de Gaulle, as the latter acknowledged.[38]

General de Lattre de Tassigny was another moderate element whose presence in North Africa enhanced Free French prestige.[39] He had served before the war in Africa under Giraud and at one time had the then-colonel de Gaulle under his command. After escaping from France to England in September 1943, he was put in touch with the Americans and the British. Following a three-hour conversation with de Lattre, Stark wrote to Eisenhower: "I felt I had really met a great French patriot. Broad gauged, tolerant, reasonable, no axe to grind, force-ful—well, I'd better stop or I might overdo it, but I was very much taken by the man. . . . I believe you would enjoy and get much out of an interview with him." And he reported to Knox: "The man has a splendid personality and a great fight-ing heart, and a lot of common sense" (15 December 1943). In a lengthy inter-view with Winant, the general stressed the radical changes in France following total German occupation, France's "great affection for and unbounded trust in America," de Gaulle's role as symbol of the Resistance, and French hope for a "complete and cordial agreement" between Washington and de Gaulle. The mil-itary were once again better informed about the true state of France than either the president or the State Department, and that understanding was to play a considerable role as the liberation of France neared.

Maurice Couve de Murville, de Gaulle's future foreign minister and premier, had been until 24 March 1943 a high official in Vichy's Ministry of Finance, responsible for negotiations on exchange and financial matters with the Ger-man Armistice Commission.[40] Despite Couve de Murville's well-known pro-American sentiments, Henry Morgenthau had refused to deal with him following his appointment as commissioner of finance for the French National Committee because of his past connections with Vichy. In November Pierre Mendès France, another future premier, replaced him, apparently because Couve de Murville had been reluctant to take effective action against the finan-cial groups that had collaborated with the enemy.[41]

The presence in Algiers of men like Couve de Murville, René Meyer, and Jean Monnet, representatives of big capital and financial interests, had a sobering effect on the French National Committee, further reducing their extremism and the role of the London Free French. Some historians have argued that the im-pact of the new arrivals marked the end of any romantic notions concerning the Resistance's revolutionary role. These moderating elements were there to sup-port the French military in efforts to end the bickering among the French. Ca-troux, who bad ambitions of his own, was especially critical of the situation. In conversations with Robert Murphy he recommended that "the British and American Governments, possibly through Admiral Stark, take a definite stand, making it clear that they support fully the idea of French unity but that they oppose de Gaulle's drive for personal power."[42] Murphy felt that Catroux wished to replace both de Gaulle and Giraud, which "might not be an unhappy solution as he is an intelligent and able person who is well disposed and reasonable." But de Gaulle, Murphy told the president, "as you know, is another cup of tea. He suspects Catroux and has no intention of permitting Catroux to supersede him. I doubt seriously that Catroux will be able to overcome de Gaulle's energy, am-bition, and his intention to appeal for popular support by using every trick dear to the heart of a demagogue who believes in his own publicity."[43]

In an effort to solve the Giraud controversy, on 28 March 1943 Catroux proposed a compromise to de Gaulle: De Gaulle would preside over the executive and legislative branches of the Empire and would select the committee's members in consultation with Giraud. Giraud would become a constitutional head of Fighting France with the title lieutenant general of the Republic. He would assume command of the army, promulgate the laws, and represent France's provisional power vis-à-vis the Allies. De Gaulle rejected the proposal, asserting that Giraud was unfit for the task.[44]

In June 1943 the French National Committee consisted of four generals (Giraud, de Gaulle, Georges, and Catroux), five banking or financial representatives (Monnet, Pleven, Meyer, Diethelm, and Couve de Murville), and two labor leaders (Philip and Tixier). This was hardly a revolutionary group, and Murphy could confidently recommend its recognition to the president.[45] Later changes in the National Committee's composition did not alter its basic conservative configuration. Meeting in Quebec on 26 August, Roosevelt and Churchill extended limited recognition to the French National Committee, which received the news with "enthusiasm and gratification."[46]

When Giraud resigned from the National Committee, the U.S. command was relieved it no longer had to deal with his inefficiency and lack of realism. He was not "a big enough man to carry the burden of civil government in any way," Eisenhower had warned the Combined Chiefs of Staff. Concern that Giraud's ouster would strengthen the position of radical elements within the committee was soon dissipated, for the contrary happened; the ouster marked the real beginning of de Gaulle's "de-radicalization" process.

More and more representatives of the "old society" and the old "general staff" (military, administrative, political, economic) who had supported Giraud saw no alternative to supporting de Gaulle. Many of these people had much more practical experience than the Free French "amateurs," and they began to convert some of the Free French round de Gaulle to their own way of thinking; the extreme "radicalism" of the Resistance, strongly influenced by the Communists, scared many Gaullists, and they began creating round de Gaulle himself a new political atmosphere which was different from the "pure Gaullism" of the London days, with its uncompromising hostility to Vichy. More important still was the Army; there were about 400,000 French troops (though only about one half of them armed) outside France, and most of them had originally been "Vichyite" and not "Free French." Even in the famous Free French Division under General Leclerc, which was the first to enter Paris, less than half of all the officers and soldiers were originally Free French; the rest were most ex-Vichyites.[47]

The impact of the army on de Gaulle was also decisive, as Claude Bourdet explained:

De Gaulle, man from the Right, long close to the Action Française, turned republican by osmosis, because surrounded by republicans, but also as a reaction to Vichy's fascism, had been suffering for three years rejection by his social milieu and especially by what had been truly his family, perhaps his only political party: the Army, the officers' corps. The possibility of rejoining this milieu taking advantage of Giraud's collapse, to reestablish broken ties, to become the only possible leader, even if some accepted him reluctantly, was far more important than remaining only the head of the anarchic Resistance he was already suspecting and of those Free French fighters whom he certainly loved, but who were only a handful.[48]

Symbolic of the new orientation[49] was General Juin's appointment as commander of the army. Released from German captivity having given his word of honor not to fight the Germans again, faithful to his oath of allegiance to Pétain (who considered him, as he told Leahy, "the ablest soldier we have in France"), he had met with Goering to coordinate the defense of Tunisia with the Nazis. He had placed himself successfully at Darlan's service, then Giraud's, and was finally at de Gaulle's.

By rejoining the fold as a right-leaning general, de Gaulle eased Washington's fears of disorder and revolution in liberated France. His ambiguous position on the Resistance, which he needed for the legitimacy it conferred but which he also mistrusted as a potential challenge to his authority, gave further reassurance. De Gaulle was extremely concerned, or so the U.S. military believed, about the radical and communist elements supporting him both in France and Algiers; their extremism had sobered him.

Although Roosevelt continued to suspect de Gaulle, the U.S. military had come to trust him completely. De Gaulle was particularly anxious to ingratiate himself with Eisenhower, whom he respected. He absolved Eisenhower of responsibility for U.S. recognition of Darlan and subsequently of Giraud, blaming Murphy, and he frequently expressed his admiration of Eisenhower's military ability.[50] De Gaulle was a changed man, too: "Ike had recognized this before he left Algiers, which accounted for a love fest with de Gaulle before leaving for Washington."[51]

According to de Gaulle, on 30 September Eisenhower told him:

You were originally described to me in an unfavorable sense. Today, I realize that that judgement was in error. For the coming battle, I shall need not only the cooperation of your forces, but still more the assistance of your officials and the moral support of the French people. I must have your assistance, and I have come to ask for it. . . . Now I can assure you that as far as I am concerned and whatever apparent attitudes are imposed upon me, I will recognize no French power in France other than your own in the practical sphere.[52]

Eisenhower left North Africa to prepare for the landing in France. In Washington, he visited with the president three times to discuss Franco-American relations, the last visit taking place on 12 January 1944. That there was a meeting of minds is doubtful, since the immediate concern for Eisenhower was military necessity, not abstract notions of legitimacy or de Gaulle's views on the future. Roosevelt's perspective was on the long term; Eisenhower's, on the short term — his attention was focused on one of the largest military operations in history. Military necessity was gradually defeating Roosevelt's plans.

10

France Is Free

As the year 1944 opened, with the dawn of Europe's liberation after four years of Nazi rule appearing on the horizon, Roosevelt's instructions to Edwin C. Wilson, recently appointed U.S. representative to the French Committee of National Liberation, represented a fresh review of U.S. policies toward France. The document mentioned the military reasons that dictated the government's decision to maintain *"official*—I stress the word official" relations with Marshal Pétain: to prevent the fleet from falling into German hands and to keep the Germans out of North Africa. Never did the government "by word or deed imply that the policies sponsored by Marshal Pétain and his collaborators had American approval." Relations with the French were at all times dictated by military considerations. "In spite of frequent public pronouncements the policy pursued by this government in North Africa since November 1942 has been even more misunderstood, if that is possible, than its previous attitude toward the Vichy regime." One policy was the continuation of the other, the final target being France's liberation.

Concerning relations with the National Committee, the president admitted that "many of the developments in North Africa were contrary to what we would have wished," but the military exigencies of dealing with Darlan

in no way affected our fundamental aims. . . . Military considerations in the prosecution of the war against Germany are and must remain paramount. Although the soundness of this principle should be self-evident, it is unfortunately a fact that certain French elements have come to accept an Allied victory as the foregone conclusion. They have consequently permitted their attention to be diverted from the main task and have devoted themselves primarily to political activities which retard and are a constant threat to the Allied military effort.

The president reasserted his government's readiness to support all French citizens willing to fight and not to recognize any individual or group as representative of France and the French Empire before the French people had had an opportunity to express their collective will. He had been "deeply disturbed" to notice, instead of the union of all French in the war, "an unrelenting struggle for political power." "General de Gaulle and his associates have attempted to arrogate to themselves the credit for resistance to Germany, ignoring or belittling the efforts of other Frenchmen and the enormous assistance being rendered the cause of France by the United States and the other Allies."

Roosevelt clearly resented de Gaulle's taking credit for the liberation of France, since French efforts were actually quite modest compared with those of the United States. This was one more reason for Roosevelt to deprecate de Gaulle's campaign against the United States as well as his futile and "most disheartening" efforts to drive a wedge between Washington and London and between the Anglo-Saxons and Moscow. "Nothing but disaster can come from a policy which strives to unite Frenchmen by subtly inculcating in them a sense of grievance against foreign countries in general and their friends and allies in particular."

After warning that the National Committee's efforts to present itself as the government of the French Republic "possess no validity" as far as the United States was concerned, the letter concludes, "No people in the world look forward more than the people of the United States to the day, drawing ever nearer, when France will emerge from the shadow with new strength and vigor to resume its rightful place and to contribute its genius to building a just and lasting peace."[1]

Roosevelt's instructions demonstrated a freezing of attitudes toward France while eluding a fundamental question: Between D-Day and such time as the French could hold elections, who would administer the zones being progressively liberated? In the fall of 1943, the three participants in the Moscow Conference – the United States, Great Britain, and the Soviet Union – had stated categorically that the supreme commander would have no dealings with the Vichy regime "except for the purpose of liquidating it,"[2] and he would keep no person in office who had willfully collaborated with the enemy or deliberately acted in a hostile manner toward the Allied cause. This policy, reiterated in direct instructions to Eisenhower, meant there would be no repetition of the North African experience, where the Vichy structures were kept in place.

With Vichy excluded, two alternatives were left: the Anglo-Saxons or de Gaulle's National Committee. The military had made it clear that administering France was beyond their means and their competence; it would have meant treating France, not as an ally, but as an occupied country, the same as Italy or Germany. In early April the president had directed that the supreme commander be left free to deal with the French National Committee or any other group that might prove helpful. Eisenhower feared this instruction might result in a competition among factions that would lead to civil war. The British shared

Eisenhower's concern that dealing with groups other than de Gaulle's might result in the emergence of another Darlan.

The State Department had by that time moved a step ahead of the president. On 9 April Cordell Hull praised the French Committee of National Liberation as a valuable symbol of resistance and stated that the United States would permit it to "exercise leadership to establish law and order" in liberated France, so long as it operated under the supervision of the supreme commander. Hull made it clear that the United States had "no purpose or wish to govern France or to administer any affairs save those which are necessary for military operations against the enemy. It is of the utmost importance that civil authority in France should be exercised by Frenchmen." De Gaulle considered the speech constructive provided two conditions were respected: maximum assistance to the inter-Allied command and full respect of French sovereignty on French soil.[3]

Roosevelt, who had not underwritten Hull's statement, still had reservations. As an example of what might happen in France, he discussed the possible action to be taken if the mayor of a given community appointed by the National Committee proved unacceptable and his presence led to disturbances. "General Eisenhower, because he is responsible for the safety of his rear, has the authority, of course, to put in who would maintain peace, the same way as he would have the right to put in troops to maintain the peace. . . . The military element is of course paramount because we want peace in France, not just throwing the Germans out."[4]

The president's thesis on France sounded rather impractical to the military, who would have to deal with the French situation on the spot. His insistence that the French had no way of making known their preference clashed with the evidence gathered by various intelligence services that a majority of the French would follow de Gaulle. His instructions to Eisenhower in particular, authorizing him to deal with de Gaulle on military but not on political matters, could simply not be implemented. The military had no choice but to circumvent Roosevelt's instructions, thus opening a new chapter in American relations with the French. Almost imperceptibly, by force of circumstances he could no longer control, the president gradually came around to the military's point of view. As we shall see, this reversal had a considerable impact on U.S. policies concerning France.

As D-Day neared, Allied headquarters in London repeatedly alerted Washington that strict application of the president's instructions would result in compromising the success of the operation. In an 11 May message to the Joint Chiefs of Staff, Eisenhower warned that the limitations under which he was operating in dealing with the French were "becoming very embarrassing and producing a situation which is potentially dangerous." He made it clear that the only body or organization that could effectively assist the Allies in the fight against Germany was the French Committee of National Liberation. He also asserted that he understood Washington's policies well enough to be able to reach a "working way" with the Committee. "From a military point of view," Eisenhower insisted, "coordination with the French is of overriding importance." He constantly requested that "this matter be treated as [one] of the utmost urgency, and that it be considered, as far as possible, on its military aspects."[5]

In a separate message of the same date Eisenhower wrote that his command had conferred with military and naval representatives of the French Committee on matters such as the following: (1) formation of security battalions to guard lines of communication; (2) billeting, labor requirements, and distribution of civil supplies; (3) the initial approach to the French people; (4) reconciliation of the French people to the necessity for the U.S. bombing program.[6] Obviously, technical issues such as these had political implications. As Eisenhower's chief of staff, Walter Bedell Smith, explained in a message to Marshall, "No one who has dealt with a foreign government, at close range as we have, can fail to realize that when a military commander is operating on foreign soil there is no clear cut line of demarcation between military and civil or political questions."

Addressing the president directly, Eisenhower assured him that he would "carefully avoid anything that could be interpreted as an effort to influence the character of the future government of France," but he added:

However, I think I should tell you that so far as I am able to determine from information given to me through agents and through escaped prisoners of war, there exist in France today only two major groups, of which one is the Vichy gang, and the other character-ized by unreasoning admiration for de Gaulle. This may merely be an indication of the "shell shock" to which you refer, but its effect will be a practical one when we once shall have succeeded in liberating areas that will fall outside the strict military zone, and should therefore be turned over to local self-government. It is possible that we shall then find a universal desire to adhere to the Gaullist group.[7]

Eisenhower insisted it would help if the president's wishes for France, "of which I am already aware," came to him as a joint directive of the American and British governments (15 May 1944). Eisenhower was acting not as an American but as the Allied military commander responsible to both Washington and Lon-don, and he needed and expected the two capitals to coordinate their instruc-tions.[8]

Roosevelt informed Eisenhower through Marshall:

I still think he [Eisenhower] does not quite get the point. . . . He evidently believes the fool newspaper stories that I am anti–de Gaulle, even the kind of story that says I hate him, etc. All this, of course, is utter nonsense. I am perfectly willing to have de Gaulle made President, or Emperor, or King or anything else so long as the action comes in an untrammeled and unforced way from the French people themselves.

The president added that "it is awfully easy to be for de Gaulle." He declared that the French must have a chance to freely choose their leader: "Self-determina-tion is not a word of expediency. It carries with it a very deep principle in hu-man affairs."

The president had once again circumvented the real issue. The problem was not what the French were free to do after the Germans had been driven out, but what to do until then. Eisenhower shared Roosevelt's "deep principle," but in the meantime he needed the cooperation of the Free French. Churchill was equally convinced of this, as shown by several notes to the president. He wrote on 14 April, "I am very conscious of the dangers of an unfriendly France on the morrow of its deliverance by the English-speakers."[9] On 12 May: "We must take care that our joint troops do not suffer heavier losses owing to the fact that no agreement has been made for the employment of the French resistance groups."[10] And again on 26 May: "I feel . . . that we should be in a difficulty if it were thought that more British and American blood was being spilt because we had not got the French national spirit working for us."[11]

Lack of close coordination with the French Resistance was also upsetting to Eisenhower. He deemed it urgent to furnish the French general Koening, who was under his command,[12] with "certain general information in connection with forthcoming operations . . . in order that arrangements can be made for coordinated action by French resistance groups." Effective coordination required U.S., British, and French intelligence organizations to work in close contact. This proved difficult because a directive issued by the Joint Chiefs of Staff before the North African operation against "tripartite intelligence" had not been revoked. General Donovan found the directive compromised the opportunity to increase the amount of useful military intelligence coming out of France in addition to hampering OSS activities and operations within France. Donovan told the Joint Chiefs that

the various Resistance Groups and organizations offered by far the greatest immediate possibility for the securing of intelligence and the carrying on of the other activities within the scope of the work of the OSS, provided proper contact and lines of communications could be established with them. . . . Close collaboration with the British and Free French Services would assist us in maintaining and developing the lines and operations of our own independent service, as well as give us an additional source of original intelligence material through the Fighting French.[13]

Lack of cooperation in the intelligence field had worried Cordell Hull. He complained to the Joint Chiefs that arming the resistance groups had become an important issue in the eyes of the French; however, "the impression seems to have gained general credence that what is being done in this field is being done by the British and that the United States not only has played no part in the matter but is even opposed to arming the 'underground' for political reasons . . . if not actually hostile to the resistance groups in France."[14] Humors soured further when, on 21 April, de Gaulle expressed satisfaction at British efforts to get arms into France, stressing that they were solely British efforts. "This statement is just the sort of thing that we have been hoping to be in a position to combat," Hull complained to Marshall.[15]

Hull's concern reflected a widespread malaise resulting from the feeling that opportunities had been lost. The administration was receiving increasingly well documented evidence of the true state of affairs in France. Stark had come into possession of a secret memorandum detailing plans for a national insurrection in France; this he made available not only to King but also to Eisenhower, Winant, and Undersecretary of State Edward R. Stettinius. The memo, issued by the Central Committee of the French resistance movements, provided instructions for a "national insurrection" to take over all administrative offices and to eliminate all prominent collaborationists in the interval between the departure of the Germans and the arrival of the Allied forces in each French region. A quotation by de Gaulle headed the text: *La libération nationale est inséparable de l'insurrection.*

The committee's instructions included the following:

(a) Definition of national insurrection on "J-day" [D-Day].
(b) Preparation for J-day and command arrangements for the insurrection.
(c) Revolutionary action:
    (1) Military action.
    (2) Technical activities (procedures for seizing control of public administration and local governments.)
    (3) Political action, or action of the masses.
(d) Plan for the insurrection.
(e) Launching of the insurrection (in connection with and following Allied landing operations).
(f) Special point.
    There can be no liberation without insurrection. The action which the resistance has prepared and which it owes to itself and to its martyrs is something more than a *coup d'état*, a palace revolution for a simple change of administration. . . . The only way to produce a complete clarification of the French situation is to proceed with the national insurrection or revolution in order to make it a striking demonstration of a genuine popular will under the leadership of the resistance movements and all the resistance forces in the country. This insurrection must be brought about in the short period of time which will elapse between the departure of the Germans (or their complete disintegration) and the arrival of the Anglo-Saxons.

The insurrection was intended to paralyze simultaneously the German defense organization and the Vichy command; guarantee the immediate revolutionary repression of treason; replace Vichy officials with Resistance appointees; assure international recognition of the *de facto* government of de Gaulle; and base Resistance action on the national will and not on any consideration of diplomatic opportunism. The document described in considerable detail the administrative apparatus to be set up by the Resistance, closely following the plan for the administration of liberated regions used by de Gaulle in Algiers. It also contained a warning: Although full assistance was to be offered to the Allied landing forces, the cooperation of the resistance movements and the authorities to be set up by them would depend upon the degree to which the Allied command recognized these authorities as the only administration qualified to deal with the Allied military command.[16]

This and other documents made clear the price the Allied forces were expected to pay for the collaboration of the French Resistance. The Allied command was willing and ready to accept these terms, for it dreaded the responsibility of administering France. It obviously interpreted "military necessity" differently than did the president and inevitably drew the conclusion that was in its own best interest. Apparently the president had decided not only on a military government for France but also on Allied supervision of the general elections that were to return "legitimacy" to France. Secretary of War Stimson was greatly disturbed by this prospect. He wrote in his diary:

America cannot supervise the elections of a great country like France. . . . I am deeply concerned lest . . . we get dragged into a situation where we ourselves will assume the responsibility in part or more for its execution according to Anglo-Saxons ideals. That would result in terrific dangers and would be likely to permanently alienate the friendship of France and the United States. . . . It is better not to run the risk of bickering now which will serve not only to divide us from de Gaulle but will divide us from the British who more and more are supporting de Gaulle. . . . We have thus far been unable to agree with them upon a directive to Eisenhower as to his conduct in setting up French authority in the operations of France which he is liberating. He is the general not of the United States but of the two allied governments, and he is in a dreadful position when those two governments differ and get deadlocked on such an important question.[17]

Stimson did not contest the president's view that de Gaulle was a "narrow-minded French zealot with too much ambition for his own good and some rather dubious views of democracy"; he was nevertheless convinced of the military importance of effective working relations with de Gaulle and his supporters. He found that "de Gaulle is bad, but not to deal with him is worse."

"Personally I have a great distrust of de Gaulle," he wrote, "and I think that the President's position is theoretically and logically correct, but . . . [it] is not realistic." During a telephone conversation with Stimson, the president expressed the belief that de Gaulle would crumble and that de Gaulle's British supporters would be confounded by the progress of events. "This is contrary to everything that I hear," Stimson replied. "I think de Gaulle is daily gaining strength as the invasion goes on and that is to be expected. He has become the symbol of deliverance to the French people."[18]

De Gaulle's behavior in the Middle East strengthened Roosevelt's suspicion that the general was an apprentice dictator, speaking more democratically than he acted. In November 1943 de Gaulle reacted to Lebanese and Syrian demands for independence by suspending their constitution, dismissing the parliament, and imprisoning ministers. Churchill saw in these "lamentable outrages" a "foretaste of what de Gaulle's leadership in France means. It is entirely contrary to the Atlantic Charter. . . . Everywhere people will say: 'What kind of France is this which, while itself subjugated by the enemy, seeks to subjugate others.' " The president, to whom these lines were addressed, told Hull: "The general attitude of the Committee and especially de Gaulle is shown in the Lebanese affair. De Gaulle is now claiming the right to speak for all France and is talking openly about how he intends to set up his government in France as soon as the Allies get in there."

The arrest the following month of three prominent Vichyites who had aided the Allied landing in North Africa strengthened Roosevelt's conviction that a France under de Gaulle ran the risk of civil war. The Free French announcement that prominent Vichyites, beginning with the marshal, would be tried and sentenced caused further anxiety. De Gaulle held he had no other choice: Accepting the compromise with Vichy meant losing his only "legitimacy"– namely, the support of the Resistance, or at least that of its most active faction, the Communists.

Roosevelt's concerns about the prospect of revolution in France had become such an obsession, according to Stimson, that the secretary was afraid it would hamper the implementation of U.S. policies. He told the president repeatedly that no revolution could occur until Germany was conquered, since the German menace was what was holding the French factions together. Should a revolution occur afterward, U.S. forces would already be out of France and lines of communication would no longer run through the country. France "has had many revolutions before now which she has been left to settle herself and that ought to be done now. But the President has worked himself into an apprehension of this."[19] The man probably closest to the president at the time, Admiral Leahy, kept insisting on the danger of revolution. Early in 1944 McCloy told the British ambassador of "Admiral Leahy's advice to the President, that Marshal Pétain was the most reliable person to whom the Allies could look for help in rallying the French, when the Allied troops entered France."[20] This was a strange suggestion, considering that, while ambassador at Vichy, Leahy had dubbed Pétain a "jellyfish."

Roosevelt's fear of a French revolution was not totally unreasonable. Civil war would break out in Yugoslavia, and the British army would fight the communists in Greece. The French Resistance was facing not only the Germans but the ferocious Milice and often the Vichy police as well. The opposing camps were about equal in strength. Furthermore, there was evidence that Pétain's popularity was undiminished. When he visited Paris unannounced on 26 April 1944, a mere month and a half before the landing in Normandy, he received an enthusiastic, spontaneous reception. Wherever he went, huge crowds acclaimed him. Saint-Etienne, for example, which he visited on 6 June, the day of the landing, received him in triumph. It was not illogical to assume that Pétain's followers might fight it out with the Gaullists the way they had at Dakar and in Syria. Should civil war break out after the Americans had left France, the problem would be for the French to resolve; but if it commenced before that time, the lines of communication across the country bringing men, armor, and supplies to the front lines would be endangered, forcing the American army to intervene to reestablish freedom of transit. The president was so concerned by this possibility that he at first refused to situate the American zone in southern Germany precisely to be free of dependence on France. He would have preferred a zone of occupation in the north, relying on Belgian and Dutch ports.

Roosevelt's worries became most acute at the time he decided to run for an unprecedented fourth term in 1944. Victory over Germany was in sight, and his main concern now was the shape of the postwar world. When he had met with Chiang Kai-shek in Cairo and Stalin at Teheran, he exchanged views with them on the future of the Pacific area and Europe. Stalin had agreed with him that French pretensions in the new global context were out of touch with reality. Threats by the newly self-proclaimed provisional government of the French Republic to turn to the Soviets left the president unimpressed. Stalin had made it clear that he did not think much of the French in general, de Gaulle in particular; he also agreed to oppose restoration of the French Empire to France. "The entire French ruling class was rotten to the core," Stalin told the president, "and . . . was now actively helping the enemy."[21] He felt it "would be not only unjust but dangerous to leave in French hands any important strategic point after the war." He further agreed that Indochina, New Caledonia (which threatened Australia and New Zealand), and Dakar, which "in unsure hands" posed a direct threat to the Americas, should be placed under trusteeship and United Nations control.

Efforts to curtail his authority only served to strengthen de Gaulle's determination to be the one and only person representing France and French sovereignty. The issue of supplementary currency for use by the Allied armies in France offered a test. According to de Gaulle, the currency printed in Washington was "false money," since he claimed only he, as head of the provisional government, had the right to validate currency. He spoke in the name of a sovereignty that neither the president nor anyone else, for that matter, recognized. "General Eisenhower, Supreme Allied Commander, is the only authority with the power to issue currency," Roosevelt told the press. "Such inherent power of a commander of an expeditionary force is well recognized by international law. As soon as there is an appropriate French authority recognized by the Allied governments, we will of course fully accept any currency which it issues."[22] To be legitimate, French authority had to be recognized rather than self-proclaimed, Roosevelt felt. De Gaulle's "unreasonable attitude" did not disturb him because "if for any reason our supplementary currency should not be accepted by the French people we can use the yellow seal dollar and British Military authority notes without any adverse effect except depreciation of the French franc for which the Committee will have to bear full responsibility."[23] A supporting statement by de Gaulle was to no avail. "Provided it is clear that he acts entirely on his own responsibility and without our concurrence he can sign any statement on currency in whatever capacity he likes, even that of the King of Siam," Roosevelt told Churchill.[24] De Gaulle's attempt to control currency was the assertion of a sovereignty Roosevelt was not prepared to recognize. Churchill felt differently, since he was under severe pressure from Anthony Eden, other members of his cabinet, and Parliament to recognize the French National Committee.

Clearly, the British and the Americans had different views concerning the future of France. The British were anxious to preserve a buffer between their realm and Germany and the Soviet Union. Roosevelt, for his part, could never shake off the suspicion that the British wanted de Gaulle as an ally in imperialism and old-fashioned colonialism more than anything else. He found confirmation in de Gaulle's frequent references to the French Empire and his seemingly imperialistic actions in the Middle East.

Roosevelt's refusal to recognize de Gaulle's right to speak for France meant that as D-Day approached, Eisenhower was continually without instructions on how to deal with the French general politically. De Gaulle took advantage of this fact to create a stir. He probably felt that once the invasion was under way, it would be too late for him to get what he wanted. The heads of the European governments in exile in London were to prepare radio addresses inviting their peoples to support the Allies in their sweep through the Continent. They all cooperated, their addresses being recorded for delivery on D-Day. The invitation had been extended to de Gaulle, but he refused to deliver a message that Eisenhower's headquarters had prepared on the grounds that it too strongly stressed obedience to the Allied military command and made no mention of his own Algiers committee. His deportment during the dramatic hours preceding the liberation of France was responsible for what one military historian has called "a comic opera prelude to the invasion": Washington was alternatively informed that "General de Gaulle will speak," "General de Gaulle will not speak," and "General de Gaulle has changed his mind."[25] Churchill considered de Gaulle's gumption "remarkable, as he has not a single soldier in the great battle now developing."[26]

More than 180 French officers, out of some 550 Eisenhower had indicated would be needed, had been in training in London; out of pique over his lack of recognition, however, de Gaulle decided that only 20 would accompany the invasion. Fortunately, the French liaison officers awaiting assignment with the American and British civil affairs detachments were less concerned with political sovereignty than with getting the civilian affairs of the liberated areas back into operation. Thanks to these officers, de Gaulle's lack of cooperation with the Allies proved less damaging than had been feared.

De Gaulle's lack of appreciation, or even concern, for the young Americans who would shortly be discharged upon the beaches of France to engage in one of the bloodiest battles of the war did not go down well with the military. "De Gaulle's highhandedness provoked one of Marshall's especially memorable explosions of anger," Forrest C. Pogue wrote.

"I got hold of de Gaulle's chief officer Lieutenant General Émile Bethouart, [chief of staff of the General Staff of National Defence] and raised the devil," he recalled. To another French representative he raged that what the General had done was a "contemptible thing." He told Foreign Secretary Eden that de Gaulle's actions were "outrageous," and that "no son of Iowa farmers would fight to put up statues of de Gaulle in France." Shock waves of the explosion lapped at Washington, where Stimson noted that "when Marshall gets indignant it usually makes a profound impression."[27]

Morgenthau quoted Marshall as saying, "If the American people could know . . . what de Gaulle has been doing to hamper the invasion – the actual military operations, if that ever leaked out, it would sweep 'the whole damn thing aside.' "[28] Marshall told Stimson he feared "that all this attack on the military effort, the troops, directly by de Gaulle, and indirectly by Eden's support of de Gaulle, was playing with the most dangerous kind of fire; that as soon as the American people learned that the cause their boys were dying for was being obstructed by the French, there would be a tremendous explosive reaction against the French themselves which would play right into the hands of isolationism and make our people anxious to drop France altogether and drop her for good."[29]

Despite his outrage at de Gaulle's behavior, Marshall felt that the need for Anglo-American cooperation during the invasion made it necessary to find some way to resolve the problem of the French general's recalcitrance. As Marshall had feared, de Gaulle's last-minute cancellation of orders to the French liaison officers to proceed to France was resented throughout the United States and checked the steady rise of public sentiment in favor of full recognition of the Free French. The decision was viewed as irresponsible temperamentality, amounting to near sabotage of the Allies at a critical moment.

In the end, de Gaulle agreed to broadcast a radio message to the French from London. It was a moving call for full French commitment in the war, delivered in the general's inimitable style. He mentioned Great Britain but not the United States or the authority of the supreme commander, calling on the French to follow the instructions of the French government (he omitted the word "provisional") and of the leaders authorized to give orders. Eisenhower, too, had a proclamation for the French people, to be posted in captured territory and dropped from planes in leaflets one or two days after the start of the invasion. De Gaulle objected to Eisenhower's failure to mention the French National Committee, but the text had already been printed and it was too late to modify it.[30]

The cause of de Gaulle's pique was the exclusively Anglo-Saxon character of the operation. During strategy discussions in Washington in the summer of 1942, Tixier had been instructed to make it clear that "General de Gaulle must participate directly in the elaboration of inter-Allied plans of operations in Western Europe." Tixier was told to add that de Gaulle was all the more resolved to obtain satisfaction, since "his confidence in the perspicacity and strategic ability of the Allies is open to doubt"[31] – as cheeky a statement as the general ever made. De Gaulle had stressed the same point in a note to Admiral Stark requesting that the French command be party to all plans and decisions on the European invasion.[32] He later mentioned his hurt over France's not having a representative to the Combined Chiefs of Staff. He always spoke as if France's power were on a par with that of the United States, Great Britain, or the Soviet Union. In December 1943 he told Ambassador Wilson that "if in the plans of operation in France, north and south, participation of our armies was not planned in a manner we consider consistent with the national interest, we would recover our armies and freedom of action."[33]

On the eve of the invasion the atmosphere in London was one of tension and confusion. Sir Alexander Cadogan entered the following in his diary on 5 June: "Cabinet 6.30. We endured the usual passionate anti–de Gaulle harangue from PM [Churchill]. On this subject we get away from politics and diplomacy and even common sense. . . . Roosevelt, PM, and – it must be admitted de Gaulle – all behave like girls approaching the age of puberty. Nothing to be done."[34]

During the months that preceded D-Day the fate of French acquaintances for whom he felt esteem was a source of much concern to Roosevelt, especially following the Riom trial. His repeated efforts to get Edouard Herriot out of the country were of no avail. His heart went out mainly to Léon Blum, for whom he felt esteem and affection. In mid-June he had received a letter from Félix Gouin, a socialist who had acted as Blum's counsel at the trial, urging him to join Churchill in addressing a solemn warning to Hitler should the Nazis make an attempt on Blum's life. The president had already intervened on Blum's behalf. In a 30 April 1943 letter to Roosevelt, Blum had written, "I have learned, by unmistakable and repeated tokens, of the great interest which you have taken in my personal situation; and I must let you know how precious these indications of your sympathy have been and are to me."[35] And in September, writing to Madame Suzanne Blum-Weill to thank her for an inscribed copy of Blum's writings and speeches, the president stressed his "great interest in and approval of the splendid record your father made."[36]

While a powerful army was being assembled along the southern coast of England for the assault on Fortress Europe, France was awaiting developments with a mixture of hope and fear. Hope and joy for the masses, concern for a certain portion of bourgeoisie that feared, even more than the destruction, the civil war and disorder that could follow in the wake of the liberating armies. Toward the end of 1943, with the Red Army advancing rapidly along the eastern front, the question was being widely asked, "Who will get to Paris first, the Russians or the Americans?"

Some of the French deluded themselves that Roosevelt might prove more reasonable than Churchill and realize the mortal danger facing civilization. Portugal, Spain, and the Vatican, greatly fearing the spread of communism in the wake of disorder that could accompany the Allied advance, advocated a peaceful compromise to enable the Germans to contain, and possibly defeat, the Soviet Union. They were concerned that Germany's "unconditional surrender" would play into Stalin's hands. The president, however, never deviated from his position that no Darlan-type deal would be made with a German general.

Vichy's hopes that the president would see the light were thus disappointed. Undoubtedly Roosevelt would have preferred a different leader for France than de Gaulle, one whose ideas about the future were more in tune with his own; it can even be assumed that despite his real affection for Churchill, he might have rejoiced at the Labour party's postwar electoral victory, which paved the way for a resolution of the Indian and other colonial problems that had set the president at odds with the previous British cabinet; it can also be assumed that he might have wished for an honorable exit for the old marshal–but all these assumptions were never borne out.

The official U.S. position had repeatedly been made clear to the French. During the months following the Allied landing in North Africa, and even more insistently after D-Day, rumors were afloat about American "plots" against de Gaulle and efforts to salvage what was left of Vichy. They were the product of inflamed imaginations.

In January 1944 the French National Committee had formally been informed that the U.S. government had no intention of having any further dealings with Vichy. The president's 15 March instructions to Eisenhower in the event of occupation of French territory were categorical: "You will have no talks or relations with the Vichy regime except for the purpose of terminating its administration in toto."[37] A few days later, on 21 March, a statement by the State Department denounced the "absurd reports" that the U.S. government would have any dealings with the Vichy regime except for the purpose of abolishing it.[38]

These instructions were carried out by American agents despite the tendency of some of them to cause confusion with unauthorized initiatives and statements.

Even before D-Day, French spokespersons for various anti-Gaullist causes were active in efforts to influence the Americans. In May 1944, for example, Lemaigre-Dubreuil, who had assisted in Giraud's escape to North Africa, showed up in Madrid with what he purported were American views on the future of France. Considered a "dubious Frenchman," "representatives of the State Department have been directed to have no transaction with him" (OSS Bern, 31 May 1944).

Concerned that its own disappearance might lead to a Communist takeover in France, Vichy turned repeatedly to the United States for salvation. On 8 June 1944 the OSS's Bern office informed Washington it had been approached by Dr. Menetrel, Pétain's physician and confidant, who stated that the marshal "was prepared to receive recommendations of Americans if there is anything that can be done to assist France." Menetrel admitted that Pétain had suffered a serious loss of prestige following the North African invasion.

Another message for transmittal to Roosevelt was carried by a Pétain envoy to Bern on 6 July:

France today looks to and expects much from America. America can shield France from disorders, destruction and civil war, thus enabling her to participate peacefully in the European equilibrium. Negotiations could intervene in order that the territory occupied by the Anglo-Saxons be submitted to a regime that will not inevitably lead to civil disorders. It would even be desirable if, in order to anticipate all eventualities, a secret envoy of the Marshal were accredited with the American authorities. It is hoped that the American Government's attitude concerning the issues mentioned in this note be made known as soon as possible.[39]

On 12 August Pétain tried once again to influence the Americans by empowering Gabriel Louis Jaray, president of the Comité France-Amérique, to contact on his behalf the American diplomatic authorities accredited in Switzerland in order to "acquaint them with French political problems and inform them of my intentions at the moment of the liberation of the territory with a view to safeguarding the principle of legitimacy that I embody." Jaray was to "seek a solution that would prevent civil war in France, relying to that effect on President Roosevelt's high authority."

Laval had also been active. One Jean Fabry had been directed by him to contact the U.S. embassy in Bern to convince the Americans that de Gaulle was a communist stooge who should be kept out of France if civil war was to be averted. The ambassador refused to see him. The Americans had hoped that a "publicized hands-off policy of the State Department in connection with Frenchmen like Fabry and Dubreuil ought to forestall any further efforts by people of this character to contact Americans" (OSS Bern, 4 July 1944). It apparently did not, if one "considers the attempt by an under-cover agent of Pierre Laval in Madrid to negotiate with diplomats of the Allies," an attempt which was "disdained" (OSS Bern, 6 August 1944).

On 24 July OSS Bern enquired in Washington about the veracity of reports that the United States was supporting a Chautemps government. Two days later came the reply:

Authorize you to make the unqualified statement that the American government does not endorse any political group or organization until such time as the French people are liberated and have chosen their government. Secretary Hull has made a public denial of continued Vichy-inspired propaganda indicating that the United States is ready to negotiate with Vichy-France. . . . The United States officials can readily appreciate the hostile attitude of the active resistance groups toward Bonnet and Chautemps. There is absolutely no foundation to the rumors circulating from France to the effect that the American government supports Chautemps.

Meddling by unauthorized agents was at times responsible for rumors of U.S. support for Vichy. A typical example is the mission to Portugal undertaken late in 1943 by one Colonel de Gorostarzu, who had been sent to Lisbon by Pétain in the hope of contacting Leahy. He was refused access to the American ambassador, who turned him over to Colonel Robert Solborg, the military attaché. Solborg was described by French sources as "chief of American intelligence services in Europe," when in fact he was not. Donovan had dismissed him as OSS chief of operations in June 1942 for indiscipline; at the time of the incident in Portugal Solborg was not involved in intelligence.

Solborg is reported to have told his visitor that Washington wanted Pétain to stay out of affairs of state and retire somewhere so that while freeing French territory the Allied armies could at the same time free him who represented French legality and legitimacy.[40] In all the 1943–44 reports by Solborg at the National Archives in Washington there is not a single document relating to France. The colonel in fact had no authority to speak for the president, and the opinions expressed were his own, not Roosevelt's.

In the overheated atmospheres of Algiers, Vichy, and Paris, Vichy's efforts to give the impression of Roosevelt's support were the source of many rumors, some of which were presented as fact by de Gaulle himself in his *Mémoires*. He wrote of Laval's having learned through Allen Dulles in Bern that "Washington would favor a scheme that included to silence or set aside de Gaulle."[41] He mentioned a "political project pursued by Laval, favored by Roosevelt," an absurd assertion if one remembers how the president felt about Laval. The reference was to a project, concocted by Laval and involving Herriot, which provided for returning to the National Assembly the powers it had conferred on Pétain, thus making possible the formation of a government that would welcome the Allies in Paris. The source of the allegations of U.S. involvement in the plot was Jean Tracou, a follower of Pétain's whose story de Gaulle accepted without question.[42] André Enfière, a close friend of Herriot's who contributed to arranging the "plot," was alleged to have been in contact with Dulles; however, there is no mention of Dulles or the Americans in Enfière's own account of the events or in available contemporary accounts.[43] So taken was de Gaulle by this legend that he believed Eisenhower had been instructed to await the conclusion of the "plot" before giving the green light for the assault on Paris on 22 August!

The Gaullists had mistrusted Allen Dulles ever since he offered to lend material support to the Resistance. Following de Gaulle's rejection, the OSS office in Bern concerned itself almost exclusively with Germany and Italy, while OSS operational activities in France were operated from Madrid. In its political reports to Washington, Bern consistently stressed de Gaulle's increasing prestige in France and the danger in America's underrating this reality:

13 June 1944: "In denying recognition to the CFLN [Comité Français de Libération Nationale] they [the Americans] are delivering a dangerous weapon to the enemy, since such a refusal is construed as an indication that the French Resistance is not trusted."

30 June 1944: "A campaign of unheard-of violence has been started in various resistance groups against Roosevelt and against the Americans. . . . De Gaulle is

being presented as the obstinate defender of the life of France, who is being hounded by American capitalists."

16 August 1943: "The growth of de Gaulle's prestige in the last few months has been extraordinary. He is backed by a strong popular current in favor of a democratic France with pronounced Socialist tendencies. The French resistance movement finds it impossible to comprehend America's attitude toward the National Committee of Liberation, which has a dangerous tendency to strengthen pro-Russian sentiment among the French." This report, as we saw previously, found its way to the President's desk.

These few samples give an idea of the mood prevailing at the OSS station in Bern. De Gaulle had really nothing to fear from Allen Dulles.

The only pro-Vichy American initiative that *might* have occurred was recounted by Jean Tracou, Pétain's last *chef-de-cabinet*. He wrote of receiving an envoy from the U.S. legation in Bern bringing a message from Marshall for Pétain. Marshall had known Pétain well during World War I while in France as an aide to General John J. Pershing and, according to his official biographer, had a "high regard" for him.[44] Even though no document was found in U.S. archives to bear this out, it is not impossible that Marshall might have wished to send a farewell message to the soldier who for him must have remained the hero of Verdun.

Washington's instructions barring any dealings with Vichy were categorical, and there is not the slightest evidence that Eisenhower or any other U.S. official violated them. To dispel possible misunderstandings, Marshall made the following points in a statement to Eisenhower:

We hear persistent stories from Algiers that the United States has some sort of tie-up with Marshal Pétain and Vichy.

One of the rumors is that the United States favors the constitution of a Chautemps government under the auspices of Pétain of which Mr. Fabry would be a member.

You may be assured that the United States Government has no agreement of any kind with Pétain or the Vichy Government, that the United States has no secret agreements with anybody in regard to France and no ulterior aims.

The United States does not favor any particular government for France to be formed by Chautemps or any other person.

The United States Government is of the definite opinion that a democratic form of government would be best for France and hopes, that when the Nazi invaders are driven from France in defeat, the French people will choose for themselves without any foreign assistance or influence a government which in their opinion is best suited to their needs.

It is my desire, and I believe it is the almost unanimous desire of the American people, that immediately following the liberation of France by a defeat of the Nazis, American troops and American officials involved in the liberation effort be returned to America at the earliest possible date, leaving to France complete liberty of action to organize its government and to start without foreign assistance a rapid march toward its previous position of influence in the civilized world.[45]

II

FDR: A Fresh Look at France

On the day the Allies landed in France, it was announced that Admiral Raymond Fenard, a French naval representative in the United States, had arrived in London with a personal message from the president inviting de Gaulle to visit the United States. The previous April the president had told Churchill that he would be "very glad" to see de Gaulle, provided the latter intimated a desire to come. Roosevelt added that he would "adopt a paternal tone," which was hardly likely to go down well with the general.[1] Churchill was anxious for the success of the visit, for he thought "it would be found that de Gaulle and the French National Committee represent most of the elements who want to help us. Vichy is a foe and there is a large middle body who only wish to be left alone and eat good meals from day to day. The energizing factor of de Gaulle must not be forgotten in our treatment of the French problem."[2]

De Gaulle had repeatedly expressed a desire to meet with Roosevelt. He said his only purpose for going to Washington was to convey France's homage to the president and to the American people and armed forces. He would not ask for recognition of his provisional government, considering the matter of no importance. He also planned neither to undertake nor to accept to negotiate on any current subject.[3]

Shortly before de Gaulle's visit the president received a memorandum from William Donovan opening with the following sentences: "The achievements of French resistance since D-Day have far exceeded expectations. Shaef, 21 Army Group and Combined Chiefs of Staff in London have credited French resistance with much of the delay in the build up of German forces in Normandy." Hundreds of rail communications had been cut; all long-distance telephone lines from Paris and most of those close to the battle area were cut off; roads were sabotaged in many places and ambushes carried out against troops on the move, staff cars, dispatch riders, and so on. The diversion of enemy forces proved of crucial importance:

In the north and east of France the Resistance has remained clandestine – small groups executing sabotage missions against selected targets. In the center, south and west of France, guerrilla activities flared up openly, resulting in bitter fighting between German and Patriot forces, tying down substantial German forces and giving resistance forces control of fairly large areas.

As the Allied landing in Normandy got under way, the Resistance was effectively used to harry and disrupt the enemy's communications; but as the battle progressed, it became feasible to "build up and expand resistance forces to the point where they can keep the enemy fighting, not only along orthodox lines against invasion troops but also in the greatest depth possible in order to retain control of the rear." An official OSS document stressed the "enormous importance of the French resistance as a source of accurate tactical intelligence."[4] On 17 June Marshall declared his satisfaction with the role of the Resistance in France.[5]

In the seven areas of France substantially controlled by the Resistance, 41,000 men and women were mobilized, of whom 14,000 were armed and 24,000 were to be armed. American assistance to the Resistance had political implications, Donovan explained in a memo to the president:

Creation of an "interior front" in southern and western France would give large masses of the French people their long desired opportunity for National self-expression. While the effort would be under the leadership of General de Gaulle and General Koening, it would produce and give lustre to other military and political leaders. The net political effect would be the creation of a large number of potential leaders for the French people to appraise and select and the building of a national self-respect vital to a strong and democratic France.[6]

Roosevelt had justified the Darlan deal on military grounds to save American lives. The activity of the French Resistance detailed by Donovan also contributed to saving the lives of American soldiers. But to support the Resistance on military grounds also meant supporting, directly or indirectly, de Gaulle's political ambitions. The secretaries of war and the navy had reached that conclusion long before. Admiral Stark had played an important role in informing the Pentagon of the realities of the French situation, a role much appreciated not only by the military, but also by Eden and Winant in London, and even by de Gaulle.

In a letter to Undersecretary James Forrestal, who made no mystery of his dislike for the French general, Stark wrote:

De Gaulle is difficult for a foreigner to understand as he is the type of Frenchman we see least, and yet he is deeply and typically French. . . . You have heard the story about his telling the Prime Minister in a fit of rage that he was Joan of Arc, that the British crucified

her, and that they could go ahead and crucify him. He is, I would say, rather filled with
the Joan of Arc Mission to save France. The British say he also has Joan's feelings toward
England. . . . Referring again to Joan of Arc, I think he feels that he is the only one who
can bear the Torch. He has always played for high stakes. He has staked all on practically
every throw. For one who has finally arrived where he has, I think it is only fair to say
that he must have shown considerable diplomatic skill while at the same time being
apparently so rigid. . . . The name of de Gaulle is a symbol . . . probably many Frenchmen hardly know that there is a man by that name . . . what it means to them is non-
collaboration and resistance . . . and as such it is popular. (10 July 1944)

In an earlier memorandum, Stark had written:

It is impossible to foresee how [de Gaulle] will evolve. It can be argued plausibly that he
has many signs of incipient dictatorship, but he is intelligent, so he may see France's
dislike of regimentation, and he is genuinely devout, while most dictators are cynic on
religious matters. My tentative and intuitive guess is that the worst danger of a xeno-
phobe de Gaulle dictatorship has passed. (20 June 1944)

With de Gaulle's arrival in Washington imminent, it became evident he
should be given some sort of recognition. On 5 July 1944 Morgenthau suggested
to John McCloy that Eisenhower issue a directive recognizing de Gaulle as a "de
facto authority." Morgenthau believed the phrase might suit Roosevelt better than
Stimson's suggestion of "provisional" recognition. McCloy agreed to join
Morgenthau in recommending it to the White House. Hull was in favor of it as
well. "We should like to suggest to you a fresh approach to the French situation,"
they wrote the president. The United States should deal with the French Committee either as the "civil authority" or the "administrative authority" or the "de
facto authority" in France "to reach agreements on civil affairs administration
along the lines of those reached with Belgium, the Netherlands and Norway."
The agreement would be temporary, but it would enable the French National
Committee to become the issuing authority for the supplemental franc, thus
eliminating a bone of contention with de Gaulle. The president designated his
preference for "de facto authority." Morgenthau found that while awaiting de
Gaulle the president was "unusually malleable." He was "very pleased" that the
currency question had been settled, relieving Eisenhower of a major irritant.[7]
De Gaulle arrived in Washington on 7 July, stepping from the automobile
"with an air of arrogance bordering on downright insolence, his Cyrano de
Bergerac nose high in the air."[8] With the war raging, but the outcome certain,
Roosevelt had turned his attention increasingly toward the shape of the postwar
world. His main purpose for meeting with the general was to bring him around
to his point of view; but since this view concerned France, it could hardly be
acceptable to de Gaulle. In Roosevelt's scenario France was not to be one of the
great powers entrusted with preserving the peace, nor would the country retain
its empire. The president considered himself the "trustee" of the American continent, whose security would eventually depend upon French, British, and

Dutch bases, especially in the Pacific. He was most interested in Dakar. The only version of their conversation available is the one given by de Gaulle in his *Mémoires*, which although colored by the general's aversion to Roosevelt, appears genuine.

The French issue had been the source of much controversy in the United States, and having accepted his party's nomination for a fourth term, Roosevelt did not overlook the political advantage he could derive from de Gaulle's visit. The independent liberal voter held the balance of power in the forthcoming election, and Roosevelt was eager to present an image of himself free of the early stigma of appeasement and opportunism. Liberal Americans had resented the Darlan deal as an insult to the very values the country had entered the war to defend. They had consistently supported the Free French and opposed the Vichy policy. The exploits of the French Resistance had received a great deal of publicity, Americans appreciating whatever help their soldiers at the front received in the war against the common enemy. The Resistance was fighting not only Germans but also French Fascists, and much as Roosevelt feared both the outcome and new civil strife, he supported anti-Fascist causes that placed him at odds with Churchill's prop for monarchy in Italy, Yugoslavia, Belgium, and Greece. "To Winston any King was better than no King," Lord Moran wryly commented.[9]

Having received sufficient reports indicating that the French identified de Gaulle with the Resistance, Roosevelt cannily answered reporters enquiring what he would discuss with his guest during their first meeting: "A great many things. Well, for instance, I will talk to him today about the operation of the underground . . . within France, a great deal of it down in Southern France. We have a good deal of information from our own sources. We will compare notes about that."[10]

Washington's reception of de Gaulle was exceptionally cordial. Not only the president, but Hull and even Leahy went out of their way to be pleasant. Cordell Hull "found that de Gaulle was now in a much more reasonable frame of mind." Referring to their conversations, the secretary said that the general had visited the Allied bridgehead in Normandy and was filled with admiration for the thoroughness of the invasion preparations and their magnificent execution, as well as for the fighting ability of the American troops. "His visit to Normandy," Hull wrote in his *Memoirs*,

and his conversations with French leaders there also convinced him that Britain and the United States were far more popular in France than he thought, and that the old Parliamentary parties in France still had considerable strength. By now he was confident that the allies would not deal with any group in France other than Committee of National Liberation. At any rate he went out of his way to make himself agreeable to the President, to me, and to other members of the Government, and to ensure us emphatically and repeatedly that he had no intention of forcing himself or his committee upon France as the future Government."[11]

Leahy, whose hostility toward de Gaulle is evident throughout his memoir, *I Was There*, finally "discovered" the Frenchman. "At our first meeting," he wrote, "I found him more agreeable in manner and appearance than I had expected. . . . De Gaulle made a very good impression upon the people he met during his brief stay in our capital, including myself. I had a better opinion of him after talking to him."[12]

The trouble in dealing with someone official Washington did not know how to handle, especially in this case, where the host made it a point not to help matters in the least, assumed tragicomic proportions at a dinner Cordell Hull hosted in honor of the general. That dinner was so illustrative of the malaise felt on both sides that Attorney General Francis Biddle's recollection of the event is worth quoting.

At this dinner for the French General the American Secretary had little opportunity to judge, for he spoke no word of French and his guest was totally deficient in English. . . . So the Secretary and the General sat stiffly in informal silence, the American drooping a little, the Frenchman solemnly and forbiddingly erect, all the six feet six of him, balancing a chip like an epaulette on each martial shoulder because he had not had his twenty-one guns on arrival.

After dinner Bill Bullitt . . . brought up several of us to be introduced to him as he sat in isolated dignity, unsmiling and showing no interest in our tentative remarks. Sol Bloom, chairman of the House Committee on Foreign Affairs, was among the first, and Bill must have murmured in his ear a word or two about the desirability of breaking the ice, an exercise for which Mr. Bloom was eminently qualified. . . . Mr. Bloom, bent at all costs on a *rapprochement*, produced a trick cigar from some inner recess, and offered it to the General, who for a moment hesitated. "Take it, take it," the New Yorker insisted. But when General de Gaulle put out his hand the cigar disappeared in Sol's sleeve, withdrawn by some invisible elastic mechanism—"Now you see it, General, now you don't . . ." Puzzled, suspecting that he was being laughed at, the General turned to his aide. "What does the American statesman wish?" he inquired. The other did not seem to know. It was not a successful evening.[13]

The only concrete result of the visit was recognition of de Gaulle's National Committee as the "temporary *de facto* authority for civil administration in France."[14] The term *authority* was clearly meant to remind the French that it was much too early to speak of government, even provisional. De Gaulle's conclusion was that "France must count only on herself."

The visit did not dispel the president's mistrust of de Gaulle. In Roosevelt's view de Gaulle was always the right-wing general with the Fascist leanings, boasting of the *gloire* and *grandeur* of a France who alone among the countries at war with Hitler had made a deal with the enemy and whose contribution to the war effort was quite modest. De Gaulle felt that irrespective of the importance of France's role in the war, a new Europe without a strong France was inconceivable and that France would reach great-power status whether it deserved it or not. He would see to it that France did achieve that status.

The two men's public discourse did not reflect their real sentiments. During a press conference de Gaulle expressed confidence that resolution of the problems between the two countries would be reached more easily, "for now we understand each other better." In an exchange of letters Roosevelt told de Gaulle that "you and I have become so much better acquainted and see alike in regard to the larger problems before us." De Gaulle responded by expressing the hope of being able to "resume and carry further [our] unforgettable conversations." But de Gaulle was under no illusion of having modified the president's views even though he found it "difficult to contradict this artist, this seducer, in any categorical way."

What de Gaulle could not detect was the subtle way the president's views were evolving. In the postwar period, peace could be kept only by four Big Powers acting in concert, with the main responsibility resting on the United States and the Soviet Union. But with the end of the war in sight, Allied unity showed cracks that threatened the president's plans. Roosevelt was particularly concerned about Soviet expansionist ambitions, though he did not advertise this as part of his proclaimed wish to come to terms with Stalin. He was also worried by Great Britain's evident exhaustion and the prospect of Churchill's unbending defense of empire weakening it further. China was close to collapse and obviously could not be relied on to be an effective fourth partner. Things were not turning out the way the president had hoped; still, he insisted on the need for the Big Powers to have at their disposal a number of bases from which to move quickly to reestablish order when necessary. Two of the bases in his program were Dakar and Indochina, both French controlled, and both of which posed the problem of the future of the French Empire.

A major reason for Roosevelt's hostility toward de Gaulle was precisely their contrasting views on colonialism and empire. Whereas Roosevelt considered both a source of the instability that led to war, de Gaulle viewed them as necessary to France's grandeur. Roosevelt was convinced the world would never be at peace as long as one country or people was subjected to foreign domination. He once told Truman he was more concerned about what the French and British empires might do after the war than by what the Soviets might do.[15] He considered Western sway over much of Africa and Asia no less threatening to world stability than German expansionism. "There has never been, there isn't now, and there never will be, any race of people on earth fit to serve as masters over their fellow men," he declared. "We believe that any nationality, no matter how small, has the inherent right to its own nationhood."[16] Confronted with Winston Churchill's emotional outbursts in support of the "White man's burden," Roosevelt feared that all colony-possessing powers would join in an unholy alliance and that the basic reason the British supported de Gaulle was that they had found an ally in imperialism whom they owned "body, soul, and britches."[17] "I have tried to make it clear to Winston – and others," the president told his son, Elliott, "that while we are their allies, and in it by victory by their side, they must never get the idea that we're in it just to help them hang on to the archaic, medieval Empire ideas."[18]

At the signing of the Atlantic Charter, Roosevelt told Churchill the dissolution of the British Empire would have to be contemplated; the United States "could not and would not underwrite colonialism or undertake to defend imperialism as against movements in various places – like India – for independence," he told Rexford Tugwell. Roosevelt suggested that India be accorded a degree of independence and then asked to join the British Commonwealth.[19] A furious Churchill threatened to resign: He had not become the king's first minister in order to preside over the liquidation of the British Empire.

Roosevelt's objections to British imperialism were mild when compared with his condemnation of French imperial ambitions.[20] He had particularly strong feelings about Indochina, where "after 100 years of French rule . . . the inhabitants were worse off than they had been before." He suggested a twenty- to forty-year trusteeship arrangement leading to independence.[21] Meeting Chiang Kai-shek in Cairo, Roosevelt tried to interest him in the territory. The first thing he asked him was, "Do you want Indochina?" The Chinese leader did not.

For Roosevelt, anticolonialism was a question of principle: One people simply did not have a right to hold sway over another people. He did not contest the evidence, however, that on occasion colonialism had been fruitful. Referring to Martinique, for example, he said:

Martinique is a French colony and they have a very interesting form of government for nearly all Negroes. They get on extremely well with the small number of French white people who are down there. They never have any trouble. They have a low standard of living but that is so throughout the West Indies. They are happy, cheerful people, and surprisingly, they have much better education among the Negroes of Martinique than we have in most of our states in the South. Now, that is an interesting fact and that is a French colony. The same thing applies to Guadaloupe.[22]

Asked at a meeting of the Pacific War Council whether the Moroccans liked the French, Roosevelt replied that "they do; that French Morocco is as a general rule well administered; that the inhabitants are allowed to live as they see fit without undue interference and that the French have made important contributions – good roads and other material improvements. . . . [I believe] that the Moors are glad to learn all they can from the French and to benefit from their administration until they feel strong enough to shift for themselves."[23] The president was, in contrast, highly critical of French administration of New Caledonia. He "personally felt very sympathetic to transferring control of those islands to Australia and New Zealand."[24]

Abolishing colonialism would thus serve the double purpose of leading dependent people to independence and providing the Big Powers, the United States in particular, with strategic bases. The problem was that the other Big Powers considered the strategic bases plan utopian; in addition, the State Department did not support it. During 1941–42 the United States had confirmed on at least seven occasions that "French sovereignty will be reestablished as soon as possible throughout all the territory, metropolitan and colonial, over which flew the French flag in 1939." Originally taken to reassure Vichy, this position was officially reconfirmed by Robert Murphy, the president's personal representative in North Africa, to General Giraud and Admiral Darlan. At a 7 January 1943 meeting of the Joint Chiefs of Staff, "the President said Mr. Murphy had given certain written pledges to Giraud to restore France and the colonial possessions of France after the war. He said that in doing this Mr. Murphy had exceeded his authority and that he as President was not prepared to make any promises." Roosevelt did not officially intervene to repudiate Murphy, and the agreement was left standing.

On Indochina, too, official America did not always speak with one voice.[25] At the same time Roosevelt was informing Eden of his trusteeship plan, in March 1943, Sumner Welles was assuring the British that "Indochina should be returned to France" if the French promised eventual independence. Cordell Hull never objected to full restoration of the French Empire.[26]

Roosevelt was seriously concerned that the colonialist powers did not realize what was awaiting them. He expressed his doubts about Asia's future in a 12 October 1944 conversation with the French admiral Fenard:

Following Japan's defeat, the situation of the white race in the Pacific will be more critical than in the past. The ideas of independence have become more familiar to the populations so far submitted to the authority of European countries. This applies to India, to Dutch possessions, and to Indochina.

I believe if we do not wish to be thrown out by those people, we must find a general formula to resolve the relations between the White and the Yellow races. This could take the form of a general organization in which each country would continue taking care of the territory it now occupies.

But a common general line of action for all colonial countries should be established as of now, providing that within a given time span colonies become independent. Delays could vary considerably according to the degree of evolution of the various territories.[27]

The Labour government in Great Britain was in tune with these views and eventually granted independence to India and other territories; but France was not, and both the French and the world would pay dearly for France's stubbornness.

By the time the Big Three met at Yalta, the colonialism issue had been pushed into the background. Churchill, who kept proclaiming he would not yield a square foot of the British Empire, was reassured by the Americans that the issue of trusteeship[28] concerned only some Japanese-mandated islands. The British also wanted the French to recover Indochina, and Roosevelt preferred not to make them angry by refusing to go along. "Better to keep quiet just now," he told reporters off the record. Following de Gaulle's warning that unless assisted in recovering Indochina France risked falling under Soviet domination, Roosevelt ordered the U.S. Air Force to assist the French. The president's project on strategic bases was practically buried.

The president had by now acquired a new understanding concerning France.

The Soviets were a few miles from Berlin, and it was obvious they intended to exert continued influence over the areas reachable by their military might. The British had made clear their inability to maintain a substantial military presence in Europe. Roosevelt was convinced the American people and Congress would not tolerate U.S. troops' being kept in Europe for more than two years. Only France could fill the void in the West.

France had been liberated by a rapid sweep of the Allied armies through its territory, and de Gaulle was now solidly in power. Roosevelt was still concerned that the controversial general's politics would invite civil strife not only in France but also in France's possessions overseas. On the very day that Germany surrendered, 8 May 1945, the French army massacred between 6,000 and 15,000 Algerians who had dared to revolt in the Constantine region. The subsequent bloody fates of Indochina and Algeria are history. Not unreasonably, Roosevelt believed a resurrection of the French Empire to be an element of instability for Europe and for the world.

The president had for some time been under pressure from the people around him to take a fresh look at France's position. The military had gone its own way, practically ignoring Washington's directives. The military's policies in fact contributed significantly to consolidating de Gaulle's power. Eisenhower proved understanding and supportive of the French general, realizing what a deep scar the defeat of 1940 had left on the French. The two French commanders, generals Juin and de Lattre de Tassigny, got along with their American counterparts except for occasional irritations due to an excess of *amour propre*. The American military had given de Gaulle a free hand in France, and the general had taken full advantage of the situation.

In Washington there was also change. Cordell Hull had waited for the results of the presidential election to tender his resignation. His almost irrational degree of hostility toward de Gaulle had abated. He had met the general in Algiers on 19 October 1943 on his way to the Moscow Conference and had been rather charmed.[29] Hull had joined Stimson in calling for the recognition of the French National Committee and had gone out of his way to be ingratiating when de Gaulle visited with Roosevelt in July 1944. Further, the Pentagon had proved to be realistic and unemotional when dealing with the French situation. Military personnel in the field knew they could count on the support of the secretaries of war and the navy.

To replace Hull Roosevelt chose the former's deputy, Edward E. Stettinius, Jr., a conservative selected primarily for the purpose of selling the United Nations to the Senate. The new secretary had played no part in the at times acrimonious debate over France, and he felt strongly about the country's importance to future European equilibrium. His position is reflected in a briefing paper prepared for the Yalta Conference:

American interests require that every effort be made by this Government to assist France, morally as well as physically, to regain her strength and influence, not only with a view toward increasing the French contribution to the war effort, but also with a view toward enabling the French to assume larger responsibilities in connection with the mainte-nance of peace. It is likewise in the interest of this Government to treat France in all respects on the basis of her potential power and influence rather than on the basis of her present strength. . . . It is recognized that the French Provisional Government and the French people are at present unduly preoccupied, as a result of the military defeat of 1940 and the subsequent occupation of their country by the enemy, with questions of national prestige. They have consequently from time to time put forward requests which are out of all proportion to their present strength. It is believed that it is in the interest of the United States to take full account of this psychological factor in the French mind.[30]

The president came to accept the new language, thanks mostly to Harry Hopkins's untiring efforts on behalf of France. It may be useful for an under-standing of the president's change of heart to examine Hopkins's role in some detail.

After meeting de Gaulle at the Casablanca Conference Hopkins's reaction consisted of three words: "I like him." Roosevelt's State of the Union message of 6 January 1945 included, at Hopkins's "strong instigation,"[31] a passage referring to the "heroic efforts of the resistance groups . . . and of all those Frenchmen throughout the world who refused to surrender after the disaster of 1940." The liberation of France, the message concluded, "means that her great influence will again be available in meeting the problem of peace. We fully recognize France's vital interest in a lasting solution of the German problem and the con-tribution which she can make in achieving international security, resuming her proper position of strength and leadership." Meeting the pope on 30 January, Hopkins expressed his "admiration for the valiant French general."[32] He was convinced that "France must be restored in its proper dignity, not only as its just historical due, but because stability in Europe was inconceivable without a strong and influential France."[33] After leaving government he wrote:

France is another country whose strength and power are selfish assets to the United States. . . . Our foreign policy toward France should not be governed by the personalities of the people who happen for the moment to be in executive power in either of our countries. General de Gaulle has done some tremendous things for France. One thing he did was to make her people hold their heads high again and be proud they were French-men, and to forget the humiliation of defeat in planning for the future. It is equally true that General de Gaulle has not always been the easiest man to get on with in diplomatic affairs. There is no use of now trying to place the blame for personal differences between President Roosevelt and General de Gaulle, but the important thing to the American people is not the temporary head of the Republic of France, but the forty million people who make up that great country.[34]

On 24 October 1946, a few days before his death, having read the result of the elections in France, Hopkins would write de Gaulle:

The election showed to the world the great vitality of French democracy and I think that much of the credit of this orderly outpouring of the French people to express their convictions at the polls is due to your patient and determined handling of your nation's affairs during the past dark and trying years.

France and the French people are emerging now into their own heritage, and, while I have no doubt that the path ahead is going to be trying and difficult, I am completely confident of the outcome as you have always been.[35]

On 16 January 1945 the French formally notified the U.S., British, and Soviet governments that participation in the conference to be held at Yalta was, in their eyes, "necessary in matters relating to problems concerning the general conduct of the war, as well as those, the settlement of which concerns the future of peace – problems in which the responsibility of France is obviously engaged." The missive was never answered, but the president had by then approved in principle a number of strategies that would place France on an equal footing concerning Germany. At the Quebec Conference the preceding September Roosevelt had indicated his readiness to allow France to have a zone of occupation.

Anticipating anger at the Big Three's refusal to accept France as a fourth partner, Hopkins went to Paris in the hope of smoothing ruffled feathers. De Gaulle had blamed Roosevelt for the lack of an invitation, and given his obsession with finding fault with the president, it would have been surprising had it been otherwise. Nearly three years after the event, on 12 November 1947, de Gaulle told the press: "All was really up to President Roosevelt. Churchill was favorable to the presence of France at Yalta. But the Marshal [Stalin] was not. Thus everything depended on the third ally, that is, President Roosevelt, and President Roosevelt decided that the Yalta Conference would be limited to three powers." Actually, de Gaulle had it all wrong. Stalin probably would not have minded de Gaulle's presence, since he thereby hoped to gain an ally to check the Anglo-Saxons; however, Churchill told Eden that "France is not on the same level as the three of us"[36]; he may have consented to de Gaulle's presence at a later date "when decisions, especially affecting France, were under discussion."[37] Churchill's proposal was adopted by Hopkins, who duly informed the French. But with de Gaulle it was all or nothing.

Hopkins left London in a gay mood after spending some time with the prime minister. Churchill, he wired the president, "says that if we had spent ten years in research, we could not have found a worse place in the world than Magneto [Yalta] but that he feels that he can survive it by bringing an adequate supply of whisky. He claims it is good for typhus and deadly on lice which thrive in those parts." Hopkins found the mood in Paris extremely somber. He met first with Foreign Minister Georges Bidault, who gave a most cordial welcome to the "devoted, loyal friend and assistant of President Roosevelt." Franco-American relations were at "a pretty low ebb" for a variety of well-known reasons, Hopkins told him, and it was his ardent desire to contribute to correcting the situation.

He was to speak with de Gaulle later in the day: Had the minister any suggestions? "General de Gaulle," Bidault warned Hopkins, "believes that Frenchmen always try to please the man to whom they are talking. He thinks they overdo it and he adopts a different attitude. He makes no effort to please."

Hopkins was soon to discover how right Bidault had been. In an "icy mood," de Gaulle proceeded to unload on his visitor years of accumulated resentment. According to Hopkins, de Gaulle told him,

The United States of America has done an enormous number of helpful things for us. You have armed and equipped our troops that are at the front; you have helped us in a number of material ways; but you always seem to do it under pressure and grudgingly. Perhaps your policy has been the right one and mine has been wrong. Perhaps you have been justified in anything you have done. Perhaps you are right to do things for us only at the last minute and grudgingly; and you are right if France is herself incapable of rising again, of standing on her own feet eventually, of resuming her place among the great nations; but you are wrong if she does rise again, does stand on her feet again, and does eventually resume her place among the great nations.[38]

After this tirade, there was nothing left for Hopkins but to reiterate his desire to eliminate existing tensions and restore the traditional cordial relationships between the two countries.

In his *Mémoires* De Gaulle has given a more moderate version of the conversation.[39] He mentioned to Bidault that

we have no interest in giving [Hopkins] the impression that we are hurt or annoyed at not taking part in the upcoming conference. First of all, it is much too late to participate under good conditions. We shall also be far freer to deal later with the European imbroglio if we have not participated in the upcoming rigmarole [bafouillage], which might end in rivalries among those present.[40]

Bidault, also, made a point of minimizing the importance of the conference. "I told Hopkins that I wish him luck," he reported to de Gaulle.

The day following his meeting with the general, Hopkins mentioned to the foreign minister Roosevelt's desire to meet with de Gaulle on his way back from Yalta. He added that arrangements could be made for de Gaulle to attend the final stage of the conference, which would deal with European matters. The minister was anxious to know whether de Gaulle would be invited to Yalta, for cabinet members were worried about the general's reaction if he were not. Hopkins's proposal implied that France would not take part in discussions on military strategy. Despite tales to the contrary intended to build up French morale, France's role in the war against Germany had been quite modest.

The French army had originally consisted of six divisions totaling 230,000 troops, of whom 150,000 were colonial, nearly all African; thus fewer than 80,000 were French.[41] At the time, the U.S. Army had over 3 million troops on the Continent.[42] By the end of 1944 the Africans, having suffered heavy casualties and being incapable of enduring the rigors of winter, had to be repatriated in large numbers. "The French have practically no army," Churchill told Eden;[43] "the French divisions have at present, except for one, a low combat value. . . . French divisions are always a questionable asset," Eisenhower cabled Marshall;[44] and in Stalin's view "the French contribution at the present time to military operations on the Western front is very small."[45]

The French army commander, General Jean de Lattre de Tassigny, reluctantly had to admit that his situation was far from ideal. In a letter written on 18 December to de Gaulle, he complained that the nation had ignored and abandoned its soldiers. "The deep cause of this malaise resides in the apparent non-participation of the country in the war." Because of casualties and "various evacuations," the army's numerical strength was reduced by 50 percent. "The few reinforcements received consist of hardly seasoned natives. They do not include any Europeans. The combatants from the Italian and North African campaigns see their comrades fall around them without that ever a French from France comes to fill the void. They do not understand why the country, at last liberated, should be unable to call to the colors the troops needed to replace those who disappear." De Lattre was concerned that the situation might prove "particularly filled with consequences for the North African who has more and more the impression of being *alone* to sacrifice himself for France" (emphasis in original).[46] Stalin wondered at Yalta why the contribution of so few divisions should entitle France to share military decisions when in the final assault on Germany the Yugoslavs had had twelve divisions and the Poles fourteen.[47]

"It would have been impossible to let de Gaulle take part in the military aspects of the Yalta Conference," Charles Bohlen wrote. "Britain and the United States had some 86 divisions in Europe; the most France could have mustered at any time was about three divisions, with two in reserve. It was obviously impossible to let a country with virtually no military weight having an equal voice with countries carrying most of the burden of the fighting."[48] On 1 January 1945 de Gaulle had written to Roosevelt of France's "ardent desire" to increase "powerfully and rapidly" her military forces, but the new units would not be ready for combat before Germany's final defeat. Meanwhile, the United States had to consider other, more urgent priorities.

At the Yalta Conference the president had to surmount not only his own prejudices but also the hostility bordering on contempt that Stalin felt for the French. The Soviet dictator surprised Roosevelt by saying it was Pétain rather than de Gaulle who represented the "real France." "There was no doubt in Roosevelt's mind on this and subsequent occasions," Sherwood wrote, "that Stalin considered the collaborationists more important than the fighters of the resistance movement in expressing French sentiments."[49] On another occasion, "Stalin again expressed himself on the subject of France whose ruling class, he felt, was rotten to the core. . . . He did not consider that France could be trusted with any strategic positions outside her own borders in the postwar period. He still seemed to attach little importance to de Gaulle as a political factor in politi-

cal or other matters."[50] When the United States suggested that France be represented in the Reparations Commission, Stalin told Hopkins that

this he felt was an insult to the Soviet Union in view of the fact that France had concluded a separate peace with Germany and had opened her frontier to the Germans. It
was true that this had been done by Pétain's Government but nevertheless it was an
action of France. To attempt to place France on the same footing as the Soviet Union
looked like an attempt to humiliate the Russians.

Stalin objected to France's being granted a zone in Germany: "The control commission for Germany should be run by those who have stood firmly against
Germany and have made the greatest sacrifices in bringing victory."[51]

Roosevelt tended to agree with Stalin, but he finally yielded to the entreaties of
both his own advisers and the British. Even though Churchill made it clear that
"he had been against the participation of France in the present conference," believing that "it would be inconvenient to add France to the present group of
major allies," he and Eden "fought like tigers for France," with Hopkins working
constantly from his sick bed to support them.[52] Finally, the issue was whether
France should have, besides a zone of its own, a place in the Control Commission. Although he shared Stalin's negative attitude toward the French, Roosevelt
informed him through U.S. ambassador Averell Harriman of his decision to side
with the British, as Hopkins had strongly urged him to do.[53] He felt "it would be
easier to deal with the French if they were on the Commission than if they were
not."[54] Finally, it was agreed that France should be a permanent member of the
projected United Nations Security Council, with veto power.

France emerged from the Yalta Conference as one of the Big Powers, a status it
would not have achieved without the concurrence and consent of the United
States. Nonetheless, de Gaulle was not happy. United States ambassador Caffery
found him in a "sulky mood." "He apparently expected a bigger role for himself
to come out of the communiqué," the ambassador wired Hopkins.[55] Bidault,
who was himself quite pleased, told Caffery that at the latest meeting of the
Council of Ministers he had encountered ferocious resentment and hurt feelings – so much that two of the ministers left the room while he was speaking. "I
shall have to make some more explanations but in the end everything will work
out all right," he said. "A part of our people are still suffering from a 1940 complex and are sensitive in the extreme."[56]

Failure to invite France to Yalta was not part of a diabolical American conspiracy (as the French seemed to think), according to Harriman. There were other
reasons, as he told his French colleague, General Catroux:

The meeting of the Yalta Conference, from which the future of the war and of France
depended, was in the final analysis tied to the realization of an agreement among three
men, three conceptions, three temperaments, who had understood one another rather
badly during their meeting at Teheran. Later, the ice was broken, Stalin had abandoned

his prejudices against Churchill and Roosevelt. The prospect for an understanding among the three was favorable. The introduction of a fourth partner who had not lived through the previous vicissitudes could have threatened that understanding. That is what we hoped to avoid, without nourishing any disobliging intentions toward General de Gaulle. In the end, the agreement between Stalin, Churchill and Roosevelt was fully successful and France has derived great advantages from the Yalta conference.

Catroux drew the conclusion that "the United States and Great Britain meant to face Stalin two against one and feared that our presence and our participation would undermine this intention thus strengthening the already advantageous position of the Soviet partner. There may lie the reason for our eviction."[57] Harriman's explanation was diplomatic, but it did not tell the whole story.

Bidault had informed the president via Caffery that de Gaulle would be delighted to meet him any place and at any time he designated. Roosevelt, who had told Churchill how "envious" he was of his "visit to the great battlefronts,"[58] had often expressed a wish to visit with his soldiers in France. But Churchill had made it clear that Great Britain should come first: "We would feel it very much and a very dismal impression would be made if you were to visit France before you came to England: In fact it would be regarded as a slight on your closest ally."[59] He assured the president that he was "going to get from the British people the greatest reception ever accorded to any human being since Lord Nelson made his triumphant return to London." The British people, he told Samuel Roseman, "all love him for what he has done to save them from destruction by the Huns; they love him also for what he has done for the cause of peace in the world, for what he has done to relieve their fear that the horrors they have been through for five years might come upon them again in increased fury."[60]

Shortly before the Yalta Conference adjourned, a rumor reached Paris that Roosevelt proposed to visit France on his way home. These reports put Paris in a quandary. No measures had been taken to prepare an official reception, nor had the police prepared security measures. Authorities were also puzzled by a newspaper report that the Allied military headquarters, Shaef, had made arrangements to receive the president. Had Roosevelt gone to France for the sole purpose of visiting his soldiers, de Gaulle would have felt insulted. The situation soon became clear. The president had instructed Caffery to inform de Gaulle that he had been "eagerly looking forward to meeting with him on French soil," and that it had proved impossible for him to go to Paris "in accordance with his much appreciated invitation," but he hoped that the alternative of Algiers would be satisfactory. A second message suggested the date of 18 February: "I hope very much that the General will have lunch with me on that date on board the ship on which I am staying and have a good talk with me that afternoon." By proposing a meeting on a U.S. ship, Roosevelt was making sure he met de Gaulle on what was technically American soil. Caffery did as instructed and was received "frigidly" by the general, who enumerated reasons – "none of them important enough," commented the ambassador – for turning the invitation down.[61] "I have done everything to make him go," Bidault complained afterward, "but you don't know how stubborn he is. He has changed his mind and won't go."[62]

The president was understandably angry with the man who had previously offered to go anywhere at any time to meet him, but Hopkins pleaded with him "not to lower [himself] to such a petulant level" by engaging in a polemic. This perceived insult to the president after he had made it possible for France to resume its place among the world's major powers was highly resented throughout the United States. "The dreary story of de Gaulle's gaucherie came to its melancholy climax today," Lord Moran entered in his diary on 15 February.[63] Upon returning home Roosevelt stressed that nothing the "prima donna" did could surprise him any more. "He does not seem upset over de Gaulle," Eleanor Roosevelt wrote. On 1 May Roosevelt received a group of French journalists, including Jean-Paul Sartre, who assured him of a tremendous reception if he visited France. He downplayed the incident with de Gaulle, saying that when the general was in Washington the previous summer, they had gotten along beautifully and had a good time. Roosevelt assured the journalists that he hoped to be able to visit Paris one day, adding that he wanted to see the rest of France as well.

The president had no illusions that Yalta had solved all the world's problems. "Adolf," he told Undersecretary of State Berle, "I don't say that [the] result was good. I said it was the best I could do." His all-consuming concern was now organizing the peace. Like Wilson before him, he felt he had no right, before the country and history, to send American soldiers to their deaths in Europe, the Pacific, and Asia if it was not to build a better, more secure world. He planned to concentrate on the United Nations project and looked forward to welcoming the delegates and delivering the opening speech at San Francisco, where the organization's charter was to be signed. Working on a message to be delivered 13 April, Jefferson Day, he wrote what were perhaps his last written words: "The only limit to our realization of tomorrow will be our doubts of today. Let us move forward with strong and active faith."

After San Francisco he told Frances Perkins, "We are going to England. Eleanor and I are going to make a state visit. . . . We owe it as a return visit, and this seems the best time to go."[64] The president had been thinking of a European tour for quite some time. On 27 September 1944 a "most secret" message from Churchill informed Stalin that "the President intends to visit England, and thereafter France and the Low Countries, immediately after the election, win or lose."[65]

Roosevelt did not live to realize his final wish. "The fears and hopes of hundreds of millions of human beings throughout the world had been bearing down on the mind of one man, until the pressure was more than mortal tissue could withstand, and then he said, 'I have a terrific headache,' and then lost consciousness, and died."[66]

"He was the only person I ever knew – anywhere – who was never afraid. God how he could take it for us all," exclaimed a young congressman. And his soldiers wrote in their magazine, *Yank*: "He was the Commander in Chief, not only of our armed forces, but our generation."

Conclusion

As the end of Nazi Germany neared, the victorious powers recognized that Europe could not be rebuilt from the ruins of the war unless France resumed its place as a great power. France was treated as if it had already attained that status, even though it would be some time before the assumption matched the reality. This policy was consecrated at Yalta, France being the country that profited most from the conference.

For the United States to accept France as the "Big Fifth" meant shelving policies Roosevelt had pursued since the tragic summer of 1940, when France's collapse had signified for many the advent of a new Dark Age. Roosevelt had formed a particular idea of France, nurtured by his youthful trips through Europe and his experience during World War I, that events had destroyed, leaving in their wake bitterness and a feeling of love betrayed.

The Roosevelt presidency spanned one of the most dramatic and tormented periods in French history. France had proved to be a mass of contradictions that American leaders had great difficulty in sorting out. It can even be said that France caused more problems for Roosevelt than perhaps any other country, problems not of magnitude but of quality. It was obvious that Hitler's Germany had to be destroyed; it was obvious that Japan could not be allowed to extend its empire through the Orient and the Pacific; it was obvious that the British would never surrender and that Stalin would impose Soviet rule on Eastern Europe. But nothing was ever obvious with France. There was not one person speaking for France, but several offering opposite advice and solutions; not one clearly defined interest at stake, but several. Roosevelt had to deal with only one Germany, one Great Britain, one Japan, one Soviet Union; but with more than one France, each claiming to be the "true France," each insisting the other "Frances" were composed of traitors. Americans were ill prepared to cope with so complex and contradictory a situation.

Roosevelt had hoped assistance to Great Britain and the Soviet Union would prove sufficient to defeat Hitler, freeing the United States from the need to intervene. When Pearl Harbor put an end to that hope, Roosevelt had willed that the now inevitable defeat of the Axis be followed by his country's making a major contribution to shaping the postwar world. In his approach to France, the president was influenced to a large extent by considerations that transcended the country and its people. He judged France and formed his policies toward it according to whether that country assisted or hindered his postwar plans. Thus France became for Roosevelt far more an object than a subject of history.

Roosevelt felt France had sunk so low it would be a very long time before it could resume its previous status. De Gaulle's claim that *his* France was ever the France of Jeanne d'Arc and Georges Clemenceau, endowed as in the past with *gloire* and *grandeur*, sounded shrill and somewhat ridiculous to Roosevelt. Roosevelt was not prepared to see, as others around him did, that there was a certain nobility in the general's defiance, that he felt he spoke not for the France of the present but that of the past and the future—*la France éternelle*—as if the present were no more than a historical accident.[1] De Gaulle resented France's dependence upon the Anglo-Saxons. "England's grievous offence in de Gaulle's eyes is that she has helped France," Churchill commented. "He cannot bear to think that she needed help." How much more "grievous" was America's "offence," on which de Gaulle was bound to rely for his country's liberation and survival! The president was seldom in the mood to make allowances for Gallic pride. "And, as Winston said," Lord Moran wrote, "de Gaulle is the quintessence of an inferiority complex."[2]

Roosevelt was the prisoner of an ideological vision that convinced him he was a Jacobin, acting on principle, and in so doing serving France's real interests by refusing to influence France's freedom of choice. He tried to impose Anglo-Saxon values based on strict observance of the legal, constitutional process, intended to ensure continuity within the universally accepted framework, to a country most of whose historical experience had been revolution and change. Roosevelt would not heed the warning that France was not an Anglo-Saxon country with a stable frame of political reference, like the United States or Great Britain, but one that should have been left to handle its coming revolution the way it had the revolutions of the past. Legitimacy was the stumbling block, Roosevelt rejecting the notion, so alien to the American tradition, that legitimacy could seek its justification in history rather than in legality. Roosevelt seemed to ignore the fact that none of the more than one dozen structural changes France had undergone between the French Revolution and World War II had resulted from free elections. The republics, monarchies, and empires that had succeeded one another over the 150-year period had issued from revolutions, wars, and coups d'état.

Roosevelt hated the notion of violence as a necessary part of history. Born in a loving, sheltered, patrician atmosphere surrounded by wealth and comfort, at a time when life was regulated according to the strictures of the Victorian age, he trembled at the thought of disorders, class conflicts, and revolutions. His European ideal was the well-ordered society he had encountered in his youth. His France was the one he had so much admired during World War I, emerging from the conflict solid and strong. The European governments that had taken refuge in Great Britain after their countries had been overrun by the Nazis also represented to him the well-ordered societies he remembered from his youthful travels. Those governments were all legitimate, unsoiled by compromise with the Nazis. In France, however, the Gaullists would not be able to establish their own legitimacy, their right to govern, until they had wiped out Pétain's pretensions to legitimacy. The surviving legitimacy was destined to emerge from a civil war that Roosevelt feared would threaten European stability. If forced to choose, Roosevelt preferred order to democracy, as North Africa demonstrated. Throughout World War II Roosevelt's French policies were a reflection of his concern that contested legitimacy might lead to anarchy. His attitudes toward both Pétain and de Gaulle cannot be understood unless this premise is kept in mind.

The liberation of France only partly reassured the president that disorder could be contained within tolerable limits because he did not feel confident in the solidity of French institutions. Soviet ambitions, Britain's exhaustion, and China's civil war conspired to confirm the need for a strong France; much as he continued to mistrust de Gaulle, Roosevelt had concurred in, and sometimes initiated, decisions favorable to France, especially as concerned its role in control over partitioned Germany.

The president had realized more quickly than other world leaders the importance of the rise of the United States and the Soviet Union as superpowers. Only they had emerged from the war with enough muscle to impose their will; the future of the world would be marked by the state of their relationship. Under the circumstances, adding France to the list of major powers would not make that much difference; in the end France would count as much or as little as Great Britain or China, and consequently it would be in no position to appreciably affect international relations. Roosevelt accepted the new balance of power as a temporary arrangement, for he looked forward to that "permanent structure of peace" that would spell "the end of the system of unilateral action, exclusive alliances, and spheres of influence, and balances of power and all the other expedients which have been tried for centuries and have always failed."[3] This almost biblical vision of swords being beaten into plowshares was the future to which Roosevelt had looked forward to dedicating all his energies.

France had become by common consent a great power – in theory. This newly acquired status was also theoretical, for France could not nearly match the countries that had become known as superpowers, a description that stressed the inequality among the Great Powers. To believe that there existed no disparity between France's theoretical status as a great power and the country's actual condition at the end of the war required a great deal of pretending.

Wartime France had its heroic moments, but it had unsavory moments, too.

Roosevelt was aware of the exploits of the Resistance,[4] but also of the thousands of Jews turned over by the French police to the Nazis and the extermination camps; of the Milice, no less brutal than the Nazi SS; of the Charlemagne Division fighting alongside the Germans against the Russians. It was only natural for de Gaulle to try to shield with his towering figure such unsavory events so they would be wiped from the people's collective memory. Roosevelt could pretend, like everyone else in his administration, that the slate was now clean, but he could not forget that France, alone among the countries at war with Germany, had had a foot in both camps: Had Hitler won, Laval would have become president and the traitor de Gaulle shot; but the Anglo-Saxons won and the opposite came to pass.[5]

The other occupied countries had had problems of various sorts, but none kept talking about abstractions such as *gloire* and *grandeur* when in fact the overwhelming majority of the people were primarily concerned, quite naturally, with survival. As Georges Pompidou, who succeeded de Gaulle as president, wrote: "The true heroes, those who voluntarily and deliberately took all the risks without hesitating, are quite few, just as rare as the conscious and resolute traitors."[6]

De Gaulle's supreme achievement was to transform the assumptions and the legends into realities – and to build a mystique around them. In this role he has been an unsurpassed master, for he enabled the French to forget the defeat of 1940 and to start anew. In so doing he unquestionably rendered an immense service to his country; at the same time, however, by assuming that France had already bridged the gap between the theory and the actuality in terms of power, he ran afoul of the United States because he insisted on the existence of a nonexistent condition of parity. He did not accept until much later the idea that a superpower is not merely a power bigger than the others, but one endowed with the responsibility of maintaining a certain degree of world order. De Gaulle held the "spirit of Yalta" responsible for the division of the world into spheres of influence. That definition served his purposes but was unrealistic; postwar history has shown that world equilibrium was maintained when the superpowers had an understanding and was threatened when they did not. Yalta strengthened Roosevelt's conviction that an understanding with the Soviets was a precondition for world order and that a major task for the United States was to learn how to deal with the Soviet Union. There was no previous example for the superpowers to follow; the ability to coexist had to be gained through trial and error without the lessons of history to help. A man close to the president, Rexford Tugwell understood that Roosevelt's "geopolitical sense made him very certain that if the U.S.S.R. and the U.S.A. had a firm understanding nothing else mattered very much."[7] In Roosevelt's time "there was as yet no absolute weapon from which to argue that there was no alternative to peace."[8] De Gaulle's insistence that France was the equal of the United States proved to be a source of disagreement not only with Roosevelt but also with the presidents who followed him.

Churchill once stated that "the Almighty in His infinite wisdom did not see fit to create Frenchmen in the image of Englishmen." Apparently, he also did not see fit to create the French in the image of Americans, nor Americans in the image of the French. Differing traditions, ways of life, senses of history, cultural heritages—all conspired in Roosevelt's time to negate any notion of similarity. And this, more than anything else, was the source of the misunderstandings the repercussions of which are felt to this day.

History will judge Roosevelt not so much for his foreign policy as for his decisions to mobilize the country's resources, aid the Allies even when the end seemed near, and engage American soldiers on every front and on every continent. Let us recall that in the tragic summer of 1940, when Europe appeared lost for generations to come, Churchill stated at a secret session of Parliament that the fate of England might depend on the result of the American election. Let us recall, too, Stalin's statement at the Teheran Conference that without America's substantial assistance, the Soviet Union could not have resisted the Nazi invasion.[9]

Roosevelt's true triumph was that had he not been there, Hitler would have won the war.

Notes

The following abbreviations are used in the Notes to refer to various collections and archives.

FDRL   Franklin D. Roosevelt Library, Hyde Park, N.Y.

FDRL: PPF   President's Personal File

FDRL: PSF   President's Secretary's File

FDRL: OF   Official File

FMFA   French Ministry of Foreign Affairs, Paris. Most documents from the French Ministry of Foreign Affairs dealing with the United States for the period up to 1940 are in "Série B-Amerique, 1918–1940." Unless otherwise indicated, the number following the date accompanied by the acronym FMFA refers to the volume in this series. In French documents "T" stands for "Telegramme."

CRC   Churchill-Roosevelt Correspondence

LC   Library of Congress, Washington, D.C.

NA   National Archives, Washington, D.C.

USNA   United States Navy Archives, Washington, D.C.

FRUS   Foreign Relations of the United States (an indispensable collection of diplomatic documents)

The following books, cited in the Notes, are referred to by the author's name followed by volume and page numbers.

Winston S. Churchill, *The Second World War* (London, 1947–51), six volumes

Anthony Eden, *Memoirs* (London, 1960–65)

Cordell Hull, *The War Memoirs of Cordell Hull* (New York, 1948)

Charles de Gaulle, *The War Memoirs of Charles de Gaulle* (New York, 1955–60). De Gaulle's original French edition, *Mémoires de Guerre* (Paris, 1954–59) is referred to as de Gaulle *Mémoires*, also followed by volume and page number.

INTRODUCTION

1. Rexford G. Tugwell, *The Democratic Roosevelt* (New York, 1957), 346–47; Sumner Welles, *The Time for Decision* (New York, 1944), 50.

2. "When Roosevelt took office, the country, to a very large degree, responded to the will of a single element: The white, Anglo-Saxon, Protestant property-holding class. Under the New Deal, new groups took their place in the sun. It was not merely that they received benefits they had not had before but that they were 'recognized' as having a place in the commonwealth" (William E. Leuchtenburg, *Franklin D. Roosevelt and the New Deal* [New York, 1963], 332). "The depression produced, among other things, a profound shaking-up of American society: It led to a general discrediting of the older ruling classes, locally as well as nationally, and a sudden opening of opportunity for men and ethnic groups on the way up in the competition for position and power" (Arthur M. Schlesinger, Jr., *The Age of Roosevelt: The Politics of Upheaval* [Boston, 1960], 696).

3. Quoted in William R. Emerson, "F.D.R. (1941–1945)," in Ernest R. May, ed., *The Ultimate Decision: The President as Commander in Chief* (New York, 1960), 169.

4. Walter Lippmann, *Foreign Affairs* (June 1937).

5. Pascal Ory, "De Boudelaire à Duhamel: L'improbable rejet," in *L'Amérique dans les têtes* (Paris, 1986), 66.

6. Raoul Roussy de Sales, *L'Amérique entre en guerre* (Paris, 1948), 295.

7. Geoffrey C. Ward, *Before the Trumpet* (New York, 1985), 37–38.

8. Letter reproduced in Raoul Aglion, *De Gaulle et Roosevelt* (Paris, 1984), 259.

9. Arthur M. Schlesinger, Jr., *The Age of Roosevelt: The Crisis of the Older Order, 1919–1933* (New York, 1957), 410.

10. Elliott Roosevelt, ed., *F.D.R.: His Personal Letters* (New York, 1948), II, 25.

11. Tugwell, *The Democratic Roosevelt*, 318.

12. Joseph Alsop, *A Centenary Remembrance: FDR* (New York, 1982), 28.

13. Elliott Roosevelt, ed., *F.D.R.: His Personal Letters*, II, 942.

14. Christopher Dawson, *Understanding Europe* (New York, 1952), 149.

CHAPTER 1

1. Orville H. Bullitt, ed., *For the President: Personal and Secret: Correspondence between Franklin D. Roosevelt and William C. Bullitt* (Boston, 1972), 227. 7 September 1937.

2. G. Henry-Haye, *La Grande éclipse Franco-Américaine* (Paris, 1972), 73.

3. Geoffrey C. Ward, *Before the Trumpet* (New York, 1985), 152–53.

4. Joseph P. Lash, *Eleanor and Franklin* (New York, 1971), 79.

5. Frank Freidel, *Franklin D. Roosevelt: The Apprenticeship* (Boston, 1952), 306.

6. David F. Trask, *Captains and Cabinets: Anglo-American Naval Relations, 1917–1918* (Columbia, Missouri, 1972), 64.

7. Ibid., 65.

8. Archives Centrales de la Marine SS ea 99.

9. Elliott Roosevelt, ed., *F.D.R.: His Personal Letters* (New York, 1948), II, 403.

10. Ibid., 406.

11. Ibid., 407.

12. Ibid., 409–10.

13. Ibid., 411.

14. Ibid., 413.

15. Ibid., 417.

16. Ibid., 428–29.

17. Ibid., 439.

18. FDRL: Assistant Secretary of the Navy, 1918–1920, Container 191.

19. Archives Centrales de la Marine SS ea 99.

20. Lash, *Eleanor and Franklin*, 234.

21. Freidel, *Franklin D. Roosevelt: The Apprenticeship*, 360.

CHAPTER 2

1. Geoffrey C. Ward, *Before the Trumpet* (New York, 1985), 147.

2. Elliott Roosevelt, ed., *F.D.R.: His Personal Letters* (New York, 1948), II, 240.

3. Kenneth S. Davis, "FDR as a Biographer's Problem," *The American Scholar* (Winter 1983–84), 107.

4. Frances Perkins, *The Roosevelt I Knew* (New York, 1946), 148.

5. 26 January 1934. Several dispatches from the French embassy in Washington were published by the Nazis in "Comment Roosevelt est entré en guerre," 1944. They are undoubtedly authentic. Some of them were found by the author in the Archives of the French Ministry of Foreign Affairs.

6. Quoted in Rexford G. Tugwell, *The Democratic Roosevelt* (New York, 1957), 561.

7. John Morton Blum, ed., *From the Morgenthau Diaries: Years of War, 1941–1945* (Boston, 1967), 342.

8. Adolf Hitler, *My Battle*. Abridged and translated by E.T.S. Dugdale (Cambridge, 1933). At the top of the title page Roosevelt wrote "Franklin D. Roosevelt, The White House, 1933."

9. A "Dear Herr Hesse" letter from the Pacific Palisades in *The Hesse/Mann Letters: The Correspondence of Hermann Hesse and Thomas Mann, 1910–1955* (London, 1975).

10. FMFA: 23 February 1933. Claudel to Paul Boncour, 303.

11. FDRL: PSF London Economic Conference.

12. John Morton Blum, *From the Morgenthau Diaries: Years of Crisis, 1928–1938* (Boston, 1959), 460.

13. Sumner Welles, *The Time for Decision* (New York, 1944), 53–54.

14. FMFA: T322 to T324, 31 March 1933.

15. Ambassador de Laboulaye to Foreign Minister Delbos, 1 March 1937, reporting on his farewell meeting with the president on 11 February.

16. FMFA: T404 to T408. Laboulaye to Paul Boncour.

17. FMFA: T33 to T37, 26 April 1933.

18. FMFA: T508 to T511, 16 May 1933. De Laboulaye to Paul Boncour.

19. Blum, *From the Morgenthau Diaries*, 9 May 1933.

20. FMFA: T519–520, 16 May 1933. De Laboulaye to Paul Boncour.

21. FMFA: Premier Edouard Daladier to Norman Davis, 8 June 1933.

22. FMFA: De Laboulaye to Barthou, 22 February 1934.

23. FMFA: T747 to T749, Henry to Barthou, 11 September 1934.

24. Hull, I, 524.

25. Harold L. Ickes, *The Secret Diary of Harold L. Ickes: The Lowering Clouds, 1939–1941* (New York, 1955), 218–19.

26. "Our historical experience of a hundred and fifty years seems to me to prove that we are drawn into a European war when Great Britain is a belligerent and that we stay out when Britain is neutral. We were drawn into the Napoleonic wars. We were drawn into the World War. We stayed out of the Austro-German war, the Franco-Prussian War, and the Balkan wars. The reason for this is evident. Our connection with Europe is the North Atlantic Ocean and Great Britain is the dominant maritime power in Europe. If Britain is at war, she closes the seas, and in the past, we as neutrals, have either to fight her, as we did in 1812, or fight her enemy, as we did in 1917. When Britain is neutral, it is easy for us to be neutral. For Britain and the United States together then have the same interests, and no European power is strong enough to defy our combined power" (Walter Lippmann, "America and the Possible War," *New York Herald Tribune*, 26 December 1933).

27. FMFA: T1140 to T1145, Roosevelt to Pierre Laval, 20 December 1935.

28. FMFA: T29 to T33, 6 January 1936.

29. FDRL: PSF Straus, 13 February 1936.

30. FDRL: PSF 42 Straus.

31. Ibid.

32. Robert Murphy, *Diplomat among Warriors* (New York, 1964), 68.

33. Welles, *The Time for Decision*, 61.

34. Ickes, *Secret Diary*, III, 217.

35. MPB 3 October 1939. Quoted in Joseph P. Lash, *Roosevelt and Churchill: 1939–1941* (New York, 1976), 75.

36. FDRL: PSF 41/France 33–39.

37. FDRL: Hopkins Papers, Box 337; FRUS: *Yalta*, 923. Between 4 September 1896 and formation of the Pétain government at Bordeaux, France had 101 governments!

38. FDRL: PSF 43 Bullitt 36, 24 October 1936.

39. Ibid., 8 November 1936.

40. NA: OSS File entry 106, Folder 107, Box 35; full text in Suzanne Blum, *Vivre sans la patrie* (Paris, 1975), 119–121.

41. FDRL: PFF 5155.

42. FMFA: 317 Neutralité, 3 March 1937.

43. FDRL: PSF 42 France 44–45.

44. FDRL: PSF 42 France 44–45, 28 November 1944.

45. FMFA: 306, 14 April 1937.

46. FMFA: 307, 11 October 1937.

47. FMFA: Ibid.

48. FMFA: 307, 2 December 1937.

CHAPTER 3

1. FMFA: 308, 22 March 1938.

2. Pierre Billotte, *Le Temps des armes* (Paris, 1972), 232.

3. FMFA: 308, 11 June 1938.

4. "The United States enforces its union, does not permit secession, and extends majority rule even over those areas where consent would not voluntarily be given. The principle of self-determination, if applied in the United States, would long ago have bro-

ken up the nation. On one occasion it almost did" (Rexford G. Tugwell, *The Democratic Roosevelt* [New York, 1957], 565).

5. FMFA: 309, 14 September 1938.

6. FMFA: 309, 18 September 1938.

7. FMFA: 309, 29 September 1938.

8. Earl of Halifax, *Fullness of Days* (London, 1957), 242.

9. FMFA: Dossier Georges Bonnet, 27 November 1938.

10. FDRL: PSF 43.

11. Ibid., 20 May 1938.

12. The acquisition of planes and other material required credit for which France did not qualify. The Johnson Act barred countries in arrear in their debt payments from floating obligations or negotiating loans. To bypass this obstacle, France proposed turning over to the United States 10 to 15 percent of the gold reserves of the Bank of France, an amount equivalent to $300 million. On 19 May Morgenthau read to Jean Monnet the following message from the president: "The formula which you and I discussed is an interesting basis for further discussions – to be kept in our safe ready at a time that looks more propitious." The president added that he did not "want to take money out of France at this time." For a full account of U.S. assistance to France, see John McVickar Haight, Jr., *American Aid to France, 1938–1940* (New York, 1970).

13. Joseph Alsop and Robert Kinter, *American White Papers: The Story of American Diplomacy in the Second World War* (New York, 1940), 30–31.

14. FMFA: 310, 6 February 1939.

15. FMFA: Etats-Unis 362, 2 February 1939.

16. John McVickar Haight, Jr., "Roosevelt as Friend of France," *Foreign Affairs* 44 (April 1966): 520.

17. FMFA: 311, 16 April 1939.

18. Harold L. Ickes, *The Secret Diary of Harold L. Ickes: The Lowering Clouds, 1939–1941* (New York, 1955), III, 37.

19. Hull, 736.

20. FMFA: 319ter, 9–10 February 1940.

21. Ickes, *Secret Diary*, III, 146.

22. Lord Lothian to Lord Halifax, 3 September 1940.

23. FMFA: 319ter, 9 February 1940.

24. Ibid., 17 February 1940.

25. Ibid., 5 March 1940.

26. Adolf A. Berle, *Navigating the Rapids, 1918–1971* (New York, 1973), 292.

27. Sumner Welles, *The Time for Decision* (New York, 1944), 86.

28. British Foreign Office, 117 FO 371/24406, 1807, 18 March 1940, as quote in Orville H. Bullitt, *For the President: Personal and Secret: Correspondence between Franklin D. Roosevelt and William C. Bullitt* (Boston, 1972), 404.

29. Welles, *The Time for Decision*, 134.

30. Ibid., 76.

31. FDRL: PSF France, Box 43. "Morgenthau told me . . . that when Welles came back from the trip to Europe . . . he told me personally that Mussolini was the greatest man that he had ever met" (Ickes, *Secret Diary*, III, 464–65).

32. Hull, 741.

33. FDRL: PSF 43 Bullitt, 23 March 1939.

34. Ickes, *Secret Diary*, III, 123–24.

35. USNA: Chief of Naval Operations, Box 232.

36. USNA: Sec Nav/CDN Confidential Correspondence, 1940–41, Box 32.

37. Raoul Roussy de Sales, *L'Amérique entre en guerre* (Paris, 1948), 70.

38. Ickes, *Secret Diary*, III, 199.

39. De Gaulle, III, 9293.

40. Albert Kammerer, *La Verité sur l'armistice* (Paris, 1944), 157.

41. Charles de Gaulle, *Lettres, notes et carnets: Juin 1940–juillet 1941* (Paris, 1981), 443.

42. Frederick Pottecher, *Le Procès Pétain* (Paris, 1980), 75.

43. William L. Neumann, "Franklin Delano Roosevelt: A Disciple of Admiral Mahan," *U.S. Naval Institute Proceedings* (July 1952), 719.

44. Tugwell, *The Democratic Roosevelt*, 37.

45. CRC: R-7x, 14 June 1940.

46. FMFA: 319 bis.

47. FMFA: Papiers 1940; Reconstruction Fouques-Duparc No. 26, 16 June 1940; Sir Llewellyn Woodward, *British Foreign Policy in the Second World War* (London, 1976), I, 270.

48. Decades later the French would overwhelmingly approve of the request for an armistice. A June 1980 *Le Figaro* opinion poll found that over 60 percent of the public believed that Pétain had been right to ask for an armistice. That was forty years after the event!

49. Sir Edward Spears, *Two Men Who Saved France: Pétain and De Gaulle* (London, 1966), 161.

50. CRC: C-38x, 10 November 1940.

51. CRC: C-78x, 6 April 1941.

52. Charles de Gaulle, *Lettres, notes et carnets: Juillet 1941–mai 1943* (Paris, 1982), 167.

53. Malcolm Muggeridge, ed., *Ciano's Diplomatic Papers* (London, 1948), 57.

54. Ibid., 400.

55. Quoted in Raymond Aron, *De l'armistice à l'insurrection nationale* (Paris, 1945), 21.

56. Philippe Masson, *Histoire de la Marine* (Paris, 1983), II, 403–404; *La Marine française et la guerre, 1939–1945* (Paris, 1991), passim.

57. Général Pierre Gallois, "L'aviation ne pouvait pas suivre," *Le Figaro*, 7 August 1990. "Algeria could not manufacture a plane, a bomb, a gun, not even a knife or a nail" (Jacques Soustelle, *Envers et contre tout: D'Alger à Paris* [Paris, 1950], 356).

CHAPTER 4

1. De Gaulle, II, 141.

2. Ibid., III, 203.

3. De Gaulle, *Mémoires*, I, 82, and 22 June 1940 speech.

4. De Gaulle, II, 361.

5. It would have been difficult to contest Pétain's claim to legitimacy at the time he took power in France. He had received 569 votes to 80 nays and 17 abstentions from the National Assembly elected at the time of the Popular Front. In the Senate he won 225 votes to 1, the lone dissenter being Pierre, marquis de Lafayette, great-great grandson of Lafayette. At the Pétain trial, former premier Reynaud chose to forget that it was at his suggestion that the president of the Republic had named the marshal head of government. On 9 July 1940 the president of the Chamber of Deputies, Edouard Herriot, declared: "Around Marshal Pétain, in the veneration that his name inspires to all, our nation has

closed ranks in its misfortune. Let us beware not to trouble the unity established under his authority." The president of the Senate was equally warm: "To Marshal Pétain I declare our veneration and the full gratitude which is his due for a renewed sacrifice of his person. He knows my sentiments toward him which date from way back. We know the nobility of his soul. It has earned us days of glory."

6. The position of the United States was made clear in February 1942 in a statement concerning French islands in the Pacific: "The policy of the Government of the United States as regard France and French territory has been based upon the maintenance of the integrity of France and of the French Empire and of the eventual restoration of complete independence of all French territories. Mindful of the traditional friendship for France, this Government deeply sympathizes not only with the desire of the French people to maintain their territory intact, but with the efforts of the French people to continue to resist the forces of aggression. In its relations with local French authorities the United States has been and will continue to be governed by the manifest effectiveness with which those authorities endeavor to protect their territories from domination and control by the common enemy." This position was restated on 4 April, following the U.S. decision to set up a consulate general at Brazzaville: The American government "has treated with the French authorities in effective control of French territories in Africa, and will continue to treat with them on the basis of their actual administration of the territories involved."

7. USNA: Record of a conversation between Admiral Stark and General De Gaulle, 17 December 1942.

8. Roosevelt Press conference No. 907, 9 July 1943. The president said to a reporter: "You used the word 'French'; but I suppose 95 percent of France is still under the heel of Germans in France. . . . There isn't any France at the present time, except the five percent outside of France."

9. Arthur M. Schlesinger, Jr., *The Birth of the Nation* (New York, 1968), 250.

10. Louis Hartz, *The Liberal Tradition in America* (New York, 1955), 306.

11. Joseph Alsop, *A Centenary Remembrance: FDR* (New York, 1982), 74.

12. Ibid., 75. "Roosevelt's genius lay in the fact that he recognized – rather rejoiced in – the challenge of the pragmatic nerve." See also Arthur M. Schlesinger, Jr., *The Age of Roosevelt:The Crisis of the Older Order, 1919–1933* (New York, 1957), III, 654.

13. Eleanor Roosevelt, *L'Amitié Franco-Américaine* (Rennes, 1949), 17–18.

14. Robert Dallek, *The American Style of Foreign Policy: Cultural Politics and Foreign Affairs* (New York, 1983), 141.

15. Eden, II, 319.

16. George F. Kennan, *American Diplomacy* (Chicago, 1984), 53.

17. Ibid., 69.

18. Ibid., 46.

19. 10 November 1941. In de Gaulle, *Lettres, notes et carnets: Juillet 1941–mai 1943*, 109.

20. Eden, II, 432. The plan was suggested again at the Moscow Conference as a means of preserving the territorial integrity of Belgium. At the conference, reference was made to "the two parts of Belgium" (FRUS: I Gen., 543).

21. Eden, II, 433.

22. Ibid., 357.

23. Churchill, V, 320–21.

CHAPTER 5

1. Pierre Billotte, *Le Temps des armes* (Paris, 1972), 187.

2. Charles de Gaulle, *Discours et messages, 1940–1946* (Paris, 1946), 149.

3. De Gaulle questioned the valor of American soldiers. "United States power may increase out of proportion to their military valor," he wrote in *Vers l'Armée de Métier.* One wonders how he knew, considering he had been a prisoner of war in Germany since 1916 and therefore had no way of witnessing the contribution of American soldiers to the Allied victory.

4. Roosevelt *did* promise in a message to Reynaud all possible aid on the condition that France stay in the war. Reynaud replied on 17 June 1940: "Your reply to my last message went to the far limit of what present circumstances allow. I wish to express to you my most lively gratitude. In her immense sorrow, France knows that, because America exists, the form of civilization which is her own will not die and that one day liberty will live anew in old Europe" (FDRL: PSF 41/France 33–39).

In correspondence with other French, de Gaulle's assessment of France's disaster was more realistic: "My sentiment is that the head of government and the military chief (Daladier and Gamelin) have suffered the impact of a deplorable generalized system that crushed them. The truth is that it had become nearly impossible to govern and command in France except in appearance given the chronic paralysis of the state" (Letter to Charles Geraud [Pertinax], 17 May 1943, in *Lettres, notes et carnets: Juillet 1941–mai 1943* [Paris, 1982], 595). "You understand that if I insisted with all my strength that our disaster was only military . . . I believe as you do that at the bottom of everything there was in our people a sort of moral collapse. The loss of the Rhine in '36, the abandonment of the Czech in '39, the incoherence of policies and the mediocrity of strategy were effects, before becoming causes. The nation was tottering for a good many years" (Letter to Jacques Maritain, 7 January 1942, ibid., 174–75).

5. De Gaulle, III, 94. As Sir Edward Spears noted "the French give way more readily than other nations to the temptation to criticize their friends" (*The Fall of France: June 1940*, London, 1945). Their defeat was often attributed not to the abysmal ignorance of the officers' corps and the treason of their leaders, but to British abandonment. The French find it extremely difficult to criticize themselves; the fault must always have been somebody else's.

6. De Gaulle, II, 88–89.

7. Ibid., 113.

8. De Gaulle, III, 227.

9. Ibid., 61.

10. De Gaulle, II, 269.

11. Ibid., 212.

12. Ibid., 271.

13. J. Robert Schaetzel, "Vue rétrospective d'un Américain sur le Général de Gaulle," *Espoir*, June 1974, 58–63. Julien Green quotes de Gaulle as comparing the United States "to one of those enormous ante-diluvian monsters whose head was small compared to the body" (*L'Expatrié: 1984–1990* [Paris, 1990], 313).

14. NA: Research and Analysis Branch No. 2508.

15. Henri Michel, *Histoire de la France Libre* (Paris, 1963). Quoted in Alexander Werth, *De Gaulle: A Political Biography* (New York, 1965), III. The following editions contain no reference to "thugs." "As in all tormented periods, some adventurers and profiteers insin-

uated themselves among the volunteers" René Cassin, *Les Hommes Partis de Rien* (Paris, 1974), 159.

16. Ibid., 4th edition, 1980, 111.

17. Philippe Masson, *De Gaulle* (New York, 1972), 55.

18. Henri Michel and Boris Mirkine-Guetzewitch, *Les Idées politiques et sociales de la résistance* (Paris, 1954), 19.

19. David Thomson, *Two Frenchmen: Pierre Laval and Charles de Gaulle* (London, 1957), 167.

20. Masson, *De Gaulle*, 113.

21. Robert Aron, *Histoire de la libération de la France: Juin 1944–mai 1945* (Paris, 1959), 75.

22. Thomson, *Two Frenchmen*, 184.

23. FDRL: PSF 42 France 44–45, 13 December 1944.

24. FDRL: PSF 167. For background to the incident see Anthony Cave Brown, *The Last Hero: Wild Bill Donovan* (New York, 1982), 611–17.

25. Raoul Aglion, *Roosevelt and de Gaulle: Allies in Conflict: A Personal Memoir* (New York, 1988), passim.

26. Raoul Aglion, *De Gaulle et Roosevelt: La France Libre aux Etats-Unis* (Paris, 1984), 8–9.

27. Raoul Roussy de Sales, *L'Amérique entre en guerre* (Paris, 1948), 125.

28. Jacques Soustelle, *Envers et contre tout: De Londres à Alger, 1940–1942* (Paris, 1947), I, 372–73.

29. Members of the Vichy embassy went on to pursue distinguished careers: Charles Lucet, a first secretary, later became ambassador to Washington; Burin de Roziers, an attaché, future ambassador to Rome, was close to de Gaulle; Hervé Alphand, financial attaché, became secretary general of the Ministry of Foreign Affairs and later ambassador to Washington; François Charles-Roux, also close to de Gaulle, was appointed ambassador to various countries.

30. "Le Général de Gaulle et l'Amérique," Lecture at the Institut Charles de Gaulle, 6 June 1973.

31. Hervé Alphand, *L'Etonnement d'Etre* (Paris, 1977), 138.

32. Sir Edward Spears, *Two Men Who Saved France: Pétain and de Gaulle* (London, 1966), 154, 141.

33. Aglion, *De Gaulle et Roosevelt*, 74–75.

34. Welles, *The Time for Decision*, 125.

35. Aglion, *De Gaulle et Roosevelt*, 102.

36. De Gaulle, *Lettres, notes et carnets: Juillet 1941–mai 1943*, 80.

37. FRUS: 42, II, 517.

38. Aglion, *De Gaulle et Roosevelt*, 36.

39. Ibid., 70.

40. Aron, *Histoire de la libération de la France*, 333.

41. FDRL: Map Room 30/North Africa. Eisenhower to Roosevelt, 12 June 1943.

42. Brian Crozier, *De Gaulle: The Warrior* (London, 1973), 196, 216.

43. FMFA: Bureau d'études Chauvel 203, 14 May 1941.

44. Georges Catroux, *Dans la bataille de la Méditerranée* (Paris, 1949), 278–79.

45. De Gaulle, *Mémoires*, I, 675–76. The Brazzaville Conference (30 January–8 February 1944), often considered a turning point in French attitudes toward dependent peoples, did not depart from this traditional view of empire. It merely proposed "to es-

tablish upon a new basis the conditions for the exploitation (mise en valeur) of our Africa, of the human progress of its inhabitants and the exercise of French sovereignty." As French historian Jean-Baptiste Duroselle commented, "Not only the idea of independence, of sovereignty for the indigenous people did not appear, but all autonomy, all 'self-government' were formally excluded" (*L'abime*, 1933–1945 [Paris, 1982]), 368.

46. Jean-Baptiste Duroselle, *La France et les Etats-Unis des origines à nos jours* (Paris, 1976), 168, quoting Raymond Poli's report to the European Association for American Studies.

47. 21 January 1944. Hull Papers, Box 33, Folder 169. This argument was well developed by Harold Macmillan: "If you take the worst view of de Gaulle . . . what could do more to elevate his position in French eyes than to try to snub him . . . ? All history teaches the same lesson. The French are just as insular and proud a people as the British. As we preferred a Dutch King who was maladroit, and two Hanoverian Kings who could not speak English, to the charm and attraction of all the Stuarts – and why? Because the Stuarts depended on France for money, arms and political support. But of course the Americans do not read – or at any rate comprehend – history" (*The Blast of War, 1939–1945* [New York, 1967], 290).

CHAPTER 6

1. H. du Moulin de la Barthete, *Le Temps des illusions* (Brussells, 1945), 194. "While the Marshal had hardly any sympathy for England, he always remained loyal to the Franco-American friendship. This dates back to 1918. He had not forgotten the hostility Douglas Haig had shown toward him at the conference of Doullens. He was convinced that this hostility had caused him to be removed from the high command. He also remembered the affectionate devotion of Pershing, who had requested his presence at the head of the Allied armies" (Jacques Benoist-Méchin, *Soixante jours qui ébranlerent l'Occident* [Paris, 1956], III, 605).

De Gaulle, too, paid tribute to the "glorious General Pershing, great man who witnessed the sacred union of Frenchmen around Poincaré and Clemenceau. Great soldier who willed and did realize with Foch and with Haig the united front of the Allies in the battle of France. Great chief who stood as the symbol and the inspiration of the unitary action of the Allies in the struggle for liberty" (14 July 1942, *Discours et messages*, I, 215).

2. General Laure, *Pétain* (Paris, 1941), 416–20.

3. Jean Tracou, *Le Maréchal aux liens: Le Temps du sacrifice* (Paris, 1948), 111.

4. René de Chambrun, *Général, comte de Chambrun: Sorti du rang* (Paris, 1980), 208–215.

5. Du Moulin, *Le Temps des illusions*, 194.

6. Georges Pompidou, *Pour rétablir une verité* (Paris, 1982), 30–31. "Has the general understood that for many of his fellow Frenchmen to shout 'Vive le Maréchal' and now to shout 'Vive de Gaulle' is simply to shout 'Vive la France'. "

7. Harold L. Ickes, *The Secret Diary of Harold L. Ickes: The Lowering Clouds, 1939–1941* (New York, 1955), III, 585.

8. FDRL: PSF 4/France.

9. FMFA: Bureau d'Etudes Chauvel 203, 7 February 1941.

10. FMFA: Guerre 1939–1945, Série Z, Carton 401, 10 September 1941.

11. Ickes, *Secret Diary*, III, 277.

12. Stanley Hoffmann, *Essais sur la France: Declin ou Renouveau?* (Paris, 1974).

13. Robert O. Paxton, *Vichy France: Old Guard and New Order, 1940–1944* (New York, 1975), 67–68.

14. FMFA: Papiers 1940, 202, 23 November 1940.

15. FDRL: PSF 41 France 33–39, 28 July 1941.

16. Ibid., letter to Roosevelt, 26 August 1941.

17. Ibid., 27 October 1941.

18. William D. Leahy, *I Was There* (New York, 1950), 70.

19. Ibid., 75.

20. FDRL: PSF 4/France, 1 August 1941. "But neither side can win the war and Europe will be exhausted," he added.

21. Forrest Davis and Ernest K. Lindley, *How War Came* (New York, 1942), 76. Hitler considered Laval a "dirty democratic politician, a man who doesn't believe in what he says, who turns to us only to save himself" (Muggeridge, ed., *Ciano Diplomatic Papers*, 400).

22. Alain Darlan, *L'Amiral Darlan parle . . .* (Paris, 1952), 103. In a conversation with Leahy (21 January 1941) he expressed the belief that "the Nazi regime can not long survive after the passing of Hitler, and that the French people will then attain a position of great influence or control in a new Europe that will emerge from the war."

23. *The Ciano Diaries, 1939–1943* (New York, 1946), 457–58.

24. Quoted in Geoffrey Warner, *Pierre Laval and the Eclipse of France* (New York, 1968), 296–97.

25. FDRL: PSF 166/OSS.

26. Louis Noguerès, *Le Véritable Procès du maréchal Pétain* (Paris, 1955), 383–93.

27. Eberhard Jäckel, *La France dans l'Europe d'Hitler* (Paris, 1955), 393.

28. Llewellyn Woodward, *British Foreign Policy in the Second World War*, II, 283.

29. Raoul Roussy de Sales, *L'Amérique entre en guerre* (Paris, 1948), 365.

CHAPTER 7

1. Eden, II, 374.

2. Ibid., 341.

3. Pierre Billotte, *Le Temps des armes* (Paris, 1972), 185.

4. FMFA: Guerre 1939–1945, Londres CNF 213.

5. The Free French conducted a plebiscite in which the islanders were to mark their choice on their ballots: Ralliment à la France Libre – Collaboration avec les puissances de l'Axe" (Rallying to Free France – collaboration with the Axis powers).

6. Cordell Hull tried to convince the military of his point of view. Reporting on a conversation with Hull, General Gerow stated:

Admiral Muselier's coup d'état in St. Pierre and Miquelon, and General Rommel's recent counterattack in Libya, have stiffened the Vichy attitude. Information from secret sources suggests that unless there was a return to the status quo in St. Pierre and Miquelon, Vichy might not only eject U.S. consuls and observers in France and North Africa, but also collaborate with the Japanese in regard to New Caledonia. Mr. Hull feared that Vichy might go so far as to turn over the Fleet and bases to the Germans. He was most anxious that the Combined Chiefs of Staff should give an opinion as to the military dangers of further Vichy collaboration with Germany, in order that the British Government might be urged to take further action to restore the status quo in St. Pierre and Miquelon.

Sir John Dill agreed with the importance of retaining relations with Vichy France, particularly in view of the danger of the French Fleet and the bases being turned over to the Germans, as well as losing important information should the Consuls and observers be ejected.

The Committee . . . agreed that with reference to the crisis which had arisen in the relations with Great Britain and the United States with the Vichy Government over the occupation of St. Pierre and Miquelon, the situation was exceedingly grave in its possible military consequences, and that a further determined effort should be made to adjust the present differences, in order that existing relations between the United States and Vichy might be maintained. (CCS 092 France, subsequently circulated as C.C.S. 21/1).

The Committee did not go so far as to suggest that the Gaullists be ejected and the islands returned to Vichy.

7. Robert Murphy, *Diplomat among Warriors* (New York, 1964), 76.

8. FMFA: Guerre 1939–1945, Londres CNF 221.

9. FMFA: Guerre 1939–1945, Londres CNF 210.

10. George F. Kennan, *Memoirs, 1925–1950* (New York, 1967), 162–63.

11. Lord Moran, *Churchill: Taken from the Diaries of Lord Moran* (Boston, 1966), 292.

12. The president had originally decided to send him to London as his representative on naval matters (CRC: R-114, 4 March 1942).

13. The Free French recognized their indebtedness to Admiral Stark. De Gaulle: "I beg you to believe in the gratitude I feel for the task which you have accomplished, in the spirit of the most intimate, most confident and most fruitful inter-allied cooperation" (Stark Papers 189, Box 2). Catroux, 24 June 1943: "My dear Admiral, the letter expressing your friendship and appreciation of the work I have endeavored to bring to a successful issue has just reached me. I wish to thank you most sincerely for it and to tell you how much it pleases me. More than anyone you know the stages which had to be passed through and the difficulties to be surmounted. My task would have been even more difficult had I not been able to talk to you openly in the course of our conversations, and to receive from you the fullest and most friendly welcome. Therefore I wish you to accept the expression of my gratitude."

14. Forrest C. Pogue, *George Marshall: Organizer of Victory, 1933–45* (New York, 1973), 413.

15. Ibid., 414. See de Gaulle's version in *Mémoires*, II, 343.

16. Roosevelt had tried to convince Herriot, among others, to leave France for the United States. Herriot wrote the president on 31 August that he appreciated the latter's concern, but he wished to share his people's suffering. He added that his last act, before being deprived of the presidency of the Chamber of Deputies, was an "homage for your noble person, for the free people of the United States, for your allies who are also ours."

17. On 25 June 1940, the British had extended recognition to de Gaulle personally: "His Majesty's Government recognizes General de Gaulle as the leader of all free Frenchmen, wherever they may be, who rally to him in support of the Allied cause."

18. FRUS: 42, II, 544.

19. 10 October 1940 letter to Churchill referring to the previous day's conversation. Following Weygand's sacking from his post in North Africa, the president decided on 23 December 1941 to enquire whether he would join the Allies in case the invasion of North African territory became necessary to thwart a German move. The message was transmitted verbally by Douglas MacArthur II, of the Vichy embassy, but the response was negative. In a message to Washington dated 9 January 1942 Murphy wrote that "ever since the dismissal of General Weygand there has been effervescence on the part of individuals and groups in French North Africa who are eager to undertake action to resume hostilities against Germany and Italy." The following day, Murphy wondered whether the

"Department is in a position to give some indication of its desire regarding the policy to be followed by our officers in North Africa who are frequently approached by French military personnel and officials who desire to transfer their activity to the Allied forces" (FRUS: 42, II Europe, 227–28).

20. Harold L. Ickes, *The Secret Diary of Harold L. Ickes: The Lowering Clouds, 1939–1941* (New York, 1955), III, 510.

21. NA: CSS-0001 Free French 9-5-42.

22. At the end of 1942, the "Leclerc column" comprised about 3,300 men, of whom only 550 were Europeans, and 350 vehicles.

23. Sumner Welles, *The Time for Decision* (New York, 1944), 155–56.

24. NA: CCS 381: France 6/3/49.

25. Philippe Masson, *Histoire de la Marine* (Paris, 1983), II, passim.

26. Philippe Masson, "La Marine de Vichy, mythe ou réalité?" (Manuscript), 13.

CHAPTER 8

1. Pierre Nicolle, *Cinquante mois d'armistice* (Paris, 1947), II, 61. "General der artillerie Walter Warlimont of the OKW [Armed Forces Command] concluded after the war that the invasion of North Africa, which came as a complete surprise to Hitler, was actually 'decisive for the whole conduct of the war' for it established a 'springboard for a thrust into the groin of Fortress Europe, the naturally weak and practically unprepared south flank! One immediate result of the Allied landing in North Africa on 8 November 1942 was to force German occupation of the whole of France and add some four hundred miles of Mediterranean coast line on OBWEST [Highest German ground headquarters of the Western front] responsibility' " (Gordon A. Harrison, *Cross-Channel Attack* [Washington, 1951], 143).

2. Various quotes in Hervé Coutau-Begarie and Claude Huan, *Darlan* (Paris, 1989). This is the best and most complete work on the subject.

3. FDRL: PSF 4 France.

4. FRUS: *The Conference at Washington, 1941–1942, and Casablanca, 1943*, 186.

5. Churchill, III, 657.

6. FDRL: PSF 4/France. A belated avowal from the man who in a 10 December 1941 conversation with the Italian foreign minister, Galeazzo Ciano, had described the U.S. armed forces as "comic opera soldiers" (Muggeridge, ed., *Ciano's Diplomatic Papers*, 470).

7. Harry Cecil Butcher, *My Three Years with Eisenhower* (New York, 1946), 145.

8. Eden, II, 345.

9. "There was a general belief in Whitehall that there had been previous leakages of operational secrets from Free French sources" (Harold Macmillan, *The Blast of War, 1939–1945* [New York, 1967], 159). On 8 August 1942, Marshall suggested to Eisenhower for cover purposes to "proceed on carefully considered planning basis with de Gaulle toward a landing in the Continent this fall" (*The Papers of Dwight David Eisenhower: The War Years* [Baltimore, 1970], I, 479–80).

10. De Gaulle, *Mémoires*, II, 355. On 27 August de Gaulle confirmed this in a message to Plevin and Dejean.

11. Winston Churchill, *Secret Session Speeches* (London, 1946), 81–82.

12. Robert Aron, *Histoire de Vichy, 1940–1944* (Paris, 1945), 444.

13. Ibid., 579.

14. Colonel Passy, *Souvenirs* (Monte Carlo, 1947), I, 340.

15. Georges Catroux, *Dans la bataille de la Méditerranée* (Paris, 1949), 300.

16. Ibid., 313. General Juin also referred to the "mystique du Marechal." He congratulated, "in the name of the Marshal," the troops that fought the Allies.

17. Robert E. Sherwood, *Roosevelt and Hopkins: An Intimate Story* (New York, 1948), 681.

18. Jacques Benoit-Méchin, *De la défaite au désastre* (Paris, 1985), II, 250.

19. FMFA: Guerre 1939–1945, Vichy Amérique, Série B.

20. He was sentenced to death and executed on 15 April 1947.

21. Eberhard Jäckel, *La France dans l'Europe d'Hitler* (Paris, 1955), 348–49.

22. Jacques Barnaud in C.E. Temoignages, VII, 2311–12, as quoted in Warner, *Pierre Laval*, 352.

23. Malcolm Muggeridge, ed., *Ciano's Diplomatic Papers* (London, 1948), 81.

24. Jäckel, *La France dans l'Europe d'Hitler*, 357.

25. Catroux, *Dans la bataille*, 302.

26. CRC: C-216, 2 December 1942.

27. CRC: C-577, 13 February 1944.

28. CRC: C-227, 9 December 1942.

29. CRC: R-236, 16 December 1942.

30. FDRL: Map Room 12/1-A, 3 December 1942.

31. USNA: Stark File, correspondence Oct.–Dec. 1942, 189 Box 1, 18 November 1942. Bullitt wrote to Roosevelt on 20 December 1941 during a tour of West Africa that according to General Sir George Giffard, "it would be unwise to attempt an attack on Dakar with less than fifty thousand troops with appropriate air and sea support" (FDRL: PSF 72/West Africa).

32. Roosevelt declared:

I have accepted General Eisenhower's political arrangements made for the time being in North Africa and Western Africa. I thoroughly understand and approve the feeling in the United States and Great Britain, and among all the other United Nations, that in view of the history of the past two years no permanent arrangement should be made with Admiral Darlan. People in the United Nations likewise would never understand the recognition of a reconstituting of the Vichy government in France or any French territory. We are opposed to Frenchmen who support Hitler and the Axis. No one in our Army has any authority to discuss the future government of France or the French Empire. . . . The present temporary arrangement in North and West Africa is only a temporary expedient, justified solely by the stress of battle. The present temporary arrangement has accomplished two military objectives. The first was to save American and British lives on the one hand, and French lives on the other. The second was the vital factor of time. The temporary arrangement has made it possible to avoid a mopping-up period in Algiers and Morocco, which might have taken a month or two to consummate. Such period would have delayed the concentration for the attack from the West on Tunis, and we hope on Tripoli. . . . Admiral Darlan's proclamation assisted in making a mopping-up period unnecessary. Temporary arrangements made with Admiral Darlan apply without exception to the current local situation only. . . . Reports indicate the French of North Africa are subordinating all political questions to the formation of a common front against the common enemy. (Roosevelt press conference No. 861, 17 November 1942)

33. FDRL: A-16/6 Warfare 168 Pacific War Council. Roosevelt could say of Darlan what he said of some "friendly" South American dictators: "I know he is a s.o.b., but he is *our* s.o.b."

34. Henry L. Stimson and McGeorge Bundy, *On Active Service in Peace and War* (New York, 1948), 545.

35. De Gaulle, *Mémoires*, II, 394.

36. Passy, *Souvenirs*, I, 361–62.

37. Pierre Bloch, *Londres capitale de la France Libre* (Paris, 1986), 35.

38. Jacques Soustelle, *Envers et contre tout: De Londres à Alger, 1940–1942* (Paris, 1947), II, 37.

39. FRUS: 42, II, 540–41.

40. USNA: Record of General de Gaulle's expressions of appreciation of the American War Effort and Aid to France in conversation with Admiral Stark, 26 November 1942.

41. USNA: Knox to Stark, 25 November 1942.

42. Ibid., 27 November 1942.

43. USNA: Record of Conversation of Admiral Stark with General de Gaulle, 17 December 1942.

44. Ibid.

45. LC: Leahy Diary, July 1942–July 1943.

46. Sherwood, *Roosevelt and Hopkins*, 663.

CHAPTER 9

1. Roosevelt press conference No. 879, 12 January 1943.

2. FDRL: Map Room 12/2B. 2 January 1943.

3. NA: OPB RG 165 War Department. General and Special Staff.

4. FDRL: Map Room 30/North Africa, 24 June 1943.

5. Ibid., 4 July 1943.

6. Roosevelt press conference No. 879, 12 February 1943.

7. Robert Murphy, *Diplomat among Warriors* (New York, 1964), 176.

8. Churchill, IV, 611.

9. Gaston Paleski, "De Gaulle, la Grande Bretagne et la France Libre, 1940–1943," *Espoir* 43 (June 1983): 24–39.

10. De Gaulle, *Mémoires*, II, 441.

11. Charles de Gaulle, *Lettres, notes et carnets: Juillet 1941–mai 1943* (Paris, 1982), 517–18.

12. FDRL: PSF 41 France.

13. FDRL: PPF 9085, 1 February 1943.

14. De Gaulle believed that "a sort of permanent election" was the source of his legitimacy:

We only are and only want to be a provisional authority serving nothing more than the nation's general interests during the war. . . . We believe we are qualified to exercise this authority for three reasons. First there is no other legitimacy and the national interest demands that there should be one. Furthermore, General de Gaulle is, among the members of the last government of the Republic, the only one to be free, and who has never accepted either capitulation or usurpation. Lastly, the effective and free adherence to Free France of thousands of French citizens and of millions of French subjects, as well as the evident sympathy of a great majority of Frenchmen in France, constitute a sort of permanent election which justifies our authority. (*Lettres, notes et carnets: Juillet 1941–mai 1943*, 147)

15. Felix Frankfurter, in John Morton Blum, ed., *From the Morgenthau Diaries: Years of War, 1941–1945* (Boston, 1967), 193. Harry Hopkins gave two contradictory reports of the conversation. In a note on the first meeting between Roosevelt and de Gaulle, he wrote that de Gaulle's reference to Jeanne d'Arc and Clemenceau never took place: "This story is pure fiction" (Robert E. Sherwood, *Roosevelt and Hopkins: An Intimate Story* [New York, 1948], 686); but in a conversation with Jean Monnet, as reported by William Bul-

litt, he confirmed word for word the president's version (Bullitt, *For the President*, 568). Apparently, de Gaulle first mentioned to Macmillan the proposition that "he [de Gaulle] is to be Clemenceau and Giraud Foch" (Sherwood, *Roosevelt and Hopkins*, 691).

16. De Gaulle, II, 88.

17. Ibid., 89.

18. FDRL: Map Room 30/North Africa, 19 June 1943.

19. Henry L. Stimson and McGeorge Bundy, *On Active Service in Peace and War* (New York, 1948), 236, 547.

20. FDRL: Eisenhower to Marshall, 18 June 1943; forwarded to Roosevelt 19 June, Map Room 30/North Africa.

21. USNA: Command File World War II.

22. FDRL: Map Room 30/North Africa, 18 June 1943.

23. Eden, II, 394.

24. He once told Leahy: "I am a pigheaded Dutchman, Bill, and I have made up my mind about this. We are going ahead with it and you can't change my mind."

25. Claude Bourdet, *L'Aventure incertaine: de la Résistance à la restauration* (Paris, 1975), 411.

26. Speech at a luncheon given by the National Defence Public Interest Committee in London. De Gaulle, *Mémoires, documents* (1940–42), 277–78.

27. Quoted in Alexander Werth, *De Gaulle: A Political Biography* (New York, 1965), 136.

28. FDRL: FSF 166 OSS.

29. Henri Michel and Boris Mirkine-Guetzewich, *Les Idées politiques et sociales de la résistance* (Paris, 1954), 73

30. Bourdet, *L'Aventure incertaine*, 200.

31. 10 July 1942. Telegram to Tixier in de Gaulle, *Lettres, notes et carnets: Juillet 1941–mai 1943*, 312.

32. Jean Moulin procured a passport in the name of Joseph-Jean Mercier, professor of law at an American university. In February the U.S. consul at Marseilles, Fullerton, gave him a U.S. visa. Moulin reached London through Spain and Portugal.

33. Pierre Billotte, *Le Temps des armes* (Paris, 1972), 215.

34. Despite all the evidence to the contrary, Roosevelt continued to belittle de Gaulle's role. In a memo to Churchill, he said he thought that "the people of France are behind the Free French Movement; that they do not know de Gaulle and that their loyalty is to the fine objectives of the movement when it was started and to the larger phase of it which looks to the restoration of France. If they only knew what you and I know about de Gaulle himself, they would continue to be for the movement but not for its present leader in London" (CRC: R-275/1, 8 May 1943).

35. FRUS: 42, II, 539.

36. FMFA: Guerre 1939–1945, vol. 1215, 432.

37. FRUS: 42, II, 540.

38. De Gaulle, II, 236.

39. After the American landing, Vichy had apparently intended (on 10 November) to appoint General de Lattre to be Pétain's delegate to the American authorities in North Africa (Louis Noguères, *Le Véritable procès* [Paris, 1955], 445). De Lattre had been loyal to Pétain until the German occupation of the free zone, when he was jailed for having advocated resistance. The underground movement tried to free him, but he refused. He was quoted as saying, "No, no, I shall not escape; I am confident in the marshal's justice"

(Bourdet, *L'Aventure incertaine*, 152). After a long imprisonment he finally realized what Vichy and Pétain were really like.

40. "I greatly admired the skill with which Maurice Couvé de Murville and Paul Leroy Beaulieu conducted for Vichy the negotiations with the Germans at Wiesbaden on French-German financial questions" (Murphy, *Diplomat among Warriors*, 74). Couvé spent most of his time in Paris, but he went down to Vichy every fortnight. In Vichy he was close to Ambassador Leahy, who said of him: "He is one of my best friends and I trust him implicitly. He is all on our side." Always, according to Leahy, "he is strongly anti-collaborationist but is one of those who feel they can render greater service to France by staying and working from within than by joining de Gaulle. In fact, he thinks the Gaullist movement, in a political sense, is a tragedy." He took advantage of an official mission to Madrid to go on to North Africa and join General Giraud. Catroux to de Gaulle: "Couvé de Murville . . . will soon recognize where the wind blows. Be sure that, if need be, no one will be more Gaullist than he."

41. On 2 May 1944, Morgenthau objected naming Couvé de Murville French National Committee's representative to the Allied Advisory Council for Italy: "During my visit last fall to French North Africa, United States Treasury representatives there demonstrated to me the uncooperative and obstructionist tactics of M. Couvé de Murville. . . . Representatives of the Treasury, with ample justification from the record, made clear their dissatisfaction. . . . The Treasury Department would regard it as unfortunate if M. Couvé de Murville were again placed in a position where his attitude and sympathies would conflict with those of our Government and obstruct the close cooperation which we feel is essential to effective operations in the Mediterranean theater" (Letter to Hull, in Blum, *From the Morgenthau Diaries* 726; also see Berstein to Morgenthau, 10 November 1943, ibid., 675, and 10–12 November 1943, ibid., 216).

42. FDRL: Map Room 30/North Africa, 18 May 1943.

43. FDRL: PSF 41/France, 6 July 1943.

44. De Gaulle, *Mémoires*, II, 459.

45. Roosevelt refused to use the word *recognition*, preferring to only acknowledge "acceptance" of the committee's local, civil authority in various colonies on a temporary basis (CRC: R-321, 22 July 1943). The formula was not to Churchill's liking. "There is no use," he wrote the president, "making a gesture of this kind in a grudging form." He suggested "separate documents conveying our different shades of meaning" (CRC: C-412, 15 August 1943).

46. Butcher, *My Three Years*, 399.

47. Werth, *De Gaulle*, 160–61.

48. Bourdet, *L'Aventure incertaine*, 249.

49. Interesting in this respect is a statement by Leclerc, the only truly Gaullist general, to his troops as he formed the Second Armored Division: "One must be broad-minded. When accepting those who have betrayed and collaborated ostentatiously, we must be on guard about being too severe. They have been mistaken. From the moment they work, each within his sphere, for the common end we must simply consider them as French. We must learn to forget" (Aron, *Histoire de la libération de la France*, 324). "The offspring of a rustic noble family in Picardy, Leclerc had Jesuit schooling, a Saint-Cyr diploma, and an outspoken sympathy for Marshal Pétain's efforts to rebuild the Christian family and the values of the old France to recommend him to the old guard's forgiveness" (Robert O. Paxton, *Parades and Politics at Vichy: The French Officers Corps under Marshal Pétain* [Princeton, 1966], 419).

50. Harry Cecil Butcher, *My Three Years with Eisenhower* (New York, 1946), 321. This was so according to Kittredge, who referred to personal conversations.

51. Ibid., 473.

52. De Gaulle, II, 241.

CHAPTER 10

1. FDRL: PSF 42 France 44–45, 5 January 1944.

2. Instructions repeated to Eisenhower on 15 March 1944.

3. De Gaulle's 21 April 1944 press conference in Algiers (*Mémoires*, II, 629).

4. Roosevelt press conference No. 961, 11 July 1944.

5. NA: CCS 350.05.

6. Ibid.

7. NA: S51959, personal from General Eisenhower to General Marshall.

8. Ibid.

9. CRC: C-654.

10. CRC: C-674.

11. CRC: C-682.

12. According to a Koening aide-memoire, "It is the Supreme Commander's intention to take the head of the French Military Mission into his full confidence regarding plans for the employment of French forces in operations in France well in advance of their being committed to these operations." See Harry Cecil Butcher, *My Three Years with Eisenhower* (New York, 1946), 526.

13. NA: CCS 350.05, 4 November 1942.

14. NA: CCS 400 France Sec. 1, 20 March 1944.

15. Ibid., 26 April 1944.

16. USNA: Stark to King, 44-00074-M, 12 April 1944.

17. Henry L. Stimson and McGeorge Bundy, *On Active Service in Peace and War* (New York, 1948), 545, 549–50.

18. Ibid., 551.

19. Ibid., 575–76.

20. Eden, II, 447.

21. Relations between De Gaulle and the Soviet Union were more complex than would appear from Stalin's statements at the Teheran and Yalta conferences. De Gaulle was counting on Soviet influence to counter what he feared might become an overly important Anglo-Saxon role in Europe. In a 20 January 1942 radio address de Gaulle had declared, "In the political order, the inevitable emergence of Russia to the first rank among tomorrow's victors will lend to Europe and the world a guarantee of equilibrium in which no power more than France has good reason to rejoice." Once in power, de Gaulle repeatedly played the Soviet card to counter American influence. His objective was for France to stand in equilibrium between the superpowers. The Soviets, for their part, were courting de Gaulle in the hope of establishing the preeminence of the Communist party in France. According to their plans, de Gaulle would be the leader of French resistance outside of France, the Communist party the leader within France. De Gaulle, needless to say, did not see things that way. Another reason for Stalin's interest in de Gaulle was Poland. At Yalta, Stalin argued that the Allies had recognized de Gaulle's Free French even though they had not been elected. He did not see why the Anglo-

Saxons refused to recognize the Soviet-sponsored Polish government on the ground it was not elected. See Edward R. Stettinius, Jr., *Roosevelt and the Russians: The Yalta Conference* (New York, 1949), 156. Among the various books on the subject, the most complete is Henry Christian Giraud, *De Gaulle et les communistes: l'Alliance, juin 1941–mai 1943* (Paris, 1988).

22. Roosevelt press conference No. 957, 13 June 1944.

23. FDRL: Map Room 12/3B.

24. FDRL: Map Room 30/002 France. The currency issue proved less critical than feared. Early reports indicated that the invasion currency was being accepted by the French even without endorsement from de Gaulle. Further negotiations in Washington by Mendes-France solved the issue to France's satisfaction (de Gaulle, *Mémoires*, II, 661).

25. "Relations with Occupied Countries," in *US Army in World War II*; Forrest C. Pogue, *The Supreme Commander* (Washington, 1954), 149.

26. CRC: C-694, 7 June 1944.

27. Forrest C. Pogue, *George Marshall: Organizer of Victory, 1933–45* (New York, 1973), III, 400.

28. John Morton Blum, ed., *From the Morgenthau Diaries: Years of Crisis, 1928–1938* (Boston, 1959), III, 174.

29. Pogue, *Marshall*, III, 401.

30. "Citizens of France: The day of liberation has dawned. Your comrades in arms are on French soil. I am proud to have under my command the gallant forces of France who have so long trained and waited for this day when they can take part in the liberation of their home country. United we come to settle on the battlefield the war you have continued heroically through the years of stubborn resistance. We shall destroy the Nazi tyranny root and branch so that the people of Europe may have a new birth of freedom. As Supreme Commander of the Allied Expeditionary Force, there is imposed on me the duty and responsibility of taking all measures essential to the prosecution of the war. Prompt obedience to such orders as I may issue is necessary. All persons must continue in the performance of their present duties unless otherwise instructed. Those who have made common cause with the enemy and so betrayed their country will be removed. It will be for the French people to provide their own Civil administration and to safeguard my troops by effective maintenance of law and order. Members of the French Military Mission attached to me will furnish assistance to this end. The valour and extreme sacrifice of the millions who have fought under the banner of resistance have helped and will continue to help the success of our arms. The presence of the enemy among you has made tragically necessary the aerial bombardment and military and naval operations which have caused you loss and suffering. This you have accepted courageously in the heroic tradition of France, as part of the inevitable price we all must pay to attain our goal which is our freedom. Every resource will be required for the expulsion of the enemy from your country. Battle may inflict on you further deprivation. You will realize that munitions of war must come first but every endeavor will be made to bring to you food, medical supplies and other assistance that you need so sorely. I rely on your assistance in the final crushing of Hitlerite Germany and the reestablishment of the historic French liberties. When victory is won and France is liberated from her oppressors the French people will be free to choose at the earliest possible moment under democratic methods and conditions the government under which they wish to live. The enemy will fight with the courage of despair. He will neglect no measure, however ruthless, which he

thinks may delay our progress. But our cause is just, our armies are strong. With our valiant Russian Allies from the East, we shall march to certain victory. Signed Dwight D. Eisenhower, General Supreme Commander, Allied Expeditionary Force" (FDRL: JC534).

31. De Gaulle, *Mémoires*, II, 341.

32. Ibid., 349.

33. Ibid., 669.

34. David Dilks, ed., *The Diaries of Sir Alexander Cadogan, 1938–1945* (London, 1971), 634–35.

35. FDRL: PSF 41 France 33–39.

36. FDRL: PSF 8529. Contrary to what the president believed, Mme. Suzanne Blum-Weill was not related to Léon Blum.

37. CRC: R-506/1, letter.

38. The State Department document reads:

The absurd reports and rumors periodically occurring, which are evidently inspired, endeavoring to create the impression that this Government upon the liberation of France intends to deal with the Vichy regime or with certain individuals directly or indirectly supporting the policy of collaboration with Germany, are false on their face. The fact that this Government kept representatives at Vichy for some time for such vital purposes as combating Nazi designs, the preservation of the French fleet, and the prevention of Nazi occupation of French Africa or the establishment of military bases there, has been most amazingly and falsely represented as founded upon a systematic relationship between the American Government and pro-Axis supporters at Vichy. Every person at all informed knew that throughout the entire period just the opposite was the truth. No loyal supporter of the Allied cause would make the ridiculous charge that the United States Government, while sending its military forces and vast military supplies to the most distant battlefields to prosecute the war against the Axis powers, would at the same time have any dealings or relations with the Vichy regime except for the purpose of abolishing it.

Matthews (State Department) to Leahy, 21 July 1944: "In view of the possible bad effects on our relations with the French Committee of National Liberation, instructions were sent to our representatives to have nothing whatever to do with M. Lemaigre-Dubreuil and we recommended to both the War Department and OSS that they similarly instruct their representatives in Spain and Portugal" (Record Group 218 entry, Leahy Box 5).

39. Pierre Assouline, *Une Eminence grise: Jean Jardin* (Paris, 1986), 153–54.

40. J.H. Tornoux, *Pétain et de Gaulle* (Paris, 1964), 160–61.

41. De Gaulle, *Mémoires*, II, 341.

42. Jean Tracou, *Le Maréchal aux liens: Le Temps du sacrifice* (Paris, 1948), 366.

43. Geoffrey Warner, *Pierre Laval and the Eclipse of France* (New York, 1968), 401.

44. Pogue, *Marshall*, I, 197.

45. FDRL: 42 France 44–46, 4 July 1944. "The army during this period was making decisions which the civilian authority of one government normally would have made. . . . General Marshall bore the brunt of this responsibility and deserves enormous credit for loyally protecting the President while remaining as anonymous as he could under the circumstances" (Robert Murphy, *Diplomat among Warriors* [New York, 1964], 248).

The Joint Chiefs of Staff tended . . . to develop a purely military perspective that considered political implications chiefly with an eye to avoiding them. This perspective accurately reflected the popular obsession with winning the war as quickly and as cheaply as possible – an obsession which allowed little room for consideration of America's postwar position. One effect was to make the Joint Chiefs of Staff relatively independent of the President and State Department in formulating strategy. . . . The President generally appeared at the Allied conferences as a defender of the strategy worked out by the Joint Chiefs of Staff." (Gordon A. Harrison, *Cross-Channel Attack* [Washington, United States Army in World War II, 1951], 92)

CHAPTER 11

1. Churchill commented, "You might do him a great deal of good by paternal treatment and indeed I think it would help from every point of view" (CRC: C-653, 19 April 1944).

2. CRC: C-707, 20 June 1944.

3. De Gaulle, *Mémoires*, II, 648–651.

4. Anthony Cave Brown, *The Secret War Report of the OSS* (Berkeley, 1976).

5. Forrest C. Pogue, *George Marshall: Organizer of Victory, 1933–45* (New York, 1973), III, 405. Eisenhower also referred to French resistance groups as performing "above expectation." The German High Command did not attribute the same importance to the Resistance. "On 13 June, Rundstedt signalled that sabotages had increased 'but not in the proportion that we had anticipated.' On the 20th he signalled that agitation had decreased among the population; no serious disorder had taken place in the former occupied zone. In fact nowhere had the Resistance or the Maquis a decisive importance on the issue of the war and the worry they caused the leaders of the Reich must have appeared to them quite secondary, compared with the situation at the front" (Eberhard Jäckel, *La France dans l'Europe d'Hitler* [Paris, 1955], 466).

6. FDRL: PSF 42 France 44–45.

7. John Morton Blum, ed., *From the Morgenthau Diaries: Years of War, 1941–45* (Boston, 1967), III, 175–76.

8. William D. Hassett, *Off the Record with F.D.R., 1942–1945* (New Brunswick, N.J., 1958), 259.

9. Lord Moran, *Churchill: Taken from the Diaries of Lord Moran* (Boston, 1966), 206.

10. Roosevelt press conference No. 960, 7 July 1944.

11. Hull, II, 1433.

12. William D. Leahy, *I Was There* (New York, 1950), 244.

13. Francis Biddle, *In Brief Authority* (New York, 1962), 181–82.

14. "The gradation of the *de facto* and *de jure* recognitions are so numerous and so readily merge as to make them distinctions without any real significance" (John Gange, *American Foreign Relations* [New York, 1959], 50).

15. Bernard Ledwidge, *De Gaulle* (New York, 1982), 196. Roosevelt stresses the main point to his wife. See Joseph P. Lash, *Eleanor and Franklin* (New York, 1971), 677.

16. To the White House Correspondents' Association, 16 March 1941.

17. Elliott Roosevelt, *As He Saw It* (New York, 1945), 74.

18. Ibid., 121–22.

19. Roosevelt returned to the same subject repeatedly, citing the issue's impact on U.S. public opinion: CRC: R-132, 11 April 1942; R-172, 29 July 1942. Churchill offered to resign if it would quiet American concern over India and preserve the wartime alliance.

20. Roosevelt's attitude was not always consistent. For example, writing to Leahy on 20 January 1942 he instructed him to make clear to Pétain that "the word 'France' in the mind of the president includes the French Colonial Empire" (CRC: R-77X, 29 January 1942).

21. FDRL: A-16/3 Warfare, Pacific Council.

22. Roosevelt press conference No. 649-A, 5 June 1940.

23. FDRL: A-15/3 Warfare 168.

24. FDRL: A-16/3 Warfare.

25. On 26 July he wrote Churchill: "I have suggested to [the Japanese] that Indo-China be neutralized by the British, Dutch, Chinese, Japanese, and ourselves, placing Indo-China somewhat in status of Switzerland. Japan to get rice and fertilizer but all on condition that Japan withdraw armed forces from Indo-China completely" (CRC: R-52X).

26. "Walter La Feber, Roosevelt, Churchill, and Indochina: 1942–45," *The American Historical Review* 80 (December, 1975): 1287.

27. De Gaulle, *Mémoires*, III, 323.

28. The Yalta decision on trust territories concerned mandates of the old League of Nations, territories detached from enemy nations, and territories that desired to be placed under trusteeship. "It will be a matter for subsequent agreement which territories within the above categories will be placed under trusteeship," FRUS: *Yalta*, 977.

29. See also de Gaulle, *Mémoires*, II, 426, 595, and 607.

30. FRUS: *Yalta*, 302. This policy was also recommended, in almost identical terms, by the State-War-Navy Coordinating Committee in "Foreign Policy of the United States," 4 December 1945.

31. Robert E. Sherwood, *Roosevelt and Hopkins: An Intimate Story* (New York, 1948), 845.

32. Ibid., 848.

33. Ibid., 858.

34. Ibid., 923.

35. Ibid., 929.

36. Lord Moran, *Churchill: Taken from the Diaries of Lord Moran* (Boston, 1966), 207–208.

37. Churchill "pointed out that he had opposed inviting de Gaulle to the Crimean Conference," Edward R. Stettinius, Jr., *Roosevelt and the Russians: The Yalta Conference* (New York, 1949), 128, 181.

38. FDRL: Hopkins 337 Yalta Conference, Folder 1. Ambassador Caffery to Secretary of State, 28 January 1945.

39. De Gaulle, *Mémoires*, III, 389–92.

40. Ibid., 392.

41. During the latter part of the war, the French army comprised 241,000 troops but was short some 58,000 support troops, placing a considerable burden on U.S. forces. The regiments were down 700–800 white effectives, each having received no replacement from liberated France. On 18 December, de Lattre urged de Gaulle to place at his disposal 8,000–10,000 young French to restore his army to "its initial moral equilibrium" and "fighting qualities." By 5 February 1945 only 2500 men had reported for instruction (Marcel Vigneras, *Rearming the French* [Washington, 1957], passim). According to a 25 March 1945 report by General Juin, the breakdown of Moslem soldiers in the French army was 134,000 Algerians, 26,000 Tunisians, and 73,000 Moroccans. Eisenhower did not think much of French divisions made up of former Forces Françaises de l'Interieur (FFI): "These troops, other than those already in the battle, are so miserably equipped and unready for fighting, that they could have accomplished nothing" (Eisenhower to Marshall, Cable S738711SA699, 6 February 1945).

42. Dwight D. Eisenhower, *Crusade in Europe* (New York, 1948), 429.

43. Churchill, IV, 227–28, 31 December 1944. Churchill told Roosevelt that 80 percent of French divisions were "native divisions from Morocco, Algeria and Tunisia" (CRC: C-721, 1 July 1944).

44. Cable S/75090/sg 997, 15 January 1945. In a separate message to Marshall, Eisenhower wrote that the French "have caused more trouble in this war than any other single factor" (Eisenhower Mss., 20 February 1945). See the detailed account in David Eisenhower, *Eisenhower: At War, 1943–1945* (New York, 1986), 700.

The French made much of Eisenhower's decision to abandon Strasbourg, a decision they felt would expose the city to Nazi reprisals. Eisenhower acceded to de Gaulle's request to defend the city, but he always wondered whether he had done the right thing. "So worrisome was the episode that in later years he could recount the details of the showdown from memory – de Gaulle's sermon on Alsace, fatuous, in Eisenhower's opinion, since de Gaulle had conceded the military illogic of holding Strasbourg, and unforthcoming, since he had failed to couple this demand with a pledge of more French troops or help in subduing the German pocket at Colmar further south. In short de Gaulle had appealed for American aid, and offered little in return" (Ibid., 604). Because of the inability to clean up the pocket at Colmar, Eisenhower had to place six American divisions under de Lattre. Eisenhower invited Juin to his headquarters at Versailles "in hope of spurring the French to greater exertions." The Juin meeting failed on every account. While Eisenhower strenuously urged that "now is the time for the French to fight like fury," Juin countered that the French were "tired," that the British were "foolish" to plan attacks in the north, that the West was "exhausted," capable of little more than fighting a defensive battle (ibid., 633). With French support evaporating, Eisenhower decided that the only recourse was to bolster the attack with U.S. reinforcements. Incidentally, Churchill did not rush down from London to influence Eisenhower's decision, as some writers have maintained. In a cable to Marshall (S73871 of 6 January 1945), Eisenhower wrote, "It was a mere coincidence that de Gaulle's visit to us was scheduled at an hour when the Prime Minister happened to be in the office."

45. FRUS: *Yalta*, 623.

46. De Lattre de Tassigny, *Reconquérir* (Paris, 1985), 131. De Lattre drew Marshall's ire when on 8 October 1944 the latter visited his command.

De Lattre, noted for his histrionics and sharp tongue, seized the opportunity to denounce General Truscott bitterly. He charged that the latter's VI corps had shown up well in recent fightings because it had taken the gasoline allocated to French troops. . . .General de Lattre's attack was made not only in front of American and French officers but in the presence of Allied correspondents. The Chief of Staff was furious with de Lattre and with William Bullitt, then a major in the French Army, who stood by without saying anything. Marshall's temper flared, but he decided to avoid a scene by terminating the discussion. 'I just stopped the thing right where it was and walked out'." (Pogue, *Marshall*, III, 475–76)

47. FRUS: *Yalta*, 623.

48. Charles E. Bohlen, *Witness to History, 1929–1969* (New York, 1973), 170. Eisenhower had high praise for the French army. See in particular Harry Cecil Butcher, *My Three Years with Eisenhower* (New York, 1946), 703, 706. In *Crusade in Europe*, Eisenhower wrote: "Throughout France the Free French had been of inestimable value in the campaign. . . . Without their great assistance the liberation of France and the defeat of the enemy in Western Europe would have consumed a much longer time and meant

greater losses to ourselves" (296). For his part, General Mark W. Clark wrote in *Calculated Risk* (New York, 1950) that "a more gallant fighting organization never existed" (360).

49. Sherwood, *Roosevelt and Hopkins*, 777. Stalin told Roosevelt that he found de Gaulle "unrealistic in his estimate of France's contribution to the winning of the war" (ibid., 851).

50. Ibid., 781–82.

51. Ibid., 894.

52. Ibid., 858.

53. Ibid., 859; FDRL: Hopkins 337 Yalta Conference, Folder 2.

54. FRUS: *Yalta*, 900. "When Marshal Stalin asked the President why he favored a zone for France, Roosevelt replied that he favored it only out of kindness. Both the Marshal and Molotov, in vigorous tones, said that this was certainly the only reason to give the French a zone. The Marshal made it clear that he did not believe the French deserved a zone." (Stettinius, *Roosevelt and the Russians*, 101–2).

55. FDRL: Hopkins 337 Yalta Conference, Folder 1. Caffery to Hopkins, 15 February 1945.

56. Ibid., Caffery to State Department, 14 February 1945.

57. FMFA: Y 1944–1949 121 Conférence de Yalta, 13 February 1945.

58. CRC: R-691/1, 6 January 1945.

59. CRC: C-874, 4 January 1945.

60. Samuel J. Roseman, *Working with Roosevelt* (New York, 1972), 546.

61. FDRL: Hopkins 337 Yalta Conference, Folder 1. Caffery to President, 14 January 1945.

62. Ibid.

63. Lord Moran, *Churchill*, 257.

64. Perkins, *The Roosevelt I Knew*, 396. Eleanor Roosevelt discouraged the president from going to Great Britain and France, "believing that that would not set too well with the American people" (Sherwood, *Roosevelt and Hopkins*, 831).

65. Churchill, VI, 187.

66. Sherwood, *Roosevelt and Hopkins*, 880.

CONCLUSION

1. "If . . . mediocrity shows in [France's] acts and deeds, it strikes me as an absurd anomaly, to be imputed to the fault of Frenchmen, not to the genious of the Land" (de Gaulle, I, 3).

2. Lord Moran, *Churchill: Taken from the Diaries of Lord Moran* (Boston, 1966), 88.

3. Speech to Congress, 1 March 1945.

4. The most extravagant figures have been given by various parties, for various purposes, concerning the extent of Resistance activity. At the time of the Allied invasion, British intelligence (SOE), which was particularly well informed of the situation, gave a figure of 58,000, adding that this figure was "considerably higher" than those received from other sources. A figure of about 50,000 is probably closest to reality (FDRL: PSF 167/OSS, 7 June 1944). Following the liberation of Paris, "the competent authorities registered 123,000 requests for recognition as F.F.I. fighters when in fact their number was no more than 20,000" (Adrien Dansette, *Histoire de la libération de Paris* [Paris, 1946], 31).

5.

It is salutary to reflect on Hitler's blind arrogance. One can only speculate on what would have happened if he had been less vengeful, less wedded to forceful solutions, quicker to sense others' needs and aspirations. If he had given France enough to eat, arms to defend her empire, and the promise of territorial integrity, France might well have become the neutral 'west wall' that Pétain was to talk about later in 1942. If German dominance meant abundance, as Gide observed cynically on 9 July 1940, nine-tenths of Frenchmen would accept it, three-fourths with a smile. Hitler's arrogance of power never gave speculation a test. (Robert O. Paxton, *Vichy France: Old Guard and New Order, 1940–1944*, [New York, 1975], 134–35)

6. Georges Pompidou, in *Pour rétablir une verité* (Paris, 1982), quoted de Gaulle as saying, "Poor France! During the war she did not fight" (62). "I bluffed, for the First Army was made up of Negroes and Africans. The Leclerc division enrolled 2500 volunteers in France. In fact, I saved face, but France did not follow" (127–28). "In 1940 France was occupied. Afterwards, I could make believe that she was with me" (129).

7. Rexford G. Tugwell, *The Democratic Roosevelt* (New York, 1957), 632. In an address on 19 January 1898, Roosevelt (then age 16) had stated, "Of all the great powers of the world the United States and Russia are the only ones which have no colonies to defend" (*F.D.R.: His Personal Letters: Early Years* [New York, 1947], 180).

8. Ibid., 631.

9. Lord Moran quotes Stalin as saying, "Without America we should already have lost the war" (*Churchill*, 154).

Bibliography

PUBLISHED SOURCES, DIARIES, AND MEMOIRS

Berle, Beatrice Bishop, and Jacobs, Travis Beal, eds. *Navigating the Rapids, 1918–1971: From the Papers of Adolf A. Berle.* New York: Harcourt Brace Jovanovich, 1973.

Blum, John Morton. *From the Morgenthau Diaries.* 3 vols. Boston: Houghton Mifflin, 1959–67.

Bullitt, Orville H., ed. *For the President, Personal and Secret: Correspondence between Franklin D. Roosevelt and William C. Bullitt.* Boston: Houghton Mifflin, 1972.

Byrnes, James F. *Speaking Frankly.* New York: Harper & Bros., 1947.

Chandler, Alfred, et al., eds. *The Papers of Dwight D. Eisenhower: The War Years.* Vol. II. Baltimore: Johns Hopkins University Press, 1970.

Churchill, Winston S. *The Second World War.* 6 vols. Boston: Houghton Mifflin, 1948–53.

Dallek, Robert. *Franklin D. Roosevelt and American Foreign Policy.* New York: Oxford University Press, 1979.

De Gaulle, Charles. *The Complete War Memoirs of Charles de Gaulle.* New York: Clarion Books, Simon & Schuster, 1972.

Dilks, David, ed. *The Diaries of Sir Alexander Cadogan.* New York: G.P. Putnam's Sons, 1972.

Eden, Anthony. *The Reckoning.* Boston: Houghton Mifflin, 1965.

Eisenhower, David. *Eisenhower at War, 1943–1945.* New York: Random House, 1986.

Eisenhower, Dwight D. *Crusade in Europe.* New York: Doubleday, 1948.

Funk, Arthur L. *The Politics of TORCH.* Lawrence: University Press of Kansas, 1974.

Hassett, William D. *Off the Record with F. D.R., 1943–1945.* New Brunswick, N.J.: Rutgers University Press, 1958.

Hull, Cordell. *The Memoirs of Cordell Hull.* 2 vols. New York: Macmillan, 1948.

Ickes, Harold L. *The Secret Diary of Harold L. Ickes.* 2 vols. New York: Simon & Schuster, 1953–54.

Kimball, Warren F., ed. *Churchill & Roosevelt: The Complete Correspondence.* 2 vols. Princeton, N.J.: Princeton University Press, 1984.

Leahy, William D. *I Was There.* New York: Whittlesey House, 1950.

Macmillan, Harold. *The Blast of War, 1939–1945.* New York: Harper & Row, 1968.

Moran, Lord. *Churchill: Taken from the Diaries of Lord Moran.* Boston: Houghton Mifflin, 1966.

Perkins, Frances. *The Roosevelt I Knew.* New York: Harper Colophon, 1964.

Pogue, Forrest C. *George C. Marshall: Organizer of Victory.* New York: Viking, 1973.

Roosevelt, Franklin D. *F.D.R. His Personal Letters, 1928–1945.* Elliott Roosevelt, ed. 3 vols. New York; Duell, Sloan and Pearce, 1950.

Sherwood, Robert. *Roosevelt and Hopkins: An Intimate History.* Rev. ed. New York: Grossett & Dunlap, Universal Library, 1950.

Vigneras, Marcel. *Rearming the French* (United States Army in World War II). Washington, D.C.: OCMH, 1957.

Welles, Sumner. *Seven Major Decisions.* London: Hamish Hamilton, 1951.

Among the numerous biographies of Roosevelt are the two volumes by James MacGregor Burns, *Roosevelt: The Lion and the Fox* (1956) and *Roosevelt: The Soldier of Freedom*; Kenneth S. Davis, *FDR* (3 vols., 1972–to date); Frank Fredel, *Franklin D. Roosevelt: A Rendezvous with Destiny* (1990); Geoffrey Ward's two volumes, *Before the Trumpet* (1985) and *A First Class Temperament* (1989); and Joseph P. Lash, *Eleanor and Franklin* (1971).

FRENCH SOURCES

Aglion, Raoul. *De Gaulle et Roosevelt.* Paris: Plon, 1984.

Baudouin, Paul. *Neuf Mois au Gouvernement: Avril-Decembre 1940.* Paris: Editions de la Table Ronde, 1948.

Bourdet, Claude. *L' aventure incertaine: De la Résistance à la Restauration.* Paris: Stock, 1975.

Charles-Roux, F. *Cinq Mois Tragiques aux Affaires Étrangères (21 Mai–1er Novembre 1940).* Paris: Librairie Plon, 1949.

Coutau-Bégarie, Hervé, and Huan, Claude. *Darlan.* Paris: Fayard, 1989.

Ferro, Marc. *Pétain.* Paris: Fayard, 1987.

Gillois, André. *Histoire Secrète des Français à Londres de 1940 à 1944.* Paris: Hachette-Littérature, 1973.

Kupferman, Fred. *Laval.* Paris: Balland, 1987.

Masson, Philippe. *La Marine française et la guerre, 1939–1945.* Paris: Tallandier, 1991.

Mauriac, Claude. *Un Autre de Gaulle: Journal 1944–1954.* Paris: Hachette, 1970.

Moulin de Labarthète, H. du. *Le Temps des Illusions: Souvenirs (Juillet 1940–Avril 1942).* Bruxelles: La Diffusion du Livre, 1946.

Noguères, Louis. *Le Véritable Procès du Maréchal Pétain.* Paris: Librairie Arthème Fayard, 1955.

Stucki, Walter. *La Fin du Régime de Vichy.* Paris: Oreste Zeluck, 1947.

Tracou, Jean. *Le Maréchal aux Liens.* Paris: Editions André Bonne, 1948.

Index

About the Author

MARIO ROSSI is a former special correspondent of the *Christian Science Monitor* and United Nations correspondent for the *St. Louis Post-Dispatch*. He is the author of *The Third World* (1963) and *North Africa* (1974).